Feeling People

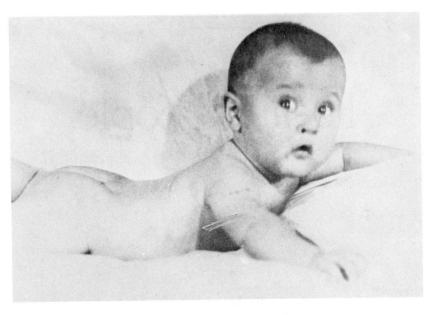

". . . and this is me, the author . . .
I lived this book with my guts . . . a book can be a rebirth . . ."

Feeling People

A Revolutionary Concept
in
Therapy, Lifestyle
and
Human Contact

by
Paul J. Hannig, Ph.D.

Anna Publishing Inc., Winter Park, Florida

DEDICATION

*To my sons, Mark and Adam, who have shown me
the beauty and innocence inherent in all of us. And to all
the children of the world, that they may never lose that spark
that makes them so special.*

TABLE OF CONTENTS

ix

PREFACE

Since the original writing of *Feeling People*, much time has elapsed and the therapy and program of which this was an accounting have also moved on. As I state in the introduction of the book, very few things in life remain stationary. So it is with the Total Feeling Process.

As the book goes to print, we are using a much more eclectic approach utilizing principles from existential/humanistic psychotherapy, behaviorism and the psychodynamic perspective. The interpersonal, psychosocial and cognitive schools are also highly relevant in our total approach, since we believe that no one school or set of theories has all the answers to the complex organism that we call humankind.

We have also moved very strongly towards improving our diagnostic-assessment capabilities combining traditional clinical procedures based on the *Diagnostic and Statistical Manual of Mental Disorders (DSM-III) Third Edition.*[1] Combining this with a system that we call Vector Analysis, we are capable of drawing up a clearly conceived working model for both the client and the therapist to work with. The Vector system is an outline of salient clinical features that depict a rather complete personality picture of each client along with appropriate treatment strategies. It is a large sheet of paper that is divided into multi-dimensional segments, each depicting a concise, clinical description of the areas that the therapy will be concerned with. The paper is continually expanded to cover the areas of growth and treatment; thus, almost giving a computer-like print out of the symptom pictures, intrapsychic materials, treatments recommended and behavioral descriptions. This type of analysis is a very specific, precise and highly detailed account of the etiology, course and progress of each client's therapy and growth. Appropriate clients are able to take their vector sheets home with them and continue to work and expand on the material explored during private and group sessions. Thus, there is very little, if any, separation between therapist and client and the client and his/her therapy. Nothing is secret and the vector material is available along with its information and insights for the client's use.

---

[1]American Psychiatric Association; *Diagnostic and Statistical Manual of Mental Disorders, Third Edition,* Washington, D.C., APA, 1980.

This method has helped us to focus on the pure clinical issues of psychotherapy, while at the same time, the other existential aspects of an eclectic approach allows us to facilitate and explore the transpersonal and transcendental facets of human existence. Thus, we are able to examine and work with deep core familial pain, while at the same time, delve into those realms that elevate the traveler to the psychological spheres of ecstasy and spiritual enlightenment. The core resting place is still deep feeling integration as a technique and with the utilization of other methods of analysis, we have evolved into a more socially oriented and interactive approach.

My objective in writing this book was to share with both the professional and lay population an experience in therapeutic living and an exploration of the roots and theoretical components of many interpersonal difficulties. Much of what I have written may cause controversy and rebuttal but it is based on sound psychological principles and personal experiences.

I believe that all growth motivated people seek to discover their own innate capacities for personal beauty while overcoming the ugliness of their own lives. This quest implies that all humans are somehow always dissatisfied with their lot in life and are thus motivated to seek new and better ways to enhance and deepen their capacities for totally loving others and being loved themselves. To overcome the pitfalls and downturns in this all too human search, it is common to slide into the existential dilemma of hopelessness. Deep core feeling connectedness puts people in touch with their buried capacities for *real* hope and, by so doing, helps them to transcend mundane suffering and eventually reconnect to the universal source of their own being. Real hope is inherent in all deep feeling and is based on the mystical and practical traditions of all true religious experience.

No book can be prepared for publication without the help of many good people. I sincerely thank the following for their unlimited suggestions, support and friendship during the writing and production of *Feeling People:* co-director and editor, Susan Ball, M.Ed., for your contributions to the writing, editing and text; Reisa Winston, my personal secretary, typist and friend who has devoted untold hours of sacrifice and stamina in the compilation of the original and edited manuscript; and Ivan

Arnove, my friend and co-therapist who has been an ear to listen as well as our cover artist and my collaborator.

To all members of the Total Feeling Community goes my thanks and appreciation for your ongoing patience, support and friendship over the years. Together we are the core of *Feeling People* and your sincerity and openness in dealing with your own emotions have made this exploration into the human condition a truly exciting, growthful one. At times we have struggled together battling the ravages of neurosis. There were moments when some of you have wanted to "throw in the towel." But for those who stuck it out, the rewards have been great.

Finally, my thanks to my two sons, Mark and Adam, who have continually been an inspiration and source of joy and enlightenment. By constantly looking into your faces and seeing the purity and innocence of your childhood, I am confirmed in my personal beliefs and fortified in my goal to eradicate the ravages of early childhood trauma and adult neurosis.

INTRODUCTION

This book is about feelings and the way in which feelings change and transform people's lives. It is also about the way in which human beings make contact with one another and how their honest, straightforward interactions bring them into full juxtaposition with their realities. This is an excursion into an in-depth, highly evolved psychotherapy and as such, the reader can travel along a pilgrimage into his own feelings, the dynamics of all types of behavior and the deep feelings of the people that he will encounter in these pages. At times, the writing style will be highly theoretical to satisfy those of us who need an empirical understanding of life. At other times, the style will be deeply moving, and hopefully, will reflect the concerns that lurk in the depths of the human soul.

I will attempt to take the reader upwards to the world of cerebration and then, intimately plunge into the hurts and longings of all of us. If you have the intention of going high and reaching cosmic consciousness and peak experiences, please be forewarned that we will also plummet into the reservoirs of anguish and pain. Thus, we will go high and deep, for man cannot exist solely with his head in the clouds while his feet are not firmly anchored to the earth. If you feel that you are traveling on a roller coaster with peaks and valleys, your perception will be quite accurate, for I do not wish to overburden you with extremes of cognitions or maudlin babblings of excessive human emotion. Life and health are a curious blend of the interconnectedness of mind, body and soul.

We will begin by examining some basic immutable truths that can stand the test of time and can also be continually subjected to inspection, modification and improvement. We, ourselves, will share in this process. Observations cited at the beginning of this book will be continuously elaborated, explored and modified. Perhaps positions will be investigated later as new and better discoveries take their place.

Like any major work, this book has been challenging to write. It has been necessary to select specific and pertinent material that may be useful and interesting to the reader as well as to the author.

Unequivocally, many who have delved deeply into themselves acknowledge that one of the supreme values for living is fully *feeling*. These individuals recognize that at the core of all human experience is a realm of powerful feelings that, when fully felt, clarify and significantly establish personal truth. These individuals do not see the Total Feeling experience as something that is transitory, but rather that it encompasses all of human experience. Many of the secondary issues of life, such as cars, money, houses, prestige, status, position, power, recognition, etc., have their base roots in the curative power of core feeling. These objects, symbols and things become more meaningful once their significance is felt on a deep level.

Through deep core feeling, these individuals come to know their own truth in all its varied forms and disguises. The Feeling Process itself becomes the means to help everyone to be fully vibrant and alive. Tension, anxiety and defensiveness melt through the onslaught of deep core feeling and the problems of living are solved at the deepest centers of human nature. It is through this same deep core feeling that one can open oneself to the entire Universe, transcend time and space and connect to evolutionary history, plus spiritual and ethical values.

> *Oh truth, Sweet Truth,*
> *You are like the fruit of the vine*
> *that cleanses and*
> *refreshes*
> *my wayward, tired soul.*
>
> *Give to me all thy juices:*
> *I am,*
> *I feel,*
> *I open.*
> *Glad for the passion*
> *of life.*
>
> *Richness is mine*
> *As I feel the essence of all holiness*
> *Wrapped in the sometime deception*
> *of my body.*
>
> *For there is nothing but*
> *true, real, deep feeling.*
> *All else is sham and superficiality.....*
>
> *I am Feeling Man*
> *That is my absolute truth.....*
> *Open your eyes*
> *All you who would drink from the vine*
> *And join me on my journey........*

Chapter 1 An Overview

HISTORY

It all started for me in the fall of 1968. I was 31 years of age and just graduating from college with a degree in psychology. In a sense I felt as if I was over the hill, but I was able to get an excellent job at Philadelphia State Hospital as a training therapist in the Mental Health Worker training program of the Psychology training section. I was very impressed with the director, Bob Martin, who interviewed me. His straight-from-the-shoulder talk actually convinced me to take the job. The following Monday morning I found myself in an encounter group with 14 other trainees, and what was to follow, would revolutionize my entire life.

I had never experienced an encounter group before but I felt immediately turned on to what was happening there. It was a new world for me, one of openness and honesty, valid feedback, care and concern from other people, as well as being able to express my innermost thoughts and feel warmth and love for other individuals. At the same time I gained incredible practical knowledge and experience in all phases of psychotherapy. It was at this point, too, that I was introduced to the world of feelings.

At the end of the one-year training program, I had a sense that with all the techniques and therapy that I had been through, I was left with one piece of knowledge and that was that I wanted to go deeper into myself. Bob, in the meantime, asked me to stay on and become a member of his training staff. I was very flattered and remained for a total of four years, gaining invaluable group experience, not only as a therapist but as a teacher, supervisor and program director.

While all this was going on, I had developed an outside practice of my own: a community-based, human relations training center utilizing existential group methods and hypnosis, plus other altered states of consciousness techniques. I had been studying hypnosis since I was twelve years of age and it seemed to me the perfect tool to be synthesized.

During the transition from 1970 to 1971, with all the techniques that I had gleaned, I was ready to begin experimenting with my own in-depth probes into myself and my patients. I can remember lying down on the floor and combining some very specific breathing techniques, with body methods, and finding myself blowing wide open. In a matter of seconds, I was writhing on the floor in agonizing pain calling out for my mother. The episode went on for quite a while and I came out of it feeling cleansed, exhilarated and magnificent. I had been through my first total feeling, primal experience.

As I continued my self-exploration, not only within my own growth center, but with some of the staff from the Philadelphia State Hospital, I met with astounding results. I didn't know it at the time but I was going through, not only a great personal transformation, but a professional one as well.

In 1972, I left the state hospital system and went into full time private practice. I had slowly given up hypnosis and the group encounter model gave way to a new method of deep feeling therapy in conjunction with total group encounter. It was an incredible combination, one that I still use today and it has come together in one of the most powerful, effective therapies I have ever seen.

During my Ph.D. training, I came across two other therapists who were into deep feeling work, Lucy Ulman and Noble Turner. We worked extensively with one another and I deepened my explorations into myself. At that time, I also became good friends with Jacqui Leichter and Mike Broder, therapists at the Center for the Whole Person in Philadelphia who helped me to further synthesize the new methods of the Total Feeling Process.

About the summer of 1974, my therapy program was coalesced and I decided to move to Florida. A number of group members followed me down in order to continue with the therapy and we began the Total Feeling Community in the South Florida area.

South Florida was really the ideal place for the Total Feeling Community to flourish. It was here that the Total Feeling Process came to full fruition. The climate and the countryside were superb and had all the ingredients for enhancing life. A casual unpretentious atmosphere flourished providing the perfect incentive for increasing body awareness, sensuality and growth.

In order to maximize growth, I have found that it is necessary for the entire staff to devote an incredible amount of energy to each individual client and the group as a whole. Every therapist within the Center knows what is happening with every client and feeling interaction is highly processed.

I have found over the past few years that there is an acceptance by deep feeling people of all disciplines and approaches that help lead one to deeper realms of feeling and more integrated lives. As an outgrowth of this, I have come to realize that there is no one right way to do therapy. Therefore, I see myself as a reluctant bystander to all the internecine wars that exist between competing psychotherapists, especially the body therapies and the so-called feeling therapies. Because I have never been fully hung up on authority, I never felt the need to attach or be caught up in any territorial battle with other psychotherapists. None of them are either fully right or fully wrong . . . each one has his own limitations and high points.

Many of the different methods and philosophies of these therapies have been useful in my own growth and practice; yet, I have come to recognize that it is total group process in conjunction with deep feeling methods that has truly *transformed* my own life and the lives of many of my patients. I see that transformation taking place at the deepest core levels and then spreading out to permeate one's entire existence.

As the Total Feeling Process emerged and developed, we were on our own search for the elements of the therapy that made it so effective. Intuitive knowledge was not enough, so we had to concretize what were the essential ingredients that made for systematic and profound change and cure. For many years we were absolutely sure of the effectiveness of the deep core, total feeling experience. We created an optimum, systematic methodology that allowed our clients to feel and integrate the deepest parts of themselves. The Total Feeling experience brought great relief, change and growth to many lives. We were certain that heavy core feeling would eventually blow away all painful, disorganized behavior. Over time, however, we came to realize that there was another element that was very important in the feeling, growth experience: this was a systematic "working through" of all symbolic, interpersonal and intra-psychic confusions that occur. We knew that we had to help people to feel all the buried deep pain but we also knew how vital it was to methodically work through all of the acting out or "off the wall" issues and behaviors.

For example, if a veteran "feeler" can lie down and get in touch with his deep core feelings yet not connect these feelings and work them through his here-and-now craziness, then he would not be fully cured. This was one of our criticisms of some primal type or abreactive therapies. They certainly knew how to blow out and exorcise someone's past, but they fell short when it came to genuinely working issues on a secondary level. Therapies that stress a predominant group orientation, err in the opposite respect. What is absolutely essential is the presence of a processing therapist who can render the attention and the skills to decode, encapsulate, role play, interpret and confront the unfeeling, adult, symbolic displacements from feeling reality.

So, we have the powerful combination of the total "blowout" feeling experience, group involvement and the systematic working through and dismantling of the patient's non-feeling life episodes. We have also developed a structural system that allows a person to continue in the Total Feeling Process for as long as it seems desirable.

CHANGE

What is to follow stems from some basic premises in life and may apply to many individuals. We will take a more in-depth look at some of these premises later in the book. The first idea we will touch upon is that most people are changeable, are in a state of change, and will continue to change throughout their lifetime. This implies that a growing person changes from what he was yesterday, the week before, and all the previous years of his life. Thus, we can expect the transforming individual to be in a different place tomorrow, the next month, and in the ensuing years.

We can further postulate that all human beings who are interested in reaching their full human potential must be in a constant state of movement, flux, recapitulation, and reassessment. That is to say that as one moves into the deeper and higher levels of consciousness, he will be rediscovering and redeveloping the very nature of his being. What may be right for him at one point, may not be right for him at another.

We will attempt to explore how individuals make the transition from believing in and being their defenses to becoming who they really are on a deep feeling level. This means that as change occurs, people will begin to recognize the extraordinary difference between *thinking* about a feeling and *experiencing* that feeling at its deepest core.

It has been our experience that in-depth, intensive psychotherapy is perhaps the most powerful tool yet devised to bring about and facilitate this change. No other vehicle approaches the potential benefits to be derived from full therapeutic, in-depth, human encounter. Psychotherapy certainly offers the best hope for mankind, because it is the only method to date that can allow each human being to go deeply into himself and reorganize his individual being at its deepest core.

THE NOW

Another important premise, inherent in all movement and change, is that there is a necessity to return to familiar or buried spaces and places to reclaim a feeling, a thought or a theme that might have been missed the first time around. This return to the past is needed in order to complete a gestalt for the present and the future.

Most people do not realize how the unfelt, buried past influences the "Now." To the extent that someone is mixed-up, troubled and confused, we may assume that something denied in the past is exerting pressure to be felt and resolved in the present. The present is thus overburdened by the painful past and all here and now actions are colored and superimposed by one's history. This type of contamination can make one's present a mixture of hell and conflict. Only by fully feeling the past does one become fully here in the "Now."

The more that one can feel his past in the "Now," the more he is freed up to exist in a near ecstatic state. This is not to imply that a perfect and continuous state of bliss is authentic. Clinicians are only too familiar with the so-called blissful denial states of drug induction, temporary insanity and the illusory ecstatic states of certain neuroses. I am referring to the general state of ecstasy that many self-actualizing people experience in their everyday responsible lives, that lies just below the perimeter of consciousness and reflects the real way that these people relate to the world.

The "Now" is the only place where people can feel that ecstasy and thus, experience full meaning in their lives. As feelings about work, family, spirit and love are resolved in a totally responsible life, then we can see the payoffs for those who would seek the self-actualizing, feeling path. There is a kind of reverence for the "Now" and when we can "Be Here Now"[1], we can experience the profoundness of the present second. It is only here and now that we can stop and feel where we are in the Universe and perhaps, recognize that we are all connected to it in some way.

The past may try to drag us down and keep us from appreciating the present moment, while the future holds onto us with anxiety

---

[1] Baba Ram Dass, *Be Here Now*. (New Mexico, Newspaper Printing Corp., 1971).

. . . Both are unlike the steadfast sureness that can be realized by cleaning up the past and completing a feeling gestalt.

So it is with therapy that we attempt to let someone feel his past fully so that he can truly be clear in the present and be free enough to move with less encumbrance into the future. There is no failure in therapy. There is only the failure to feel fully in the "Now." Partial feelings can cause those mental distortions that separate one's past and present and thus create what looks like failure in the "Now." A patient once put it this way:

> "A 'Now' life for me is an everyday,
> hour, minute and second of experiencing,
> expressing, relating and feeling all
> aspects of my being. It is an emotionally
> 'No holds barred' way of life."

THERAPY

The next premise involves a new look at the term "therapy." Webster[2] defines therapy as "curative treatment." Being curative or therapeutic implies "treatment of disease" and a therapist is one who is skilled in the "practice of therapeutics." This definition is so broad and vague that professionals have had to devise a multitude of specialities in order to define and attack a particular malady, as if it were some foreign invader. It was, of course, a great boon to mankind when Freud[3] helped to define mental disorders as an illness to be treated humanely, just like any physical disease. This was a great advance over previous attempts by society to regard deviants as agents of the devil who were possessed by demons and had to be punished, burned and tortured.

We are more sophisticated today. The demons still exist, but only as aberrations of the mind trying to deal with an overload of buried pain. A cure, or a restoration of balance, can be obtained, if one is capable of a proper ventilation, connection and resolution of blocked, unfelt feelings over a considerable length of time.

---

[2] *Webster's New World Dictionary*, 2nd College ed., 1976.
[2] Sigmund Freud, *A General Introduction to Psychoanalysis* (New York: Washington Square Press, 1960).

Therapy, as it is generally understood by the public, is meant to treat the sick or the disturbed. This means that those who would deny their own neurosis can neatly discard the term and project that only "those people" need it, not I. Hence, a therapist is one who works with those who are "sick" and "need therapy."

It is not really in the best interests of humanity to restrict ourselves to the narrow confines of traditionally understood "therapy." Any feeling conception of life must by necessity go beyond correcting socially defined sickness and include within its purview the advantages to be gleaned from current growth models and the educational process itself. Formal therapeutic procedures need to combine with a holistic approach that encompasses all of human experience and provides an avenue or vehicle to feel and experience all that is divinely human. The thesis here is that therapy is an integral part of an overall growth system that encompasses deep intra-psychic delving, emotional expression, information dissemination, counseling and seminar techniques.

We have achieved a synthesis of these methods by fully understanding the full feeling procedure within the context of extensive group dynamics research and experience. Thus, the Total Feeling Process combines the benefits of individual psychotherapy plus group processes. It is essential to understand that human beings grow intensely in a full comprehensive, extended therapeutic milieu. This mechanism must also encompass the transpersonal, ethnic and cultural dynamics of each human being.

DISTRACTIONS

It is through deep and absolute commitment to feeling, that growth becomes possible as well as feasible for the most rapid, profound and lasting changes. This value lies at the core of the Total Feeling Process and any compromise detracts from the effectiveness of the treatment.

Many individuals, unfortunately, render their lives full of distractions. This means that if one tries hard enough to trick himself, he will invent all manner of devices to distract himself from the full commitment to feeling: work, school, sex, spouses, boyfriends, girlfriends, debts, lack of money, etc. The list is endless. These can all be used to keep a person from deeply exploring his core feelings. In a clear individual, these might be used to trigger more and deeper feelings. But in the neurotic, these will be escape routes from reality and the inner self. To be a full feeling human being, one must possess that deep emotional commitment to living a full feeling life. This drive necessitates a special quality that can be stated simply by one such person:

> "All I know is that I want to feel me and feel everything that it is possible for me to feel. I want this more than anything else in the whole world. It feels good to make whatever personal sacrifice I have to, in order to put myself more into this intense feeling atmosphere."

The simple truth is that total commitment of one's full being and energy into any endeavor increases the potential for a more comprehensive, successful outcome. If energy is dissipated into various channels, then one can only be distracted from the task at hand, which is the experiencing and sharing of more feeling. We know from our own personal experience and the experiences of our patients and friends that full commitment works. It has worked for us.

In a broader sense, the whole phenomenon of dedication deserves much more attention and research than behavioral scientists have given it in the past. If one believes in something with all his heart and soul, then he will devote his life energies to it.[4] This is no small matter. Where would psychoanalysis be, if Freud had not doggedly persisted in presenting and developing his new science? Where would Christianity and Judaism be, if their followers had not been willing to fight and, in some instances, die for their well tested convictions? It is that determination and commitment that reflects, "This is absolutely right for me and this is where I want to be." Wanting to be a feeling human being becomes, in a sense, a conversion experience of "finding one's place in the sun."

It is part of a parent's job to offer support and encouragement to a child in all of his endeavors, so that he develops faith in himself and what he does. If a father offers himself to the child with a simple, warm and comforting, "I know you can do it and do it well," then the child will develop faith and confidence in himself and this will manifest itself in healthy dedications and commitments. Little children, likewise, need all their mother's support and encouragement in their endeavors to become full-functioning, creative human beings.

---

[4] Joseph Chilton Pearce, *The Crack in the Cosmic Egg* (New York: Pocket Books, 1971), pg. 12.

As responsible adults, we must recognize and differentiate life's many tasks and ventures that promote feeling growth from tasks that block and hinder feeling and act as distractions from feeling. If the task is part of an overall sick system, then it serves as a flight from feeling and belongs in the category of defenses. For example, one male who really needed more therapy and feeling time and functioned on a very limited financial budget, foolishly spent his hard earned money on a boat that he could hardly afford. He just about guaranteed that he couldn't pay for his much needed therapy by his extravagance. Thus, he set up a new struggle for himself, while using the boat and financial deficiencies as a distraction from his therapy.

We have learned, as in the above example, that if a client is not ready to go into a given area, all the pushing in the world won't get him there and may even close him down more and increase his resistance. Our structure is devised in such a way as to maximize the chances for a successful outcome. We know this in advance, because we have been through it ourselves. The beginning or the intermediate patient may not be aware of what he really needs in order to get healthy, so he may inadvertently impede his own progress. Those who have stuck to the structure of the therapy, were always the ones who succeeded. Their progress was usually quite consistent over time.

From time to time, we have had to keep an eye on the development of reified, defensive dyadic cliques. For example, one member may become overly attached in a symbiotic fashion, to another member. This could be a developing love relationship or a spouse. Unfortunately, all their struggles and energy get focused and narrowed into that dyadic relationship. This "getting lost" in the twosome serves to protect the individual from relating on an emotional level with the therapists and other group members. The two may reinforce each other's defenses in order to protect their own neurotic emotional investment in the diad.

For example, John may be defending and claim to be too tired to go to group that night. He feigns illness and evokes sympathy from his partner who stays home with him to play "mother." They get vicarious gratification from this age old game but lose the benefits of feeling something deeper that could release them from pandering on one another's guilt.

This is another familiar game as stated by one client.

"Early in therapy my cage would be rattled. I couldn't feel anything deeply, so I would be indirectly hostile and defensive and at times I would withdraw because I was afraid of the therapist and the group. I needed support for all my defensive maneuvers, so I would play on my girlfriend's sympathies and loyalties. Thus, I set up an elaborate defense system to avoid a real confrontation with all authority and ultimately, my feelings."

"I had always been afraid of authority figures, but I didn't know it. I would justify myself continuously in order to avoid a confrontation with myself and others. I know finding fault with everyone was a ploy on my part not to feel."

In the Total Feeling Process the therapy is quite explicit at the beginning. The client openly states, verbally and by his attendance, that he wants to feel more and deeper. The Total Feeling Community is a comprehensive system developed to facilitate just that. If one wishes to "act out" his needs, however, rather than feel the pain involved, it can become fairly uncomfortable relating to others in the Community who are committed to a fully feeling way of life.

This point needs reiterating. We are so geared for intense, deep core feeling that if someone chooses to get caught up in one of his acting out defenses, then he will experience some discomfort in the program. Someone may be acting out an incredible amount of unfelt feeling and trying to get everybody to buy into it. If it's a male, the only one that may fall for his manipulation might be his girlfriend. She will compromise reality in order to stay safe and accepted. But that doesn't mean everyone else will be maneuvered. When he fails at trying to negotiate an unworkable, unreal contract with people, his only move is to feel or withdraw. This does not mean that the program is intolerant. Group members are very tolerant. They may put up with someone's defenses and acting out for a long time. but they won't buy into it indefinitely.

Feelings are not just to be connected to those areas that are within the limits of a particular theoretical framework. The range of potential feeling includes everything that is locked away and buried. This implies that facilitation must be geared to open up a person to all that is inside. One has feelings about everything: God, country, the Universe, family, one's city, and one's transcendental historical potential. An individual may have developed feelings toward Christ, Lincoln, Superman, Moses, or Popeye. These people, places and things are objects of deep emotional meaning and sometimes require reconnecting and full feeling, as much as, if not more so, than mommy, daddy, brothers and sisters.

It becomes important to remember that in the Total Feeling Process, feelings are the therapy and the therapy is feeling. There is no distinction or separation between feeling and therapy. One may argue, "Well, I can feel at home and do my therapy at home." This has considerable value and is encouraged as a part of the total process. But, it is only a partial approach and remedy. One needs the inputs, interventions and the energies that are only available at a full range, comprehensive, workable therapy center. Real therapy begins when the participant makes himself as available and vulnerable as possible. Since the individual needs a virtual storehouse of feeling, therapeutic, growth resources, these resources should be available at all times and structured in such a way as to incorporate his therapeutic growth into an on-going lifestyle.

THERAPY, THEN COMMUNITY

Most people conceive of a therapy as having a given number of sessions and a certain length of time. We have found that this varies from individual to individual. For some people it is much easier to get to deep feelings and resolution than for others. The individual eventually reaches a point where his sickness is pretty much gone and no longer dominates his life. This may take anywhere from two to three years. He still may have periodic episodes of tension and distortions in living, but he can usually feel his way through them with little difficulty. In time, he slowly transcends or moves out of therapy and either leaves the program to pursue his feeling experiences in other avenues or stays in the program and becomes an integral part of a real Total Feeling Community. If he stays, that does not mean that he is dependent on the program. He has decided that this is the place where he can best fulfill his feeling capacity. That is one of the goals of the Total Feeling Process, to provide a place, a set of circumstances and experiences that will increase one's feeling capacity and potential. The more that one feels, the wider is his capacity to appreciate the horizons of life.

One trainee put it this way:

"I had been in therapy for quite a while and I felt that I could go and live my life away from the Center. I wasn't 'crazy' anymore. But then it hit me in a feeling way. I really loved being here and caring for others and feeling cared about. Where else could I have so much fun and joy and still learn so much about myself and other people? I wanted to really know others and I wanted others to really know me. This felt so good, that I decided to stay. I got to watch others and see how deep and far their feelings went. Some were into things that I never dreamed possible. And as I watched the way they lived, worked and felt, I found myself experiencing feelings that I never had gotten to when I was in my formal therapy. A whole new world was opening to me that was beyond the treatment of my neurosis."

The cycle proceeds from "I am sick and I need help" to "I am better and healthy" and finally, for some it becomes "I want to live a full, happy, actualizing life. I will be beautiful, happy and at times, ecstatic. Sometimes, I'll be a little tense and crazy."

Sometime during formal therapy, deep core feeling becomes a way of life. Full feeling is not just a means to release pain and connect to history. It becomes a welcome method of continuous, actualizing discovery. I have heard people ask, "How long will I have to lie down and feel the pain?" For some, during the initial period of intensive therapy, there is a period where they are on the floor for long stretches of time. This is probably a period of deep anguish, change and exhilaration. The paradox is, the pain is usually not experienced as excrutiating. I have heard others, from different therapies, claim that they were disgusted with being stuck in bad feelings. I have never witnessed this in the Total Feeling Process. The interventions keep the person moving deep and through his feelings, so that he gradually overcomes his blockages. A Total Feeling experience becomes something to look forward to, because there is great pleasure and satisfaction in learning some truth about one's own life.

The Community aspect of the program developed out of the shared feeling experiences of the members. It wasn't imposed from the outside by an authoritarian leader or a set of abstract principles or beliefs. Cohesion developed out of the shared history of the participants. If you were to experience your deepest truths and share them with someone or a group of people, and then have them do the same in return, a strong bond of feeling develops. This continuous self-revelation and sharing creates an atmosphere for trust to develop. The Total Feeling Community developed out of people really knowing each other's deepest feelings. They learned to listen and respond naturally to one another's pain. I really believe that people develop intimacy by getting close to another's soul.

When feeling is absent, the members often drift from one another and interpersonal difficulties develop. It is only by feeling their blockages that they come back together again. This is why so many marriages and families end in disaster, because there are no ongoing emotional bonds to nourish the growth of the parties involved. This is, also, why so many occupations and jobs are so disillusioning, because there is no provision for people to gain access to their feelings and eventually, share them with others in a contactful way. Most individuals spend the major part of their day in a work setting with strangers and then have to come home and find estrangement with their relatives.

One young man came into our program all the way from Northwest Canada, starving for some kind of human contact. He felt alienated from his wife, children and work associates. After feeling much of the buried pain of his own early existence, he could see how he had set up his present life in exact duplication of his childhood. He didn't have to be forced into his feelings of utter desolation and deprivation. After seeing the warmth and caring that real feeling people have for each other, he exploded into all the utter anguish and despair that he had been holding in and not feeling all his life. He never knew that it was possible, outside of fantasy, for people to love each other and care for him for just being himself.

The Community also developed out of the realities of being clear. It is common for members to build up tension during their everyday lives. Tension has a way of interfering with clear contact. A common outcome for group sessions is that, as feelings get worked through and resolved, the members feel alive, open, warm and loving. It is natural that they express and share these wonderful, high sensations with one another. There is gaiety, joking and natural laughter. Above all, the energy is lively and lovely. None of this is contrived, but grows out of the spontaneity that deep feeling promotes.

THE TOTAL FEELING PROCESS

We decided to call the Total Feeling Process just that, a process, rather than a therapy, because we feel it consists of more than just a system of therapy. We believe that working on pathology is only one aspect of a holistic approach. The terms "pain" and "neurosis" represent only one segment of life and certainly, a rather limited view. The word "Feelings" seems to really fit the core essence of the major emphasis of our approach and not all deep feeling is pain, anguish and suffering. In fact, revelation can be a blinding, exhilarating, positive phenomenon.

The term, Total Feeling Process, then, is a label for the totality or the sum of all the parts of the therapy. It encompasses one's history up until the present, as well as the systematic discovery of the ideas, assumptions and beliefs about the nature of man. Because it is an open-ended approach, its only limit is one's feeling capacity. We know that members have a past, present and future and that it is absolutely possible for them to lead full feeling, integrated, happy lives with themselves and others. Our approach, therefore, is definitive, well organized, practical and constantly being revised, researched and tested within the context of living interactions.

The Total Feeling Process is also the sum total of the educational and the feeling life experiences of the people who conduct and take part in it. Each individual has left his influence, however great or small, and helped to shape the on-going feeling process. This does not mean there is a haphazard application of a potpourri of techniques. Most of the interactions are based on time-tested, tried and true methods plus the excitement of ever new creative procedures that are spawned on the spot to fit the feeling needs of the participants.

Chapter 2   Energy and Feeling

ENERGY AS BEING HUMAN

A human being is a dynamic system of energy, — consisting of thinking, feeling, moving, searching, growing and all aspects of creativity and spirituality. Feeling is the driving force behind all this motion and action. A human being needs to perpetuate and facilitate this core feeling energy in order to guarantee his existence and the immortality of his family and species line. Suppression of this feeling reduces action and can even bring it to a halt. Suppression, further, turns energy inward, thus, pushing it to key organic sites such as the viscera, the peripheral body system and the thinking processes; thereby, stifling action.

By man's nature, he cannot maintain balance or homeostasis indefinitely. He must deplete his energy and thus, find ways to restore his equilibrium. As his energy system begins to deplete, he senses his mind and body going into some form of action in order to satisfy a growing need. Thus, a baby extends his lips to reach his mother's breast in order to feel fed and loved. If this action were not met with a satisfying response, he would develop random nervous activity (excitation) until he found some sort of relief of this need.

We believe that the basic human energy for cure and transformation comes from deep core feeling. No other source of energy compares with the driving force of human emotion. If natural feeling energy is thwarted, then there are marked and decisive effects on the natural human flow. We can say that neurosis will form. When human feeling energy is thwarted or blocked by suppression, we need to return to that point where the blockage occurred. It is like a landslide coming down the mountain and blocking the road, making passage impossible. Neurotics, early in their lives, could not resolve and work their way through roadblocks, so they circumnavigated the wreckage. But the time comes when they must come back and go over that road again and, lo and behold, the wreckage is still there. The job of therapy is to go back, clean up the damage, repair the road and release all the feelings that were withheld. Now the way is clear for the individual to get to where he is going.

This analogy cannot be taken too lightly. Consider what it is like

---

[1] Berne, E., *A Layman's Guide to Psychiatry and Psychoanalysis.* (New York: Simon and Schuster, 1968), pgs. 57-60.

driving a car through a busy, crowded city street during the rush hour. Compare this with the feeling of driving on a smooth uncrowded highway. The first situation will overload you with enormous amounts of stimuli, which you will have to close out in order to tolerate the situation. Finally, it becomes necessary for you to shut down and limit your concentration. You will get to your destination but you will be depleted, tense and exhausted. The second situation allows you to be more relaxed and open to the sky and nature. The relative lack of obstacles and frustrating interferences will allow you the time to express feeling and let go of defenses. The neurotic is like the man always caught in a traffic jam. He never has time to feel. The Total Feeling Process reverses all that by taking him out of the traffic jam for awhile and allowing him to feel all that he originally had to force out of his consciousness.

One may challenge the validity of the "wreckage in the road" analogy and say, "What is the difference if he goes around the wreckage, as long as he gets there." The answer is crucial. Most neurotics spend all their lives and energies circumnavigating landslides. They always take the long way around and usually get lost in the long run. Circumnavigation is fine and probably necessary at times, but it usually succeeds at the price of sacrificing some part of the person. We want to go back and get those energetic parts that were left behind the first time. The Total Feeling Process offers a second chance to be all that one was meant to be.

THE NEED TO ABREACT

It is reasonable to assume that all human beings have needs. We cannot survive and thrive if the needs for love, warmth, shelter, protection and food are not fulfilled satisfactorily. If the satisfaction of these needs becomes thwarted, then the nervous system must create a defensive structure to protect the organism from the threat of pain to the body's frail integrity. Since present day reality has created a task-oriented, rather than a feeling-oriented culture, then a new secondary need must emerge to deal with the resultant pain caused by the denial of the original basic primal needs.

We call this new need the cathartic need or the need to abreact. Catharsis or abreaction means the release of deep emotion and the hooking up or connection of insight into one's own behavior. Most individuals in our society have found appropriate or socially inappropriate ways to handle and release tension. American ingenuity has created innumerable methods to relieve, ameliorate and repress it. We have also created a myriad of ways to produce and compound tension. Technological, educational, general task orientation has manufactured an overload of information that cannot be assimilated or processed properly by a nervous system that was truly designed for more human purposes. The machine age has wreaked havoc on our tender organs. And since our nervous systems can't keep up with the information processing demands of computerized living, we must devise means to release this accumulated tension. (This tension is additional to the already heavy loads of primal, historical pain and muscular armoring residing in the body.)

All cultures have provided rituals for the relief of accumulated tension. These rituals are not intrinsically neurotic and can be quite pleasurably rewarding, but they can be used neurotically. For example, sex, sports, religion, eating, drugs, etc. are not in themselves evil, but they can be abused by the neurotic in a symbolically displaced fashion.

Unfortunately, neurotic use of the mechanisms for the alleviation of tension very often only adds more of an overload to the neural circuits. Most of the ways that people drain off tension through the neurotic use of these activities are not curative or even growth enhancing. They are simply palliative. They get these people through the task of living without providing insights into their deeper selves. These experiences are usually not cathartic, or perhaps only mildly so. One does feel better when his favorite football team wins, but the participation in the activity itself, provides no corridor to the internal areas where abreactive release has to take place. This particular level of release represents the kind of partial catharsis that most people use to help them function in their own cultural milieu. And since the culture both reflects and dictates the acceptable and the unacceptable forms of release, we can only assume that most prevailing release forms are neurotic in that they hold themselves out as ends to be pursued.

One step deeper to true catharsis lies in the traditional forms of psychiatry, psychology and religion. Through psychoanalysis, encounter groups and prayer, the corridor to true abreaction is opened a little wider. The mechanisms of control are loosened much more than those on the more superficial levels. The population that participates in self investigation, on this level, is far more select and naturally, quantitatively smaller. Hopefully, they are more in touch with themselves than the upper levelers.

Even when the first and second levels of consciousness have been penetrated and partial catharsis has taken place, the individual may still be quite neurotic. Upper level releasers are the typical garden variety, closed down neurotics who make up the mainstream of a non-feeling, technological society. In traditional clinical terms, they are the normal, well-adjusted adults who function quite well in a culture that rewards all their endeavors. They stay well within the parameters of acceptable normative values and behavioral standards. Within this group are, also, included the non-functional deviants who relate from the upper level, and yet, need to be segregated because of blatant anti-social behavior. Many convicts and mental patients are conformists who couldn't quite conform enough. So, they remain in the same level of non-feeling tension relievers as their more successful counterparts.

There are also successful and unsuccessful secondary levelers. For example, an individual may have been in psychoanalysis, growth groups or religious programs for years and still not have touched deeply into the primary, bottom line of abreaction. He may be quite closed down and as crazy as ever. Or, he can be the so-called recovered, perfect, growth-oriented person. He may look and sound good, even healthy and superior, and yet still be out of touch with deep feelings. He has learned all the current growth, therapy or religious terms and even believes that he is quite extraordinary. But he is still far from his real self.

Finally, we come to the level of abreaction or the deepest levels of human emotional experience. It is in this realm that we find the full explosive force of deep, uncontrolled, core feeling. It is the encapsulated re-discovery of one's own absolute truth. All levels converge in a total psychobiological event that encompasses the mind, body and emotion. The force of energy rises and releases from a universal storehouse of very deep and profound feeling. The transformative power of the experience arises because defensive control parameters have opened sufficiently enough to allow a flood of feeling to wash through the tissues and cleanse the total being of neurosis and tension. The quality of the gained insight is significantly different and far more profound than that which is experienced on the other two levels.

THE TOTAL FEELING EXPERIENCE

As a result, when we refer to feelings, we do not mean the same thing that the man on the street regards as "feelings". In most cases, he thinks that feeling has something to do with some mental inter- pretation of what he is experiencing at any given moment: "Today I felt lousy" or "I liked that movie". Granted, these statements can be viewed as some sort of an expression of one's emotional condition. However, this is only a partial description of that state of being. The average person really has no indication of the depths and heights of his core emotions. Do his feelings come from the very "ground of his being"[2](deep core, abreactive feeling), or from the superficial layers of his personality?

As we have read, a true deep core feeling is an intense emotional outpouring and cleansing purge of neurosis and tension. It is com- plete and transformative because it connects to powerful insightful truths, scenes, themes, memories, significant events and universal revelations. It is an all encompassing, full, organismic experience. It is total because it pulls on the biological, psychological, historical, transcendental aspects of human existence.

The following is an example of a full core feeling experience. The patient is pulling on deep buried pain and is crying deeper than she could have ever previously imagined.

> "I need my Mama more than anything in the world. I want to be held and cradled by her so much . . . (crying heavily) . . . Why doesn't she hold me and touch me right? . . . Why is she always so mad and angry? . . . I don't mean to be a burden . . . I feel so incomplete and empty in- side . . . I know in my heart that I've never had you, Mama . . . (crying heavier with this realization) . . . I never had you, Mama!! I needed you when I was scared and lonely. I feel so lost without you . . . I get scared and I don't know what to do!!! . . . "

---

[2] Paul Tillich, *Systematic Theology* (3 vols.; Chicago: University of Chicago Press, 1951-53), II.

Liz is crying very deeply now as she realizes how much she wants of herself and how much she does not want to be like her mother.

"...I can't live with your emptiness inside me...I'm dying because I don't have you helping me, Mama! . . . I'm so empty inside!! . . . *You* have to get out! . . . *You're* the emptiness inside me!!! . . . Get out!! . . . Don't keep me crippled like Grandma!!! . . . GET OUT!!! . . . I don't want you anymore!!!! . . . Ma . . . Ma . . . Ma . . . Ma . . . "

As Liz emerged from her core feelings, she was able to integrate the historical pain surrounding her early need for her mother and make a connection between this early need and a recent "trigger" in the group. Another female had been defending and not letting Liz get close enough to make contact. The reality of her distance set off a transferential reaction in Liz which eventually led back to the earlier primal pain with her mother. Upon coming out of the feelings, Liz was so affectionate and grounded that she found herself moving into a clear confrontation with the original female. She was able to work with her very effectively and helped her to feel her way through her own blocks to a place where she could reach out and make contact, not only with Liz, but with all the group members as well.

The internal power of deep core feelings is a monumental catalyst for change and growth. Not only does it transform the emotional, physical and practical life of the person who is feeling, but its effects can reach out and dramatically influence those individuals and situations that are on the periphery of his life.

Chapter 3   Opening Up

CONSCIOUSNESS

As I have stated previously, all human beings who are desirous of reaching their full human potential must be in a constant state of movement and change. This change implies a certain degree of consciousness as to one's being and inner dynamics. We can postulate, therefore, that consciousness is the state of becoming awakened to reality and feelings are the mechanism or tool to bring about this change. To become conscious is to know, feel and understand one's reality fully. It goes beyond the mere possession of one's senses, however, and involves the full emotional tying in and anchoring of inner meaning and expression.

In the Total Feeling Process, participants learn first and foremost to listen to the slightest rumblings of feeling. They begin to orient themselves toward a consciousness of rising core emotion, so that what develops is a feeling awareness that will help one to work through all areas of consciousness. For example, one woman found her voice trailing off in conversations to a very low, weak pitch. All her life she had been prone to depression and her low, weak mumblings were further attenuated by her circuitous and fruitless conversations with people. She never was able to speak from her heart and feelings and, as a result, felt alienated from others. If children are never allowed or encouraged to talk or relate from their hearts, then they will develop distant, alienating styles of communication. As adults, it is difficult to find "them" in their rambling, circular conversations.

Relatives, especially children, will often develop a similar or adaptive, complimentary manner of speaking. This woman's daughter also conversed in a weak monotone, adopting the same circular, interpretive style as her mother. Whenever her mother would speak, the daughter, instead of reacting with feeling, would try to analyze and interpret what the mother was saying. So. the conversation consisted of two monotones droning on to one another, each trying to interpret the other's flat words. This behavior, as a way of avoiding real contact, had gone on for years until they finally were confronted and made conscious in group of their non-affective style. This led to a full, explosive interaction and the real feelings came pouring out.

The message from this kind of dynamic is "If you are using a lot of words to say something, then you are not really saying it". Emotional expressions that emanate from the heart are relatively simple and yet, powerful. After these women became conscious of their emotional "flatness" and the real feelings came out, they had a language and a pitch that was totally different from the original, disguised, defensive tone. The sound and words were strong and direct and they established firm feeling contact.

Feeling consciousness has to be developed, because most of us were raised in non-feeling environments where performance, rather than feelings, was rewarded. A neurotic household reverses values and places supreme priority on performative tasks rather than on who one is and how one feels. Rewards are not given for how one grows emotionally but rather how one performs tasks that have high prestige value. These homes are emotionally dead. Its members don't experience feelings, they interpret and analyze them, which leads to an emotionally dull, lifeless approach to existence.

This situation leads to a double bind, because if the individual performs tasks such as keeping his room neat or running errands, doing chores and washing dishes and he does not get the loving contact, warmth and understanding that he needs, then he becomes "crazy" and closed down. He can't win, because if he obeys like a "good little child", he sacrifices and denies his *real* need for a loving parent. And, if he rebels and rejects the performance orientation, he will lose his parents' superficial acceptance. This is the insanity of a performance-oriented rather than a feeling-oriented home. A child who is made to do things without the nurturance of a truly loving home will eventually rebel by passive resistance or flight. Power struggles may ensue as both child and parent obscure the reality of the underlying pain and stay locked into a symbolic, non-feeling, unconscious struggle.

Unquestionably, behind the difficulties inherent in parent-child performance struggles is an incredible well of unfelt and unresolved painful feeling. Releasing these feelings brings the buried reality fully into the open for total realization and integration. As the feelings emerge, many of the behavioral symptoms of the performance demands begin to dissipate.

Most of our therapy is conducted with adults who have internalized the insanity of their parents' performance demands. The therapy is not done with the real characters of the original drama, but with the stimulus value of recalled memory as well as displaced and projected stimulus figures. Interventions are aimed at disentangling clients from heavy, transferential, symbiotic relationships. First, through confrontation and interpretation, the client is made aware of the nature of his conflicts and interactions. His own self-inflicted, debilitating behavior provides him with a source of feedback about himself. Second, through heavy abreaction, he relives and integrates the suppressed feeling. And finally, he moves on with his life while making discernible changes in the way he lives and relates.

Through the Total Feeling Process patients are brought to a consciousness as to how it feels to be in their old and present environments, without the lifeless facades that have deadened them to themselves and their families. Feeling brings them to life and, quite often, they find it difficult to live in their former situations without the presence of ongoing feeling. Their value priorities change. Emotional contact with self and others becomes the principle goal and all performance expectations are relegated to support a full feeling life.

Working with an adult's memory processes takes time, however. In some cases, we have worked with adolescents and children while the parents were actually present in the session and the results have been quite dramatic and astonishing. Here, the child is reacting from his feelings with the real primary figures actually being present and the intensity of the feeling level can be dramatically greater and deeper than feelings experienced when they are absent. This is probably only true in a therapeutic setting where the safety of the therapist's presence acts as a catalyst to unlock long repressed feelings and ease past the defensive blocks. This method shows promise, because the patient has the benefit of working off the stimulus value of mommy or daddy to reach deep core feelings, while at the same time, correcting some of the disturbances that exist in the intra-family living situation of the participants. The support and reality influence of the therapy teams can help this family to uncover and correct some of its insanity.

One young girl, who was still living at home with her parents, came in with her mother for a therapy session. Both parents had been fairly antagonistic toward the therapy but had allowed it to continue at the youngster's insistence. Her obvious difficulty in relating to others as well as a sense of deep bereavement at the recent loss of a favorite grandfather further strengthened her position for therapeutic intervention.

The mother arrived at the session complaining of a lack of cooperation with chores around the house. By helping the young girl to tune into her deeper core pain, it was uncovered that she was feeling very alienated and alone in her living situation with her family and that, in fact, her grandfather's recent death had stirred up old, buried feelings of early abandonment and desolation.

"Momma, I'm alone, I'm dying
without you. (heavy sobbing). Momma,
. . . . . I need you so much. Where are
you? Why have you left me??!!. . . "

It seems that the mother had left her with a babysitter when she was just a few months old while she went off to resume her career. The intense feelings of desertion and loneliness were carried around inside of her for years until a fresh desertion stirred them up again. By cleaning out all the old pain with her mother, as well as letting go and grieving for her grandfather, this young girl was able to emerge in the here and now and make full contact with those around her. She was also able to take a clearer look at her home situation and her resistance to cooperating with household chores.

Working through to the core feeling level, with the child's parents present, also has the advantage of examining whatever crazy performance demands the parents are making on the child. In the home, these demands become a source of hurt and alienation, because they obscure the powerful surge of underlying feelings and keep all members unaware of their real contact needs with each other.

REVEALING THE SELF

There is a relationship between the way a person reveals himself and his mental health. He cannot reveal any parts of himself that he is unaware of or not in touch with and he cannot bring disowned parts of himself into intimate contact with others in a direct fashion. Whatever is disassociated from consciousness will leak out in symbolic, strange ways.

In order to take a look at this, an individual will have to ask himself many questions. "How willing am I to get to know myself fully and let others know me?" "Do I make it easy for others to really see and experience me?" "How free do I feel in letting others see what is really going on inside of me?"

People are generally afraid to reveal parts of themselves that they have not fully accepted. Unfortunately, it is only possible to form an intimate relationship with someone else according to the level of self-acceptance and self-disclosure that one is willing to attempt. Therefore, deep intimacy can only be realized with more honesty, openness and self-disclosure.[1]

All of us have a secret little world of our own and it usually encompasses certain feelings, fantasies and desires. To reveal what is occurring in these secret recesses has potential consequences; thus, quite often, considerable anxiety surrounds these hidden agendas in here and now contact situations. Suppose a married woman wishes to have sex with a man other than her husband. The conditioning of a strong super-ego may make her feel guilty and she becomes conflicted. Inside her mind she creates several fantasies. She may dream pleasurably about intercourse with her fantasied lover. Or, she could go to her husband and disclose her hidden wish and thus, bring it out into the open, subject to his reactions. Perhaps she would keep it hidden from her husband and reveal the desire to the other man, thus, setting up a different chain of events. Her drive may become strong enough to act out and fulfill her fantasy and then a whole new dynamic may enter her life.

In everyday life we all experience reactions to those that we come in contact with. The full exchange of these feelings, perceptions and reactions is generally frowned upon in our society and what usually occurs is a compromise of human relations.

A young married salesman may enter a store to sell something and sees an attractive receptionist. He has an immediate positive response to her but before he communicates anything, he is subject to all the censoring influences of his entire life. There is the conditioning of childhood experiences, unfelt need towards his parents, wife and children. Will he react with his real feelings or will he allow these other factors to influence and determine his behavior? Perhaps he will be afraid of the receptionist's reaction to him. Does

---

[1] Johnson and Johnson, *Reaching Out: Interpersonal Effectiveness and Self-actualization* (Englewood Cliffs, New Jersey: Prentice Hall Inc., 1972), pgs. 9-11, 12-15, 36-39.

she show an interest in him? Will she reject him or worse yet, is her
friendliness due only to the role of the job?

MY BRAZEN HUSSY

Remind Me
Mind Me
Blind Me
Double Bind Me
What do you want?

> *I can't win*
> *I hurt*
> *I'm only human*
> *What do you expect?*

>> *You tempt me*
>> *with your crotch*
>> *staring me in the face.....*
>> *What do you want?*
>> *what do you expect?*

>>> *You wiggle your ass*
>>> *in front of my nose.*
>>> *The animal man responds*
>>> *to move close*
>>> *But, the big BUT*
>>> *grabs me by the brains*
>>> *and rings danger.*
>>> *What do you want?*
>>> *What do you expect?*

>> *The Angel Guilt God in me*
>> *says control Thyself.*
>> *Temptation and desire*
>> *pulls Me to a Certain Doom.*

What a shame for Thee
my hussy
For they have made you hunger
For the love you missed
By Lusting your body in
full view of those who
have been destroyed and betrayed
by a thousand Mothers.

Would I be the long lost father
you yearned for in your deepest agony?
Forgot me not that I, too,
be deserted in my very smallest infancy.

Alone we be and yet
Never to be close and
together, for the flags of
our nation have bestowed
us a heritage of taboos.
Yea, never to warm each
other for the threat of closeness
brings the evils of possession.

     But you are succulent and juicy
     and my loins turn on to your
     fuckableness.
     My fear heightens, for the
     switch turns to "off" by
     the inevitability of alienating
     rejection.

     Alas, it was not meant to be
     for the ages win
     and I am too little to change
     the tide.
     Perhaps, all that is real
     exists as only marking time on this
     spotted planet, floating like
     a speck in the Cosmos.

Oh, such temptation to turn
to a vague afterlife filled with
the strange hope of something
better than this.
Then again, we all merge
together as victims of a massive rape.
I can find no one to blame
because we are all victims.
Where is the way out?

This censoring type of situation is common. Many men and women hide the real, true pain inside rather than risk the threat of rejection.

"When I was younger I always had a fear of approaching strangers. I was extremely shy and wouldn't assert myself except in an indirect way. As an adult, if I went to a night club by myself, I would sit silently and nurse a drink, but I would never approach a stranger, especially an attractive female. When I had a few male friends along with me, I felt and acted much braver and bolder, because there was always safety and support in numbers.

In my childhood neighborhood, I had been frightened to death. Everyone was potentially dangerous and violence was very common. I was shy and retiring and kept distant from all threatening kids and bad sections of town. It was difficult to make friends, although I did have a few whom I enjoyed and trusted.

When I took this reality to a deep core level, I got in touch with the real feeling which was that I really needed and wanted a mommy and daddy to be there for me in an emotionally supportive way. I used to demand attention on superficial levels, like food, clothes and a fairly clean house, but I never demanded what was important . . . warm, close, real emotional contact on a gut level. That's what I've always wanted and that's what I now try to get. I don't like emotional games or distance, especially with those that I cherish."

Irv is another example of hidden, unstraight contact. He always held back his real needs and feelings for women and thus, found himself in a dilemma. His wife couldn't trust him because he had cheated on her extensively, earlier in their marriage. Their level of contact and intimacy was at a standstill and yet, she threatened to leave him if he had sex with anyone else. Since he was ashamed of his neediness, he would try to hide himself from other females behind a joking and performative facade. As a result, the women that he was attracted to couldn't trust him either. He would bounce back and forth between his acting out with other females and his need for his wife's acceptance and warmth. He was engulfed in that age old incompatible ambivalence of deep need for contact and extensive guilt. Every time his wife expressed distrust toward him, he would act like a sorry little puppy dog, begging for love and forgiveness for being bad. She, in turn, would explode with her held-in anger but never revealed the true depths of her vulnerability and need for him.

When someone is hurt or violated, they mobilize the energy and emotions of the death wish or mortido drive.[2] In therapy, it is important that these feelings of hurt, rage, hate and destruction be vented in an appropriate and cleansing manner. When these emotions are fully expressed and connected, there is a softening and the life instinct (eros, affection) takes over and becomes expressed. Irv's wife would stop short of the life urge and become stuck in the feeling of basic primary distrust. This was her last line of defense before allowing herself to be fully vulnerable and little with him.

Irv, on the other hand, finally expressed his feelings and fantasies to the particular females in his group and to his surprise, he felt great relief. He cried deeply for a long time about the lack of warmth and contact in his childhood home and began to sense his fierce rage toward all women. In time, he will begin to feel enough of his own historical outrage. Then, he will be able to confront his wife on her resistance to feeling the roots of her distrust for him.

I have to reiterate that defenses are created early in life to serve a life protecting service. Therefore, it is understandable why people give up their defenses so reluctantly and begrudgingly. Nobody likes defenses because they can interfere with reality and interpersonal relating, but we cannot just blast them away without allowing for a full, integrative feeling experience. Overloads may develop and there will be random chaotic behavior attempting to alleviate

---

[2] Eric Berne, *A Layman's Guide to Psychiatry and Psychoanalysis* (New York: Simon & Schuster, 1968), pgs. 60-61.

the anxiety of rising core feeling. When both parties are emotionally ready to feel their blockages and deep core reality, they will move into an area of more intense, interpersonal contact and real intimacy will emerge.

FRIENDSHIP, AFFECTION, CLOSENESS

When a person opens up and lets another in, there is the potential for real intimacy, affection and friendship. As one's defenses let down more and more, one can permit another person to enter into his deepest recesses and together they can share in the experience of feelings. A genuine, warm bond begins to develop and they start to care for each other as separate, distinct people. This need for intimate, close human contact is very powerful and if this need is not met satisfactorily, painful alienation sets in.

One young man cries in agony, because no one ever let him in close.

"Let me in . . . let me in . . .

Don't shut me out. Let me come close.

. . . I don't want to be so far away."

He is beginning to make his move to come closer to others and at the same time, experience the feelings of early rejection and isolation.

"Please open up to me . . . Tell
me about your feelings . . . Tell me . . .
Tell me . . . I want you to care . . . I
want you to care . . . "

He breaks out in anger and screams,

"I want you to care about my
feelings . . . I want to share my feelings
with you . . . Please care."

As he jumps up and down, he is getting ready to get closer to other males, something he has longed for all his life. He wants to come closer to the male therapist and other males in his group, but first he needs to feel the pains of his own blocks to intimacy and friendship.

"I want to be someone special,
not just another kid . . . Look at me . . .
see only me . . . want me . . . me, me . . .
Look at me, please . . . "

The little boy inside pleads for contact and affection. He needs his father to look at him, to make contact with his eyes. That's what he needs to feel alive and wanted . . . just a simple affectionate glance from his father. He will feel special and cared for if daddy touches him with his eyes and his hands. If daddy doesn't let the baby boy come close to him, the child may feel mutilated and totally destroyed.

This young man will go on for hours, days and maybe weeks working on these deep feelings and, little by little, he will be making more meaningful contact with males in the here and now. He may be able to express his own needs and feelings more clearly. It pains him to realize how shallow he has been with his previous friendships and acquaintances.

Because groups are made up of people, they display the same phenomena and phases that individuals go through. When affection and closeness becomes a principal focus of individual feeling life, a new sense of excitement permeates the entire community. Affection, contact and opening up to others becomes the arena of group feeling concern. People vary in the relative degree of closeness that they desire and the limits of each person's ability to get close at any given moment must be recognized and respected. If someone tries to get close prematurely, before he is emotionally ready, anxiety will develop and ritualized defenses for coping with fear will become evident.

In many instances, an over-personal individual will make overt bids to get close and make contact, but his symptomatic behavior will effectively keep others at a distance. This is especially difficult for someone who possesses an over-abundance of buried, unexpressed rage. He wants to get close yet, at the slightest hint of rejection, evaluation or negative criticism about his behavior, he may attempt to destroy his love object, either directly or subtly. These objects always try to set the limits of intimacy with the overpersonal individual and, since the overpersonal never is satisfied with meager hand outs, he inevitably gets very angry at his so-called "rejector". When rage is suppressed and displaced, it always acts as a barrier to real contact. Thus, the angry one must learn to accept the fact that others are afraid to get very close to him. When he deals with his buried anger in a real way, then others can run the risk of relating intimately with him.

Most feeling people are very warm, loving and sensual and they can relate productively at various levels of intimacy. This does not imply that they are conflict free. Quite the contrary. The more that intimacy threatens, the more likely that there will be vacillation, ambivalence and self-protective maneuvers. Emotional intimacy involves the willingness and the capability to open up fully and let someone touch your very core soul, the very center of your being. It means knowing someone at the very deepest levels. In this day and age, many people make physical and sexual contact with others and consider this intimacy, but they never quite make full emotional contact. Life is incomplete if one cannot make deep emotional connections with at least one other person.

Since groups are a microcosm of society, they reflect the tendencies of all people and their needs. Everyone wants to get close to some degree, although usually there is some fear of doing so. Distance between people is usually established unconsciously; albeit, there are certain conscious elements involved in all decisions to become more or less intimate or distant.

First, the individual may ask himself, "Whom do I wish to get close to first?". He creates a hierarchy of most preferred to least preferred people. Second, he may make overtures that help define the kind of contact that he wants. Perhaps, he will make explicit statements indicating his desire to get closer or pull back. There will also be a strong non-verbal component to his feedback to others, whether to come closer or move away. Many people will remain silent and play it safe for awhile, before revealing where they are with other people. If someone has felt hurt or injured by someone, he may withdraw from further contact, perhaps even silently reject the violator. Unfortunately, because people do make affectional, friendship choices which follow some sort of selection procedure, some degree of rejection is inherent in all contact.

Because there is both the desire and the fear of intimacy, individuals often will hold back their thoughts and feelings or they may express themselves in mixed-up ways. They may attack or express distrust for past violations or become entrenched in a defensive system of contradictory messages.

If someone is not clear with his feelings, he may do a number of things. He may dump them directly on someone or, he may pretend that he is clear and withhold his mixed-up reactions only to later dump them, outside of the original conflict context. The latter is relatively safe to do, because he can't have his "off the wall reaction" countered and challenged, so his craziness stays intact, justified and fortified. A person who is clear will have very little difficulty expressing himself. But, if he is unsure of himself, he will be reluctant to expose anything for further testing of reality. Many persons are afraid of their own craziness and will defend because of the fear of losing control and connecting to the real sources of their transferences. Detachment, withdrawal and non-participation are the principal defenses against deep feelings, self-disclosure, honesty and reality testing. If someone appears to be uninvolved emotionally, and hides his feelings behind a non-expressive facial mask, then we can be fairly sure that he is holding back his reactions and mixing his here and now feeling with the unfelt past. Plainly speaking, the result is a "pile of garbage" that has to be dumped somewhere. We try to encourage those who are emotionally detached, non-involved and distant to recognize that they have "garbage" and that they can honestly present themselves in a non-dumping way. One can be honest about his mix-ups and express them openly without displacing all over someone. By feeling one's historical pain, one can usually become free of interpersonal blockages and grow to further closeness.

TRUST ME

You push me away
without knowing
but my body
knows.
Fear not, for I will
be there for you.
Trust me, for I am Real.
I can dance with you
in your deepest spaces
and we will truly know
one another.
As we unfold we
are strangers no more
I to your world and
you to mine as
we blend in
full humanity.

The purpose of the Total Feeling Process is to provide a therapy that allows for and stimulates maximum growth and the elimination of the vestiges of insanity. Intimacy is one area of deep feeling that requires careful working through. True intimacy is never debilitating, but mixed-up or contaminated closeness can present problems. The participants must become aware when too much intimacy becomes a hinderance to further growth and movement. When full blown neurosis is present, true intimacy is practically an impossibility. The neurotic who is overpersonal will try to rush into intimate contact while he is devouring his "victim" with unstraightness and multiple, mixed, unclear agendas. He makes his prey feel guilty for rejecting him and yet, makes it so that he must, ultimately, be rejected.

The counter-personal individual sends multiple messages also. He may say with his behavior, "I want to get close, but . . . ". The "but" is the grabber, because it is loaded with pain. He might be saying, "I can't get close, because you will hurt me," or "I don't trust you or anyone". He may have a strong primal based fear of any intense involvement.

Some find it necessary to test others repeatedly to find out if it is safe to come nearer. They are sensitive to the slightest hint of potential danger. If delving deeper into contact with self and others over-whelms these individuals, the relationship and all subsequent contact may become so threatening that the only recourse is disintegration and discontinuation. Flight becomes the only answer.

"I love you—But I'm afraid.
I know you would do anything for me
and when I'm around you, I feel that
bond between us, that warmth and close-
ness, that flow. But when I'm away from
you, I get scared and lonely and feel
so incredibly vulnerable . . . I can't
take it anymore. I want out . . . I'm
sorry. I love you. But I want out . . . "

Most people possess varying mixtures of counter-personal and over-personal traits and will display these traits in circumstances that trig-ger one or the other of these responses. There are others that may show a predominance of either characteristic and their behavior tends to be somewhat stereotypic. One individual found it necessary to return to the roots of his own counter-personal stance everytime the group reached that point of furthering intimate contact.

"They don't want to come close to
me . . . My family . . . the kids . . . the
neighborhood . . . nobody wants to come
close to me . . . Mommy . . . You're all

afraid . . . Oh, My God, you're all afraid.
The whole world is afraid to get close."
Deep core feelings that have a direct connection to intimacy are usually triggered by something in the present, such as an awareness of wanting more affection from the whole group or part of it. Maybe there is the desire to hold someone closely and make full body contact, but there is a reticence to do so for many different reasons. Someone may react when the entire group is locked in a tight, cohesive, feeling embrace. For him, this could trigger the need for his whole family to be warm, close and embracing. A female might fearfully protect herself from touching other group members because she is ashamed of her breasts and feels too unworthy to receive the affection. She may then choose to start her feelings from the present source and trace them back to their painful origins. Invariably, tracking a here and now feeling to its origins always clears it back up again in the present.

Sometimes the pain in childhood is so great that a person will develop an underpersonal[3] orientation to closeness. In this instance, deprivation of warm, loving, close contact is usually total, so he avoids closeness with everyone, even though he is desperate for love and affection. One woman with an unusually painful and traumatic birth and infancy found herself questioning a marriage where she saw her husband a few weeks out of every few months. Up until she entered therapy, she had not considered this underpersonal orientation unusual. Her only major complaints were somatic. Upon reviewing the first week of her life and the underpersonal orientation of her mother, it became clearer to her why she was so "comfortable" with distance and isolation. The following exerpt is written verbatim as the mother described to her daughter the initial moments of their relationship. The underpersonal tone is evident already.

"Mother gave birth 2½ months ahead of schedule due to hemorrhaging caused by the premature separation of the placenta and uterus. Mother spent 5 days in bed before the doctors decided to do a Caesarian to save her. Baby was delivered suffering from fetal distress and doctors were doubtful of survival. Baby was placed in an incubator and was being treated

---

[3] W.C. Schutz, "The Postulate of Interpersonal Needs: Description", *Interpersonal Communication*, Edited by Orr, C.J. and Williamsen, (Iowa: Kendall/Hunt Publishing Co., 1977), pgs. 73-90.

for hyaline membrane disease. Baby was breathing by a respirator and fed intravenously." After 16 days baby was fed by tubes through the nose and spent 4 more weeks in the incubator. At 7 weeks mother held and fed baby for the first time. Baby was released from the hospital at 7½ weeks and finally given a name."

These underpersonal individuals can form harmful relationships where distance is maintained at an unsatisfying, safe, painful cost. A schizoid/masochistic type female may form a relationship with an alcoholic who will fulfill his half of the contract by staying distant while living inside a bottle of booze. Generally, the underpersonal hates himself but may need others to love him while he works insidiously to destroy whatever potential love he may receive. He must turn others against himself in order to confirm his unlovableness. His history traps him again and again.

Avoidance of closeness can be maintained quite effectively if the person can maintain a position of potential antagonism. The posture of combativeness is a stance that has all the characteristics of manipulation and entrapment. One woman gave the impression that she really desired direct honesty and mutual self-disclosure, but whenever she would ask or invite someone to open up to her and share these feelings, she would automatically respond with attack, defensiveness and overreactive anger. Everyone avoided intimate contact with her because she would make herself unattractive on a deep intimate level. She stereotyped herself by being someone who could not receive and give both affection and honest reactions.

Children growing up in underpersonal homes never receive the necessary stroking, fondling and caressive intimacy that leads to feelings of lovableness. Eventually, they begin to feel that maybe they didn't deserve love or that it was their fault, their badness, nastiness or inadequacies that negated the reciprocal expressions and transactions of affection. As a result, they grow up with bodies and personalities that show this lack of warm, close contact.

What a different ring to the dictum: "I love you with all my heart, soul and body, simply because you are my child. You will be able to love yourself because of my love and probably love me back, not because I demand it or you owe it to me, but because I am lovable, too."

Therapists in the Total Feeling Community are emotionally available to all members for deep intimate contact, according to the patient's present capabilities. For most, it is probably the first time in their lives that they have had an opportunity for such contact and the intimacy that develops may become a model for later intimate relationships.

"All during my therapy I had built a certain rapport and trust with my therapist. The spaces I had to get to, the pain I had to feel was easier to reach since I had positively transferred onto him. He became my direction . . . virtually my life line during those early, painful spaces I went through. The times I felt I would never return from those spaces—that I would be stuck back in time—were virtually nonexistent when he was with me. I knew in order to grow I had to feel and integrate the pain but it made those 'hellish' spaces more bearable knowing there was someone who understood them afterwards. We could talk . . . I could integrate . . . there was strength and contact in all of that. It was okay to come out more often and grow and maybe learn to love and be myself after all. I was given something I had never received as an adult or a child . . . genuine caring.

My therapist has never lost faith in me . . . he knows what I am going through. Now I can grow a little more . . . maybe peek out of my shell a little more and make contact with others because I'm beginning to learn the value of people. It's strange how fulfilling my therapeutic relationship has been and how it has taught me the value of what I have in myself."

The Center for Feeling People is not just a therapy center. It is also a human relations laboratory where people can learn, through deep feeling and interaction, new ways of being, relating and behaving. Once they learn how the old ways were limiting and destructive, they experiment, reshape and re-parent themselves into newer, more natural and beautiful forms.

The therapy helps the person to successfully resolve his affectional feelings from childhood so that he is truly free to be himself and live his own life in a completely transformed manner. Close, affectional relationships with others present no problem and he thrives in such a setting. He also learns when it is wise to relate from a distance and legitimately protect himself. He may encounter situations in the future where he will not be liked, accepted or receive as much as he would desire. Likewise, there will be times when he will not be able to fully like, accept or receive someone or something else. This will not alter the fact that he is a lovable, worthwhile human being, capable of giving love and confirmation.

HONESTY

There is always the question of how honest should one be in revealing oneself and to whom. When people decide to open themselves up to others, they have to make some kind of assessment as to how appropriate their actions will be. What will be the reaction when the held back material is disclosed?

One male started dating two females at the same time and was very fond of both of them. At the beginning of the relationships he wanted to tell each one of them about his feelings toward the other female. One female allowed him to express his caring for the other, but the second did not want to hear about his affection for anyone but her. Thus, he developed a norm of honesty with one and holding back with the other. The results were not positive.

A person who is very connected to his core self will not have much difficulty expressing his feelings clearly and coherently. One who is not very clear with himself will express his needs in mixed- up ways, with unclear double messages that confuse the receiver and arouse distrust. Many people who may sound bright and quite eloquent can take a long time to express themselves and still leave the listener feeling as if there is something missing, namely himself.

When the receiver feels a sender's message in his guts, then there is full impact. If someone expresses something and it has no impact, it usually means that he is letting only a small part of himself dribble out. Someone who is boring is not really with you, making honest emotional contact. There are no dull people, only out of touch people. The relative degree of honesty depends on the kind of relationship that one is attempting to negotiate. To be honest with someone involves several aspects. A person will want to be honest if he desires to improve or define a relationship. If a problem needs solving, honest expression of feelings and perceptions can clear up a misunderstanding or solidify a growing emotional bond. Honesty can also be used to further one's own well-being. If someone is holding onto a negative reaction to someone else, he will probably feel physically and/or emotionally uncomfortable. If, on the other hand, he experiences expressing his negative emotion as desirable for him, then he will be freed up in doing so.

Many people feel better when they share what is bothering them with the person that they are having the reaction to. "I express myself to you because I believe that it will benefit both of us or even just myself." If, however, the expression of honesty is met unfavorably, then one may be reluctant to share reactions with that person again. Both individuals will then be more distant with one another and communication will be at a standstill. Usually, there will have to be an element of safety involved before one feels secure enough to open up. He must sense that if he does reveal himself, he will not be greatly punished and that his self-disclosure, if genuine, will be met favorably.

Not revealing a part of oneself can also be in one's self interest. To be too honest in an inappropriate situation or with the wrong person can be self-destructive. It is usually not proper judgment to reveal something that can hurt you or be used as a weapon against you by a hostile party. This happens with the "true confessions" type of honesty, which is not real honesty. For example, one girl thought that she was very open because she would reveal to almost perfect strangers her past sordid sexual escapades. On the one hand, she wanted acceptance for her disconnected past, while at the same time she was struggling to find her identity as a total, feeling human being. It is hard to say whether she was really being honest or just seeking male attention and confirmation for being a hot number. It might have been more revealing and honest to say how lonely she felt and that what she had done in the past was not what she really had wanted to do to get the attention and affection she so desperately needed.

It is difficult to ascertain when it is safe to reveal secret parts of oneself to others. No one can absolutely predict what someone will do with the information and what their reactions will be. It can be devastating to reveal oneself to someone who can't be fully trusted. There isn't a person alive who hasn't done something that someone else hasn't misinterpreted or overreacted to. There is always a risk that one will be misunderstood and certainly, many people have reacted in anger, repudiation and recrimination. So perhaps, it is necessary to temper honesty with good judgement.

In the type of interpersonal contact where deep intimacy is a remote possibility, many people keep everything on a sweet and light level. Deep emotional discourse is not necessary in this situation and the communication is limited to maintaining or promoting the primary purposes of exchange. For example, if two organizations are seeking mutual business benefits, the participants do not necessarily have to like each other in order to conduct their business profitably. For the most part, it is not necessary to share their personal reactions to one another. Difficulty arises however, when personal issues and feelings get in the way of organizational efficiency. At that point, the interested parties may have to either open up the channels of communication and relate more honestly or discontinue their relationship.

When conflict does arise between people and there is no resolution, everyone is left hanging and the aura of unfinished business is deadening to the interested and involved parties. No business, family, group or organization can function well, if it does not create the means of fostering honesty and managing conflict. Many worthwhile projects and relationships have been abandoned because the participants have not discovered the means of honestly resolving conflict, overcoming crises and developing a system of communication that leads to consensual validation of the experience.

There are members of the Total Feeling Community who develop relationships and then decide to start projects or businesses together. Sometimes, one of the parties will step on the other's toes or do something that threatens the relationship and the project. Perhaps, one person doesn't fulfill the other's expectations and conflict arises. When someone feels put off, rejected, hurt or angry, a deterioration sets in and then we have to decide if the whole community should get involved or leave the participants alone to work out their own issues.

Therapy can provide a forum or a vehicle for problem solving and the group can act as consultants or mediators. It has proven invaluable for the injured parties to bring these conflicts before the entire group and allow everyone to identify and bounce off the hidden pain that emerges. There are usually enormous amounts of feeling that need to be expressed and connected.

Honesty and self-disclosure can only be practiced, however, to the degree that someone has worked through and lifted their repressions. In the Total Feeling Process we define honesty in relative terms, according to the range and depth that a person has felt all of himself. Obviously, a person who has spent a great amount of time and energy at his bottom and peak lines of feeling is going to be more open and honest. Someone who has not been to the depths and the heights of his feelings will express himself in a much narrower frame of feeling honesty and his communications will be often symbolic, contaminated and distorted. His fears will move him farther away from reality and alienate him from those with whom he has not been fully honest.

In intimate ongoing primary relationships, honesty is not only the best policy, it is the only policy. To be honest with someone who is vitally important to you, means that you wish to get closer and to improve the relationship. To compromise one's honesty and integrity for the sake of controlling a fearful situation will eventually lead to the very outcome that one wishes to avoid. Those who would lie or mislead with partial truths or omissions will leave others with manufactured fantasies, disordered emotions and imminent distrust for the perpetrator of the dishonesty.

Some people "protect" a partner or close friend from the truth for "fear of hurting them". I think it is important to determine whether the parties concerned can handle the bare hard facts. Honesty of feeling always necessitates the ability to be able to perceive how another is reacting to your behavior. This requires skill and sensitivity. Whenever I am interested in someone and their welfare, I will share my feelings and perceptions with them and then go back and check on their reactions to me. I don't want anyone feeling dumped on because of my "honesty". I try to convey to them that I am interested in their welfare and their feelings and my feedback to them is an important element in our ongoing relationship.

Many times, however, the person one is "protecting" by holding onto the truth is himself. His own fear of the other's reaction keeps him locked into a dishonest facade. In this case, the relationship is usually kept at a certain safe level and true intimacy cannot develop.

In situations of extreme transference, intense anxiety may breed tendencies towards dishonesty. In Freudian terms, a client's internalized parental super-ego may threaten punishment and shame if he acts out his basic or sexual impulses. The patient may make a lover, friend, therapy group or other representations of authority into a condemning parent and his projections and displacements may force him to go underground to seek gratification of symbolic

unmet needs. This is probably the base root of all forms of dishonesty, lying, holding back and omissions.

If a client learns early in therapy about the absolute therapeutic
benefits of honesty, he will make it a daily practice to keep his peers
and authority figures up to date. This way he can allow these important persons to react as appropriately as possible and integrate
his sharings so that the relationship does not self-destruct. Keeping
up to date with everyone and working through all feelings can and
will sustain ongoing communications.

Lying, omitting, story telling and holding back will treat others
as if they were stupid. It is not uncommon when those others start to
sense the unstraightness, that they begin to feel the pangs of interpersonal betrayal and deception. This can only lead to an eventual
deterioration of the relationship and a direct or indirect abrasive effect on the affectional and love elements between the individuals. If
affection, honesty and open communication had been reinforced in
the early home, then an emerging human being wouldn't feel the
need, shame and fear that necessitates the formation of dishonesty.

Chapter 4   The Search Inward and Out

CONTACT

All therapies have, as one of their goals, the removal of obstacles and blockages that alienate a person from himself and others. This alienation is experienced as a painful separation from the core of humanity. We have already stated that a human being is a dynamic system of energies and when these energies are disturbed and distorted, there is a deadness in the contacting function that takes place between people.

Unfortunately, a person may be in the throes of deep powerful pain and distortion and not even know it. Since buried feelings exist on a gut level, they are defensively split from consciousness. As a result, a person may have his nervous system in havoc, while his thinking processes set up delusions and stories to keep him safe and unaware of his core feelings. He may erect a facade or front that is intended to keep himself and others at a distance.

A favorite quote of mine is, "To get close to another's pain and deep feelings is to get close to your own". To stay away from the insides of another human being is rather safe but unrewarding and eventually, will lead to the sickness of non-involvement. For example, take the perpetual joker. The closest that he lets others get to him is to his humor. I once asked a party-time comic what he would be like without his jokes. His reply was, "I'd have to face myself and I don't think I could stand that".

Another man was always angry and gruff with his wife and children. He could only function as a drill sergeant and yet, he longed for the love and contact of his family. His frontline behavior was a barrier between himself and the world. He wanted to succeed as a husband and a parent, but all he could manage was to turn off his loved ones. After initiating therapy, his first few sessions opened him up to his need for his son and his own drill sergeant father. He was then able to go home and spend some very lovely, wonderful times with his wife and children. Of course, getting in touch with and expressing some deep feeling isn't enough to overcome a lifetime of roles, alienation and non-feeling. He knew that he would have to go back to his core feelings, time and time again, until he cleared out all of the historical pain.

Lack of contact and alienation may be experienced by a new patient as a vague feeling that something is missing. The person may not even know that it is himself that is lost, plus all the love and

61

richness of real human contact. Dissatisfaction with one's life is an indication that the contact function is disturbed and one is not making full feeling contact with himself and others.

A non-feeling person is not really "here" in the Now. Only his facade and defenses are available to make contact. Many times the patient does not even know that he is not fully here, Now. His real self has retreated deep into some hidden recess of a particular defensive complex of symptoms or facades. One young woman was not fully "here and now" in total contact. Only little pieces of her were present and dispersed in many different places. She was not grounded deep in her real self; thus, she could not respond to life situations in a realistic, appropriate fashion. The part of her that could respond realistically was buried in an excruciating birth scene where being "here" meant facing almost certain death.

"I felt I was struggling inside a tight cocoon of little space, little air and echoing, terror-filled cries . . . I broke into frenzied screaming and sobs . . . Terror wracked my soul . . . I could only let it rise a little at a time. My rational mind wouldn't/couldn't let go fully. It felt like if I did, if I let that terror over-take me, I would go completely beserk and break into a hundred pieces. I would die. 'My body can't breath . . . I'm going to suffocate . . . God, I'm going to die'.

At this point one of the therapists moved in to assist and started a barrage of physical poking and shaking which helped to loosen up my defenses. Again, I felt a breaking up and a holding on. If I didn't hold on, I would break up into hundreds of pieces. I couldn't be whole unless I felt the smashing into those pieces and yet, I could feel myself still holding on.

In the here and now I can't let myself explode with love or sex or joy. I have to hold on even then. Exploding is so terrifying to me . . . whether in joy or in pain. I feel more pain realizing I can't explode in sexual joy with my husband, the man I love most in the world, because I'm still 'holding on'. I can't explode into the Universe and fully experience the Cosmos because I still am 'holding on'. Will I ever be able to be fully alive and unafraid and free?! Or, will I always be scattered in pieces, not whole, until I'm finally able to let myself explode in terror—and live."

Many times an individual will avoid contact by "acting out" and retreating from the real core feeling. This acting out comes from a lost place somewhere between the old, buried, unfinished feeling and the crises of Now. In therapy, a patient acts out bits and pieces of an unfinished feeling and to an observer, the behavior may seem nonsensical. However, if the acting out is scrutinized closely, a certain logic begins to appear and the part that is unfelt can be anticipated. The therapy then brings those pieces together to form the integrative feeling experience. During the feeling, connections are made and, as the separate bits and pieces come together, the individual emerges connected to his core inner self. He, then, is able to relate to the world from the grounded, authentic self and make real, emotionally honest contact.

Anchoring in the real self is not something that can be accomplished merely by doing certain exercises, such as those borrowed from Bioenergetics.[1] The body may become grounded by the energy flow through the legs, but total grounding only comes from an emotional connection to something that has been buried, albeit exerting its influence on the body, mind and behavior. Reconnecting to those disowned parts creates a true grounding in reality. The past or disowned parts are brought up to date and the person is "Here and Now".

Many people are frightened of the Total Feeling experience and they tend to defend by rationalization. They will say, "This is all in the past and why should I dredge all that up?", or "What good will it do to go back—I'm only interested in the present and the future". What they do not understand is that their fear of the past exists right now and that fear is real, even if not felt. Those pains are here and now because they are being dragged around in the present and preventing people from living fully and making contact. One may not be aware of it or feel it, but the past is exerting its insidious influence right at this moment. And the point is that its effects can be felt and undone by experiencing and contacting it fully in the Now.

If we are somewhere in between now and then, we cannot bring ourselves to cope with the problems of existence with full, clear energy. Many individuals, therefore, find themselves not ready for the emotional demands of life. Work, love, parenthood, creative productivity all require an emotional preparedness that few people

---

[1] Alexander Lowen M.D., *The Way to Vibrant Health* (New York: Harper and Row, 1971).

possess. Most individuals try to tackle these responsibilities before they are emotionally capable or sufficiently up to date with themselves. Society pressures them to work, succeed and be intimately involved in sustaining love relationships. They look, act and perhaps perform like mature, responsible adults, but inside, they are children. Once they go back and feel those old feelings, they will be better able to maintain a grounded contact with themselves in the present. Maybe this is one of the major goals of any therapy—to help a person get himself back.

"I used to think that I would be happy and fulfilled if I had cars, money, position, children and a house, but now all I want is me. That is the best I can hope for. If I have me, I'll be more than happy."

The following is extracted from a session with a young married woman with five children. She has been in therapy for about seven months and has begun to get in touch with feelings of impending doom, death and alienation. I have included this feeling experience in this section because it demonstrates some of the feelings of alienation and aloneness with their historical antecedents, that lie at the root of an unfinished gestalt.

She is stuck and lost between her past and present. As the feelings begin to rise, the pains of repression begin to crumble and her reality pours out. She then presents a living panorama of the tragedy and possible eventual triumph of her life. The reader will witness how a perfectly beautiful and innocent child can be hurt deeply and the patterns of alienation stamped in at a young age.

"Don't leave me here . . . I want to go home . . . I don't want to stay here . . . (I'm in school for the first time) . . . I don't know anybody and nobody wants to be my friend . . . " "I don't understand why nobody wants to play with me . . . Don't go!! . . . There is nothing to do here, no friends . . . There is never anything to do . . . My mother is playing cards, daddy's working . . . All I have is a maid!!! . . . People who are not mine . . . not all mine . . . I can't stand to be alone . . . Daddy, I need you to play with me!!! . . . "(loud crying) "I'm not special anymore . . . You don't love me anymore . . . Where do I go now?! . . . I never fit in anywhere . . . I try so hard. Why don't you hear me??!!! . . . I want to be with you always. I don't ever want to let you go . . . You never took the time to know me! . . . I'm your little girl, Daddy. There's no other like me . . . I'm Yours!!!" "I hurt, Daddy . . . I hurt . . . Nobody likes me out there!! Nobody ever takes the time to ask what is happening . . . I just want you to stop and listen . . . (heavy crying) . . . I feel so dumb, trying to get you to listen to me . . . Everytime I feel stupider!!! . . . I feel like a God-damn Ass!! . . . I feel like an ass!!! . . . I don't fit in my own house, anywhere!!! . . . How could you leave me out here all alone??!! I'm nothing but an outcast . . . I can't get in . . . Daddy, I Need you!!!! . . . "

For the next hour, the patient cried deeply and profusely, clean-ing out those disturbing elements of childhood. She did not com-plete this feeling during that one session, and the events that caused these problems will need continued refeeling and connecting. However, she is well on the road to resolving many of her feelings of separation and alienation and establishing meaningful contact in the here and now.

IN SEARCH OF

I named this section "In Search Of," because searching is what many therapy pilgrims are unconsciously doing. A father seeks a lost son, the son seeks the missing father. Mothers try to connect to the daughters they never have had emotionally, while the child will close down and build a strong defense against the parents' emotionally "not being there" for them. Much patient behavior can be explained quite clearly once we locate and decode the symbolism in their actions. Every scene and episode that is disconnected can be understood as some kind of search for something that was absent or lost.

We must remember that a basic premise of deep core feelings is that *a baby remembers everything.* You cannot lie to or fool an in-fant. His/her body psychoneurologically records everything exactly as it happens. Parents may try to "con" a child with deceptions, but the body always records the truth. You may confuse the head with stories and collusions but the body will eventually reveal what actually has occurred.

The patient in therapy always expresses these past inconsistencies and illogical half-truths. It is all he knows. When the therapist spots the missing pieces, he intervenes and the patient melts into the feel-ing truth.

In the preceding section, the woman in the experience eventually regressed back even further and connected to the disconcerting circumstances surrounding her birth and her true ethnic identity. The mother who had raised her was not her natural mother, although she was born to her real father and another woman of a different ethnic background.The patient was formally adopted into the legal marriage, although she was never told that she was adopted until the age of 22.

All during her childhood she did not feel "right" in her adopted mother's arms. She was finally told about the adoption, although the father insisted that her real mother was of the same religious and ethnic background. This last piece of information did not coincide with what she was feeling at a deep core level. Something inside of her knew that she was living a lie and that her father was the perpetrator of that lie. When I confronted the blocked feeling, she exploded into powerful longing toward her real mother, whom she experienced as of a different ethnicity. It seemed incredible to her until she remembered that she had known her mother intimately while being inside of her womb for nine months. She had felt and experienced her mother's moods, thoughts, and racial history.

The nine month gestation period covers millions of years of adaptive development and the neonate is sharing this experience with the mother who is the child's partner in this miracle of creation. Is it any wonder that an individual would carry a biological memory of this significant event that had been shared with her real mother and carry into adulthood the intuitive knowledge of an unfinished gestalt that laid the groundwork for a deep core feeling connection? Man's basic needs and search for integration and completion can lead him in many different directions.

Although man, basically, is on a search to find himself, he also wants to find a suitable mate to share and enhance his life. His desire for a cohesive, warm and loving family might further motivate him in this search. A longing to be connected to the Cosmos and to humanity in his own unique way, might also lead man into more profound realms of exploration. Likewise, as a social animal, man seeks identification with certain groups for mutual support, ideology, protection and gratification. And finally, the economic and success motive can be a driving force in human endeavor. People need meaningful work that helps them to be creative and expressive.

Many times individuals have searched for the recognition of these basic needs and run into difficulty because they attempted to meet a particular need out of synchronization. For instance, a young woman impulsively gets pregnant, marries and becomes interwoven with a mate before she has had other basic needs satisfied first. Twelve years later she may discover she is out of touch with who she is and wants to search and find her real self. This may put her into conflict with her family.

Similarly, a young man may become heavily involved with a female and because he never was fully in touch with himself, he cannot cope with the demands and intimacies of the relationship. Many marriages have faltered because the people were not prepared emotionally to meet the demands that accompanied satisfying that initial urge for closeness and a "loving family." Men have worked at jobs that they have hated, but stayed because they had to support a wife and kids. One dentist hated working on people's mouths, but his parents and his wife expected him to be a dentist, irregardless of the fact that he wanted to pursue a career in music. His need to placate his wife and parents in order to receive whatever "goodies" he was getting from them, led to him leading a life that was not his own.

So, it comes down to the fact that one can't search and satisfy one need if another has not been sufficiently resolved. To attempt to meet here and now needs, while ignoring the bubbling undercurrent of primal, unresolved pain, will only lead to frustration and more pain. To attempt the satisfaction of realizing a soulmate or love relationship without first reclaiming oneself emotionally leads to further insanity. "Love is not a sentiment that can be easily indulged in by anyone, regardless of the level of maturity reached by him. All man's attempts for love are bound to fail, unless he tries most actively to develop his total personality, so as to achieve a productive orientation."[2]

This productive orientation cannot be underestimated because it lies at the core of man's soul. If this growth motivation is weaker in some than in others, it is because of early stifling influences. Maslow called on psychology to not restrict itself with man's weakness and

---

[2] Fromm, Eric. *The Art of Loving.* (Holt, Rinehart, and Winston, New York, 1956), pg. VII.

deficiencies but to acknowledge his motivation for growth as well; not only to be concerned with his defenses but his growth.[3] The Total Feeling Process works through the blockages and the defenses against continuous growth. If people have themselves in a full feeling fashion, plus can support and take care of themselves, then they can find suitable mates, professions, jobs, spiritual fulfillment and appropriate membership in constructive social groups.

If a person is disordered, however, and not in touch with his early, unmet needs and feelings he may marry and become involved with someone who is very similar to the disordering, missing parent. Then he will try to make that person into the kind of loving, safe parent that he never had. This struggle to get the early need met usually fails, because the unsuspecting partner is often resisting and refusing to become the lost, loving parent. If individuals become involved in a deep core feeling way of life, there is a strong chance that they may find themselves and be real people for each other. But this takes dedication and hard work.

The following is an example of a disordered search.

Irv: "I've got a lot of need coming up . . . I'm searching again . . . I used to sleep it away . . . fuck it away or go running . . . I'm doing that now. I'm not really feeling it." (Patient then starts to cry heavily)

"Oh, God! I had some flashbacks. . . When I was little, I used to lie in bed and think what it would be like when my mommy and daddy died . . . I just couldn't think about it . . . it was too devastating! I don't want you to die!!" (Pain is wracking his body, fighting to get out. He's crying very heavily)

Don't leave me . . . Don't leave me!! . . . Please!!!" (patient falls down face first)

"Mommy . . . Mommy . . . Oh, God . . . I'm still searching!"

"Mommy don't leave me!!" (he begins to beat the punching bag)

---

[3] A. Maslow, *Toward a Psychology of Being*, (Van Nostrand, Princeton, New Jersey, 1962).

"So much inside of me, I can't get it all out!" (He is working his blockages; he cries more)

"Mommy . . . Mommy . . . I've got anger in this!!!" (He picks up the punching bag while crying. He squeezes bag, raises it up higher, and then drops it. He stands up and stretches his arms out sideways while some of his anger comes pouring out.)

"I'm finding that when I am not with my wife, I feel needy, but when I go out to date or during the day to see females, I don't feel the deep glow inside." (Whimpers)

"One time with them and I don't want to be with them anymore. I'm in more pain than before." (crying and holding his head)

"I don't get anything . . . They can't touch me . . . my heart . . . my heart is dead. I don't want to be like that!!"

Therapist: "Stay with what is happening to your heart."

Irv: "I don't want to get involved . . . no claims . . . I don't want to get close. I'll look for an affectionate girl but then, soon, I get turned off. I don't understand it."

Therapist: "Talk to the girl."

Irv: "I need so much: to feel important, wanted, desired . . . Don't hurt me!"

Therapist: "Feel how your body is fighting against the pain." (he starts crying again, touching on his bodily defenses.)

"You won't let them get to your heart."

Irv: "My heart is full of scar tissue and pain. I don't let anyone get to my heart. It's not just girls. It's everyone. I hurt so much . . . (deep crying) . . . I'm a big mouth little boy who pushes people away. I can't let people get close. It hurts me . . . I don't want to keep my heart closed."

"I'm angry because there is a part that people could really like. I hate this horrible part of me . . . "

Therapist: "Go against the wall and push."

Irv: "I'm tired of pushing people away." (He pushes with all his might while crying angrily.)

"My obnoxious pushy part won't let people see me."
(He then goes over backwards on a stool to open up his encased heart. The therapist physically loosens up the blockages around the heart and more deep feeling emerges. Blockages in the stomach and legs are loosened by pressure and feeling is coming deeply.)
"I have a lot of pain stuffed down deep. I keep it there so I don't have to feel it."
As Irv keeps pushing against the wall, he eventually connects to the realization that he used to push his mother away so she would not stifle him with her need. The patient is now at a deep level, although not bottom line. These feelings will help him to better understand his behavior and enable him to go deeper, again and again, in order to be fully free of his here and now dilemmas and disordering.

I mentioned the term "pilgrim" before because of the searching aspect of all therapeutic endeavors. As we have said, everyone is in search of something, whether it be enlightenment, the real self, relief from suffering, better communication, more feeling, etc. The list is endless. The Total Feeling Process uses deep core feeling as the road that the traveler takes to get to his inner self. Each person starts his journey in a different place and has to go back over old, unfinished spaces to get fully where he is heading.

A young father may have to feel all the things he never said or did with his own father and his son before he can feel the urgency of searching for and being himself. One father began identifying with and feeling all the pains of his own son and then, one day, he erupted with, "I gotta be me." All the years of searching and trying to reach his own child were fruitless because his own childhood had been so thwarted. Without himself, he had nothing to give but parental orders and admonitions. What he really wanted to be, with his son, was himself. So, there can be no real search until one recognizes that he must find himself.

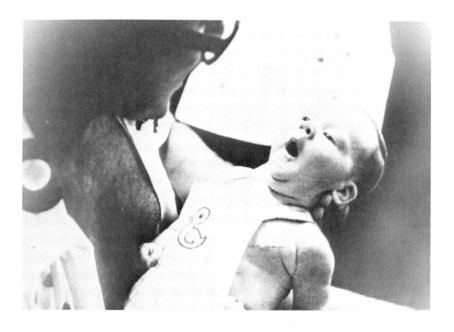

"Sometimes when I look into your eyes it's like the whole universe opens up . . . and I come to know fully who I am. I'm your Daddy and you're my boy . . . "

A mother in her forties felt alienated for seventeen years from her daughter. The more she felt of how alienated she was from her own mother, the more she realized the roots of her alienation from her own offspring. By the time that the woman realized what had happened, the daughter had built up the same kind of defenses with her. The same suspicions and mistrust that she harbored toward her own mother were being visited upon her by her child. She tried to get her daughter to relate to her in an honest, feeling way, but the years had wrought their damage and the woman was left with the knowledge that without full feeling, there can never be lasting and loving contact with anyone.

LOVE

In the previous sections we discussed how alienation from self and others leads to a painful separation from the core of humanity and an unfinished gestalt on a deep core feeling level. This, in turn, inhibits intimacy, affection and meaningful contact between individuals. One area we have not yet delved into is the element of love, which, of course, is a necessary precursor to intimacy. In this section, we will explore the elements necessary to develop a full loving relationship between two or more feeling individuals.

Love is all powerful. Much of ancient mythology and religion espouses that the Universe and Life were created in love, for love and by love. It was believed that the Goddess Venus was the deity who brought the beauty of love to one's soul and that one was then awakened to all the glories of the Universe. In many Western religions today, it is the Virgin Mary or Holy Mother who is worshipped as the vessel or divine bearer of God's Holy Love in the form of the flesh of Jesus Christ. This Holy Love has become the backbone and nurturance of Christianity, a moving social, economic and political force of the Twentieth Century.

This love drive, urge or need exists in all forms of life. Since all the elements of the Universe are interdependent and follow a pattern of attraction/repulsion, some means of guaranteeing cohabitation and survival must be found. Thus, survival, procreation and continuation of the species depends on an optimum expression, utilization and satisfaction of love. This love is the driving force that guarantees and enhances life. It embodies endearment, devotion and protection of that which is precious and sacred.

Love is so great a basic need that people will expend untold energy and effort in securing and holding onto a prized love object. People have sacrificed their lives and fortunes for love and its loss is felt as a great sadness or grief. The literature abounds with examples of "star-crossed" lovers, sacrifice and agony. Religiously, the sacrifice of Jesus' life on the cross was, perhaps, the supreme gift of love for mankind.

It is written in Luke[4] "Thou shalt love the Lord thy God with thy whole heart, and with thy whole soul, and with thy whole strength, and with thy whole mind; and thy neighbor as thyself." This is the great commandment that gains eternal life. It is as if this total love transcends time and space and passes well beyond ordinary ego boundaries. Here we have love at its grandest and fullest expression and capacity. This supreme commandment attests to complete and unrelenting love and the optimum expression of it. This is perhaps the supreme height to which love can soar and strive.

Imagine having the innate capacity to love that completely and all encompassingly. If we are capable of loving to that degree, why is it that so few people can really feel and express it as powerfully? And here lies the true tragedy: we were not allowed to. *The forces of repression not only hold back pain, but they also stifle the full development and expression of love and affection.*

If one asks a man if he can love, of course, he will reply in the affirmative. His words and beliefs confirm this. But can he really feel it to the depths that the commandment prescribes? I doubt it. In fact, most people experience only a faint glimmer of their full capacity to love. Unfortunately, repression and the holding back of feelings does not stop with anger, fear, need. It goes on to include full loving expression as well.

In the Total Feeling Process there comes a point when neurosis begins to slip away and the first full feelings of love begin to emerge and be expressed. A young trainee therapist put it this way:

"Wow! I really feel love for all of you and it's incredible. I never felt full, deep love before . . . Yet, I thought I had. Oh, my God! I've never really fully lived or felt all of life . . . I'm

---

[4] Confraternity of Christian Doctrine, *The Holy Bible*, "St Luke, Chapter 10, verse 27". (P.J. Kennedy and Sons, New York, 1950). Pg. 90.

just beginning to really live and love and I'm 30 years old. That's it . . . I never knew how to love . . . "

Most feeling people admire others for their level of feeling and tend to pull back from those who are defended and out of touch. The more that one is capable of feeling, the more loving he is and usually more accessible to other feeling people. When it is said that someone does not know how to love, we are witnessing the intrusion of neurosis on their affectual capabilities. Neurosis hinders and diminishes love. It can even destroy it. A neurotic may have an incredible internal capacity to love, yet seems to always make a mess of things.

Many people come to the Total Feeling Process incapable of maintaining a love relationship with a spouse or mate. They are often angry, discouraged and resentful. Yet, they are searching for something within themselves and with their partner that has been held out for centuries as an ultimate goal with another human being. It is our belief that romantic love is not just a dream but a practical goal anyone can attain. It takes hard work and intense committment, but it can be a reality.

What is romantic love? Poets, for centuries, have been defining and re-defining it. It is like the first blush of spring when the sky and the Universe open wide and everything is pure and innocent. The lovers cannot get enough of each other. The joy is so great—smiles abound and passions are insatiable. Exploring and getting to know one another is pursued with intense desire. The loved one wants to always be with the partner and the world takes on a new meaning.

There is a Hebrew legend that in heaven, God divided one soul in half and put each half in two partners. Through fortune and adversity, those two half souls would eventually unite and be divinely blessed for all eternity. This kind of love matures and grows and remains as permanent as the stars.

Immature and neurotic love cannot endure. Neurotics may stay together out of guilt or religious sanctions, but this is a neurotic's way of wasting his life. The love sours and drains the individual of vital life energy and creativity. If love is to flower, it must be sustained by constant growth and feeling contact. Stagnation ultimately leads to emotional death. It is the juices of emotion that keep the river of love constantly flowing. When boredom or discontent creep in, it is an indication that one is not feeling enough. Lack of feeling leaves one nowhere.

As soon as one partner in a neurotic relationship starts to feel and connect, he/she begins to realize what has been missing in their contact. If one partner decides to live a full feeling life and the other one does not, something will have to give or change. Either the person who has begun to feel will go back to living a compromised existence or he will extract himself and try to feel more on his own. The Total Feeling Process has helped to sustain and solidify some beautiful relationships and to dissolve some destructive ones.

A successful love relationship needs to have both participants dedicate themselves to their own full feeling growth and then to place the growth of their relationship as a top priority. Let me clarify this point, because it is very important and represents a workable formula for success. A non-feeling human being will always pick a non-feeling partner and love neurotically. An emotionally clear person has felt enough of himself to know what kind of partner is potentially right for him. The chemistry has to be there, of course, but it has to be connected to sanity. A grounded human being puts feeling first and is able to judge what kind of partner is going to emotionally enhance him.

"I knew from my own therapy what kind of woman was going to help me be happy. I could practically see and smell her. I also knew when I would be emotionally ready for a serious relationship. I had cleared up and resolved a lot of issues with women and I knew what emotional qualities and values would be compatible with mine."

"When I met my wife-to-be, we decided that a full feeling relationship would be the first priority. Certain values had to be realized and actualized in order for love to work. These included: dedication, committment, feeling and complete concern and respect for each other as separate, equal and unique human beings."

THE PROCESS OF LOVE AND FEELING

Generally speaking, there are several steps that people go through in forming relationships and falling in love. I will attempt to outline six distinct phases and phenomenon that overlap and interact with one another: (1) preparation, reassessment and purging; (2) search and captivation; (3) negotiation and transference; (4) committment and rededication; (5) permanence and fidelity vs. temporality and (6) regeneration and solidification. We can assume that one, more or all elements of the entire six stages may be present in different quantities in each stage. The reason for the specific labeling is because there are certain characteristics that dominate each particular level.

In the first phase, an individual will go through either a conscious or unconscious preparation for a serious relationship. Realistically speaking, a child growing up in a particular home will be prepared for a particular kind of relationship whether it be self-actualizing or neurotic. In a feeling home, where the family members are clear and solidly cohesive, this person will be real enough to know what constitutes a productive and beautiful love relationship. Unfortunately, this rarely exists in a neurotic society.

In therapy, by feeling one's own deep and high transpersonal emotions, one prepares himself for whatever future steps he may take. This would involve growth and dedication to the areas of creativity, occupational expression, family and intimacy. By feeling and integrating all of his past hurts, he will be correcting the perversions that were set upon him as he grew up. This period of preparation helps him to work through his past—evaluating, cleansing and purging it—thereby, helping him become very clear in discovering the right kind of soul mate. Thus, therapy becomes a training ground for the perfect family life.

In stage two, as patients clear out their excess neurotic debris, they begin to feel absolutely ready to seek out and fall in love with an appropriate mate. This process emerges from a grounded, clear place, free of deprived, neurotic, symbolic need. It is my contention that a clear person can and does find the perfect soul mate. Love becomes a blending of individual universes, the full flowering of spring and cosmic energies, bathed in the essence of purity and innocence. Spiritual and biological chemistries meet, mix, and merge into the total sensation of falling "head over heels." This love is total and absolute with little or no doubt.

Each partner delights in captivating and being captivated by the significant other. Absolute total immersion and full sexual exploration absorb the lovers. Passion is at its height; although not at the price of practicality, rationality, and pragmatism. No clear person ever falls in love for physical reasons alone. There needs to be some modicum of emotional, educational, physical, economic and social equality along with other common bonds.

It is not uncommon in this phase for individual identities to merge with one another without each person becoming lost. Each individual may explore, investigate, and absorb the other's transcendental causes and social interests. This latter phenomenon only exists for a short period, however, as each separate entity emerges and forms a synthesis and the creation of a new entity. As the relationship becomes more intimate and moves into deeper stages, the lovers begin to negotiate and transfer positively or negatively onto each other.

As this third phase begins, they are investing heavier amounts of emotion into one another. At this time, they begin to explore their territorial limits, boundaries and prerogatives. They may begin to experience tangling and untangling from one another's primal issues. There is a considerable amount of testing that goes on and the deeper in they delve emotionally, the more they discover that the relationship has specific themes that reveal their particular bottom line breaking points. Through experiencing the clashes of each other's history, they are provided with an avenue for discovering themselves in newer, often deeper, ways. As each crisis is resolved, the couple becomes more and more unified through the medium of feeling resolution.

Cohesion, however, exists right alongside the ever present threat of total disintegration. The relationship grows stronger by weathering certain emotional storms as each partner becomes highly involved with the other. Through this process of involvement, feeling and observing, each member discovers the rules, expectations and common experiences that help one to survive and grow with the other. Couples who cannot get beyond this stage usually fall apart because they cannot feel their way through the transference of histories onto one another. At that point they can either separate, divorce, or remain emotionally distant at the level of insanity that they have reached and failed to resolve.

As love grows, each person gains new delight in the knowledge of the other and stage four reveals each partner's strengthening and further committment to the relationship. As each new feeling is experienced and the past becomes resolved, there is rededication and reconfirmation of the incredible value of the emotional relationship. Sex is still important but it takes on a different meaning than it had in the beginning of the relationship. At the onset, intercourse brought the couple together to explore deeper levels of communication. Now sex is still wonderful but there is the added incredible joy in the knowledge of how the relationship has grown and what they have accomplished.

It is important that earlier elements of basic trust be investigated and worked through in this, as in each of the six stages. Marriage itself can take on a transcendent, cosmic meaning, as the partners become truly joined in an emotional sense as opposed to the superficiality of legal, contractual obligations. The basic trust harkens back to the earlier days, when both individuals were in total love situations with their own parents. If that ancient trust triad and it's pain has not been fully resolved, there is no way that this couple can be fully together. Thus, there can be no future, unless the past is fully cleaned up and each partner sees the other for who he/she really is.

In stage five, questions of fidelity have been worked through the previous four stages and have reached a new level, as the partners fully realize, welcome and accept the total permanence of their relationship. Their family communion transcends all time and space and assumes the proportions of universal immortality. In this phase, love is fully stabilized and lasting.

But all is not necessarily idyllic. Human beings are fallible and no one is ever completely free of the past. Minor disasters still provide a vehicle for discovering new ways of being oneself. However, fighting no longer has that life or death quality that it once had, due to the heavy contamination from the past. Conflict is merely geared towards understanding how the relationship can work better. The test of permanence reveals the couple's stamina and stability to withstand the influences of outside, crazy forces. Other people's insanity can at times pull and tug at the internal stability of this love relationship, but serious threats are no longer operational.

Finally, the formation of a family adds a new dimension for the solidification of this nuclear unit. The addition of new little members adds stresses and strains, while at the same time bringing with it pleasure and the joys of regenerated family life. Love becomes a unit of people related by blood, feeling and common experiences. Libidinal energies become reorganized and dispersed among the new members. In other words, it is not just a man and woman loving one another, but now they share and give their love to their children, as well. This offers new challenges and a chance to explore and expand new and old identities. There is a reciprocity of appreciation as mother and father confirm their love for one another, while at the same time confirming their new offspring.

Chapter 5 Soul and Ethnicity

SOUL AND ETHNICITY

Kol Nidre

As the mournful wails
ascend from the bowels
of my soul, I come to
fully know who I am.

No longer obscurred by
the frivolities of my guilt,
I am brought back by
my cries to my Center.

Forsake me not, for I
have run afoul of the track.
I have drifted away from the
mainstream of my identity.

But now I return again from
whence I came to that
natural ground that sets
me deeply in the firmament of
all that is good and holy in the
tradition of my genes.

Welcome home o sailor
tossed on the rough seas
of life. Back to the joys of
knowing who I am.
The burdens lift as I
slide into identity.

Identity, identity, identity
To know full measure
and to appreciate that which
I was borne into.
The truth doth set
me free, for I am naught
but a child who innocently

stumbles and arises again to
walk the paths of giants.

SOUL AND IDENTITY

The Total Feeling Process cannot be explained without some references to the soul of man. The soul serves as the pure center that steers man in all his endeavors. It is the immutable spirit that is basic to all human nature and serves as a connection between man and the Cosmos. It is as if the soul has a life of its own before the implantation of the sperm cell with the egg. Perhaps it is the entity or essence of life that survives before birth and after death.

The soul also seems to transcend the boundaries of the ego and inculcates the moral and emotional side of man's nature. It is his vital part, his source, heart, meaning and essence. The soul represents the fervor and very depth of core feeling. It is the basic human personage. It is who we really are before the contamination of neurosis.

In its basic form, the soul is all good, pure and innocent and totally vulnerable to the influences of life. As each soul is totally unique and individual, it can be shaped to take on all the characteristics of its environment. It is like a piece of clay, basically clear, but waiting to be molded and formed by the myriad influences of its genetic history. Since the soul is open and nondefensive, it can either be nourished or injured. The more it is subjected to the threat of violent births, unfeeling parents and other sources of pain, the more it has to use the resources of the mind and body to protect itself. In other words, the soul can be stunted and forced into extreme hiding by an unfeeling environment.

When we say that a man has soul, we mean he is expressing himself from the core of his being. We can relate to this core essence and respond to him with warmth and affection. If a person has been subjected to incredible repression as a child, he will cover up and maybe even lose his basic core self, his soul. In essence, he becomes something other than what he really is.

For example, Black people, because of exploitation and slavery have been denied access to their history and their manifest destiny to contribute fully to humanity. The Jews have been denied deliverance from their dispersion and subsequent reinstatement to the Holy Land. When someone or any particular group has been

81

denied what has been an integral part of their soul, they will build up a head of steam fueled by tension and anger.

When some need has to be held back from gratification, the intensity for satisfaction becomes greater or the need becomes reverted and re-channeled to some other goal. In the case of the individual, he may need to "forget" what has been done to him. But where does the memory go? Freud used the term "unconscious" to imply a particular area of the psyche that retains one's entire psycho-biological historical experience. Depth psychology implies that all one has to do is unlock the doors of the unconscious and buried thoughts, feelings and fantasies will come streaming out and be made available for conscious re-evaluation, insight and the modification of one's life.

We may speculate that some people have been so damaged at such an early, primary level that they may never recover their true nature. The Total Feeling Process, however, operates under the positive assumption that the core soul of most people can be reached and they can emerge into full feeling human beings.

To become who one really is, is no easy matter. The path to selfhood cannot be willed. It can only be arrived at by intensive, deep feeling work. Over time, the soul, the center of that unique feeling self, develops some very outstanding characteristics and these characteristics are dependent upon the essence of the two families that have merged their gene pools to form a totally unique human being. A person's soul is the combination of one's racial and ethnic inheritance as well as the specific birth locale with its traditional mores, and idiosyncratic specialness. All these factors combine to shape, mold and create a distinct emotional impression on the individual.

Every culture, nationality and local neighborhood has a unique soul of its own. This soul or identity encompasses whatever is loved and cherished by the collective unconscious of the group. To understand and make this identity conscious, its elements must be fully felt and appreciated. Thus, a "soul sister" refers to that characteristic of Black womanhood that exemplifies the full meaning of all that can be appreciated as Black. She is usually admired by her contemporaries because they can pick up and relate to her unique qualities of "soul."

Soul may represent the finest flowering of each group's man and womanhood. New Yorkers have developed a distinctive identity that charaterizes the quality, pride and shared experiences of New

Yorkers. The same can be said of Philadelphians, Bostonians and Kentuckians. We refer to the soul of the South when we sense a certain rhythm and manner of living that is indelibly imprinted in the hearts of Southerners. The song "Country Roads" relates to specific feelings and experiences that characterize West Virginia, while other people may find the same song touches at the core values of home and man's emotional ties to the country earth. Thus, all people are tied together by common bonds of identification that emanate from a core self. (Perhaps we are all bound together by the common bonds of the human soul, and the reason we cannot feel this bond fully is because of the influences of repression in our early primordial development.)

For example, a man is the culmination or product of his mother's and father's families. Elements of each family have contributed to who he is. The same is true of his wife's family. She would be an outsider to his family history, as he would be to hers. They are, then, at the beginning, strangers. They could come to know and experience each other and their heritage through feelings. Slowly, their separateness and boundaries would begin to disappear and they would become a new entity, combining all the unconscious elements of their respective families. Their children would be raised in a spirit and atmosphere created by the combination of their family essences.

The following is an example of an intense feeling experience which resulted in the opening up of an individual to new levels of understanding himself and his family, plus a greater empathy for his partner's background and history.

"I suddenly became aware that one of the women in the group reminded me of my dead grandmother, my father's mother, whom I have never met and who died when my father was only 11 years old . . . Oh, Grandma, I miss you. I never knew you, but you are just as real to me as any living person. You are living on inside me. A part of me is you.'
'You were a real performer . . . real
show biz . . . that ham is in me . . . . It's a
part of me . . . All of us are alive today
because of you. My poor Daddy! Oh, what
pain he has felt with no mommy . . .

83

How can my wife be a part of this?
She is not a part of my family, Blood
is thicker than water . . . '

Later in the day I felt the difference between myself and my woman dissolve.
As she experienced some of her own family
history, we became one, unified, together.
I heard and accepted all of her and felt a
new bond with the spirit of her family."

A few years ago, I was delving into myself and kept coming up
with feeling connections that answered the question, "Who am I as
a human being?". These experiences, which I later termed identity
feelings gave me a much stronger foundation and understanding of
myself as a unique individual. Every feeling was distinct yet had
certain elements in common. I would return and re-experience a
certain period of my life, usually about the age of two and earlier. It
seems that my identity as a person was very much fixed by that
time. What I needed to feel as an adult, was the goodness of that age
and the purity of my identity. This identity or soul was predeter-
mined by four thousand years of Jewish ancestry mixed in with the
richness of German Catholicism.

These circumstances of my birth were a unique combination of
my diverse ancestral heritage plus the surrounding environmental
influences of being born into a completely impoverished ghetto existence. I believe that the circumstances that surround birth have a
great influence on the type of birth that one has. When we explore
the historical circumstances that surround one's birth, we are exploring an area of intense emotion, the core factors of which may
determine one's identity for the remainder of life. It would seem
that most of the in-depth investigations of birth have paid particular attention to the actual circumstances of the birth itself,
without recognizing that this event is not independent of the
historical surroundings of the infant.

We are all accidents of birth and the cultural and ethnic heritage
into which we are born will determine the kinds of choices we may
be influenced to make within the parameters of our own cultural
expectations. I believe that a true ethnic and religious conversion
occurs when one comes to terms with, accepts and integrates what
he truly was at birth.

Many people convert to different persuasions as a reaction against early pain. They believe that if they "try on a new hat," they will feel better. In some cases, they do, but they are not really free of the past, at a deep core level. Even if one should feel all the negative feelings of earlier pain, he still needs to feel the buried richness of his own ancestry. When that richness is finally recaptured and re-owned, then one is fully in touch with himself, his soul and identity.

One woman, some time ago, had converted to Judaism from a very painful Catholic past. She had the belief and hope that being Jewish would bring her the love that she so desperately needed. Becoming Jewish was her way of escaping from the reality of an early painful environment. When she began to delve deeper into her feeling self, however, she would start to cry from her Catholic origins. She would plead, "Hail Mary, full of Grace, save me. Save me, please . . . please."

Most religious conversions are an attempt to get at something that was missed the first time around. Reclaiming what was really missed in one's own background is a rich, satisfying and unifying experience. The Total Feeling Process helps convert people to feeling and they re-convert to who they really are. If one can reclaim and feel good about what they could have been, had it not been for early trauma, then they can accept and feel proud of their Jewishness, Catholicism, New Yorkerism, Southernism, Americanism etc.

THE DIALECTIC PROCESS

When a client enters therapy, he usually gets in touch with his negative parental introjections. In other words, he begins to feel all the negativity of his early and later life. He recaptures the desolation, emotional deprivation, deadness and lack of warmth, affection and contact. It is a period of intense hurt and pain. Most psychotherapies deal with this deep core pain in some fashion or other. To stop here, however, is lopsided. Similarly, other therapies are incomplete in the opposite direction, only stressing the positive feeling experience.

Frederick Leboyer[1] speaks of the baby in the womb being overtaken by Natural Law, which stipulates that everything must become its opposite. The Golden Age phase of gestation must give way to the

---

[1] Frederick Leboyer, *Birth Without Violence* (New York: Alfred Knopf, Inc., 1975).

negative phase of painful imprisonment and birth. Maybe we can call it the Law of Reverse Effect, which implies that we cannot have a positive without a negative counterpart of equal charge. In this way we maintain a precarious balance. If the pendulum swings one way, its own weight will bring it fully back the other way.

The Total Feeling Process is not a mechanistic therapy that emphasizes only the positive or negative aspects of deep core feeling. It follows a dialectical model[2] that sees nothing as final, absolute and sacred. Everything is in an uninterrupted process of becoming and passing away. There is an endless ascending from the lower to the higher levels of feeling and vice versa. Therapy must proceed from the negative to the positive in a continuing cycle and re-cycling process. The girl who hated her own Catholicism was also hating and disowning a part of herself. When she finally begins to love who she is, then she will be able to accept being a real Christian and all that means in its true essence.

We know that the dialectic process of our therapy integrates the mixed-up, internal contradictions and culminates in a product or person that is greater than the original parts. It is these powerful, internal contradictions that create the full feeling explosions that transform and integrate people's lives. The intensity of the way a person stays locked inside his own head is matched equally by the feeling he is holding back in his stomach. When the feeling is finally released, the deadness in the face and voice tone will be replaced by an equal aliveness in speaking and looking.

IDENTITY, PREJUDICE AND FEELING

It becomes evident when working with deep feelings that patients deal with psychic material (core feeling) that is barely touched upon by traditional procedures. It becomes apparent that while for some individuals the birth experience is the most significant feeling, for others the deepest roots of human identity may lie in the realms of the racial and ethnic unconscious. Many clients, when faced with the prospect of feeling their deep ethnic, ancestral roots, encounter internal, early childhood resistances. It is as if, as Erikson puts it, "these tormented

---

[2] V. Lenin Lenin, *Selected Works, Vol. 1* (Moscow: Progress Press, 1970).

souls suffer from a painful identity consciousness or an identity in torment."[3] This occurs in certain groups because somewhere in childhood it was learned that it was not okay to be Irish, Catholic, Jewish, German, Black, etc. That which is painful must be denied.

Pride and identity, for some ethnic mentalities, is used defensively and defined in relationship to some other perceived malevolent group. Unfortunately, man's interactions with his fellow man have led individual groups to form psuedo-species, sub-groups, countergroups, special interest groups, survival groups, religious belief groups, and other social forms that are geared, in some cases destructively, to man's need to affiliate, segregate and solidify his identity. In Adlerian terms, the need to be superior manifests itself in some individuals affiliating with certain groups that profess a divine manifest destiny hinting that other psuedo-species are somewhat inferior or deserving of disenfranchisement. Erikson states that, "Man has a deep seated conviction that some providence has made his tribe or race or caste, and yes, even his religion 'naturally' superior to others."[4]

This reactionary position is untenable in an age where it is absolutely necessary for man's survival and economic sustenance to understand one's fellow man. And yet, we still find those who defensively wish to segregate themselves and others and erect barriers, that in a mythological sense, purport to maintain the survival of a particular sub-species.

I postulate that as certain societies get older, there exists the decaying tendency to protect one's own vested interest at the expense of the pain and needs of other people. The human mind exists in the error that ignoring other people's pain will somehow guarantee one's own survival and sanctity. However, we really cannot survive on this planet with each sub-group arming itself against the possible and potential incursions of other alien groups.

I also postulate that within every individual who manifests some invested interest in protecting himself from the potential harms of other groups, there lies some hereditary or psychological manifestations of that particular group which he is afraid of feeling in himself. This would mean that within every Jew is a potential Nazi, and what the Nazi fears is the Jew inside of himself. For those who

---

[3] Erik Erikson, *Identity Youth and Crisis* (New York: W.W. Norton and Co., 1968).
[4] Ibid.

would fear the Irish Catholic, the German, black, or white, I would say, "Attempt to discover your own identity and then emotionally, attempt to transcend your own barriers that exclude other groups." Pride is a wonderful thing, if it is not accompanied by some kind of abject fear and lack of acceptance for other kinds of people.

Working with many different ethnic cultures, I have come to the realization that there is a unique kind of collective guilt for just being who one is. It is hard to live down and overcome the myths and negative stereotypes of the past. Therapy provides an arena or vehicle that allows differing individuals to come together and experience pride in their own heritage, while at the same time, examining the defensive roots of each individual's prejudices. Those who would only focus on their own ethnicity to the exclusion of feeling the internal dynamics of other peoples,' rob themselves of a liberating experience, for to deny someone else is to deny that same feeling part within one's self.

It seems there is a common suffering of all human beings. We all need to feel included to some degree and hate exclusion. This is not strictly experienced as non-admission to certain clubs, hotels and neighborhoods. To be cast out of someone else's heart is the supreme painful insult. The Jew can revel in the magnificence of the German accepting and loving himself, while at the same time, being drawn closer together in a common bond of love and affection. To be deprived of that opportunity is a crime against humanity. A self-actualizing person will attempt to discover any growing hints of prejudicial tendencies in himself and will see this as a marvelous opportunity to explore something within himself which could ultimately bring him closer to other types of people.

There has been a recent trend in our society for many of us to go back and discover, historically and emotionally, our own painful and brilliant heritages. The television movies, "Roots," The Holocaust," and many other media presentations, were all aimed at rediscovering the souls of these people and hopefully making some kind of connection with a common humanity by which all of us are joined.

The human race is the *"SPECIES."* All the subdivisions have been created out of the realities of early tribal life, which necessitated a "survival of the fittest" mentality. Perhaps, it is too messianic to hope that mankind could somehow find a solution to accepting his own sub-species identities in other people. It is difficult, however, to expect to bridge the present gap that exists between American blacks and whites, South African blacks and whites, Israelis and Palestinians, Irish Catholics and Protestants, etc., given the present means for dealing with ethnic and cultural disparities. I would hope and suggest that those barriers that create warfare and tension be lowered by developing a psychological orientation for each faction to feel the Other that exists within the Self. I would hate to think of killing someone who exists as a part of me because I would be committing partial suicide.

It is in my own self interest to see that others survive in the full acceptance of who they are. This is the only way that we can prosper together without shame, guilt and identity panic. Contemporary survival demands that we transcend mythological tribal differences and tune into the special common humanity of all people.

In summary, a therapy group can be a unique family or cultural unit, based on the incredible power of emotional bonds. It accepts, investigates and explores ethnic and cultural characteristics but at the same time, draws people into one powerful and beautiful humanity. Segregation, discrimination, prejudicial practices, do not serve to solidify man's emotional life; they are merely temporary mythological expediencies. The search for the self inevitably brings each person in contact with his own defensiveness against feeling all parts of himself and those same parts in other human beings.

BASIC INSECURITY

It probably is safe to say that all human beings harbor implicit and explicit prejudices. The liberal-conservative continuum is a valuable way to explore which side of the coin is currently up with each person. There would be many liberals and conservatives who would forthrightly deny that they are prejudiced in any way or form. Perhaps, they see themselves clearly operating from a position of love; even though to observers of the opposing persuasion, this would be hard to believe.

The question arises,"Are certain hate groups motivated by love and vice versa?." It seems fair to assume that all people are motivated by buried feeling and the overt manifestations and symptomatic expressions of those feelings determine how these individuals relate to themselves and their fellow man. It would seem to me that we need a further appreciation and adoration of the human species as a whole with respect and confirmation for each individual human being's rights to personal dignity.

The explanation for prejudice seems to lie in a certain basic insecurity in one's position in life and that can only be traced back to some horrendous pains of self-denial in childhood. For if one is insecure because he has been denied the right to his identity, he will grow up either denying his own identity, defending it exclusively, or perhaps even deny and threaten the identities of other human beings. This is the tragic insecurity of our times. The job of a transcendental therapy, as I will develop later, is to allow a person to become fully who he is in an ethnic sense, help him accept those denied parts of himself, and then transcend his own boundaries to feel and empathize for all of humanity. He is, at that point, fully aware of who he is and dedicated to helping others become who they are in an ultimately non-defensive way.

We must remember that we cannot have slavery, deprivation, and annihilation without some sort of whiplash effect that not only affects the victims but the perpetrators as well. The world needs to learn that in order for one people to be fully free, all people must be free to be themselves. This means that the advantages and privileges accrued to one particular group must be made available for choice or rejection by all groups. This applies to the problems of therapy as well. If we, as individuals and therapists, find it difficult to work with a certain type or class of people, it is incumbent upon us to discuss what blockages we have to doing so. This should not be read as an impossible demand for therapists to work with anybody and everybody. But it does encourage and challenge those in the helping professions to continue working on themselves in order to overcome their own blockages and inabilities to relate to certain people.

All individuals need some sort of guarantee that there will be some emotional peace in their life. This planet survives on the precarious hope that warfare and killing will not break out and destroy us all. We exist as if we are on the perilous ledge of a volcano. Tensions that exist between groups of people simmer and smolder beneath the surface, always threatening to break out. The need for harmony is intrinsic to the creative capacities of the human species and prejudice is an ever present threat to this precarious balance between war and peace.

Since prejudice is rooted in the fear of being harmed, human beings will typically fall back on several mechanisms to deal with an impending threat. Individuals or groups will either fight, submit or flee. Subconscious forces will determine how a person distances himself. There will be attempts to control, ghettoize and segregate, based on threats to ethnic survival. One may discover fear of racial dissolution of ethnic stock, contamination of varying sorts and, with the possibility of so much intermingling, a loss of group identity followed by loss of allegiance and the ultimate destruction of the race.

I have already stated that the roots of prejudice are insecurity, fear and the anticipation of injury. Since all humans internalize, on the deep primary level, the negative introjected images and stereotypes of different ethnic groups, to overcome these prejudices requires several steps. First, it is necessary to cognitively renounce the denial that one is prejudiced and to recognize that on a deep sub-conscious level we all have fears of other people, both rational and irrational. Next, we must incorporate our own desire to do something positive with the recognition of how difficult that may be. This will hopefully lead to a letting down of our own psychic barriers towards understanding and contact. Third, by developing a positive desire to draw oneself into the emotional realities of these other groups of people, we will be allowing others inclusion rights into our emotional life, thus, immediately coming to terms with our own exclusion behavior. And finally, we can deeply feel and abreact the introjected image of the other while owning the previously disowned, negatively internalized part of the self.

I believe that feelings are intrinsically associated with the breakdown of harmful beliefs and a better existence can only be realized by the entire human race if there is an introduction of new information that shatters mythical stereotypes and facilitates more feeling integration for all people.

Chapter 6 Destructiveness

There are certain values that are placed on different kinds of feeling experiences. Some individuals think that feeling the fullness of transcendental realities is crazy, while others might consider forms of sado-masochism and self-destruction as mad. When carried to ridiculous extremes, I would agree with both sides. For instance, where a psychotic is experiencing a form of transcendence without being grounded, we would definitely have to consider him to be crazy. The same is true in the area of the sado-masochistic perversions. A rapist who goes beyond the realms of full passion and inflicts physical and psychological harm on his victim is certainly acting out a perverted need.

Just as we will examine the sublime in transcendental realities, let us also take a look at the strong tendencies in the opposite direction—the strain of destructiveness that runs through all people. This includes the harmful forces that people inflict on themselves as well as on others. These forms of destruction are present, to some degree, in most people.

But we are not only referring to the extreme or pathological forms of destruction. We are also concerned with how destructiveness operates in typical everyday life. We feel it is necessary for clients to feel and fully integrate not only their peak and transpersonal realms of feeling, but also to resolve the negative sides of their personality. Most clients are grateful for getting in touch with both kinds of feelings. To connect to all parts of one's self is to become a little more free to be one's natural flowing being.

Clinical psychology tends to view sado-masochism in the extreme, such as the sexual perversions. For the most part, it neglects the destructiveness that is part of everyday life and, in many cases, enjoys some support by society. Consider cigarette smoking. All scientific evidence has proven conclusively that cigarette smoking is hazardous to one's health, yet people are still engaging in this form of self-destructiveness, more so than ever before.[1] The body-mind split is particularly evident in the cigarette masochist. He will rationalize his behavior every time, "Oh, I know that it is harmful but I just can't

---

[1] Public Health Service, *Report on "Smoking, Tobacco and Health"*, Publication No. 1931. (Prepared by James L. Hedrick, Ph. D.)

relax without it." He completely denies the adverse effects of excessive nicotine. It seems the supposed pleasure principle always wins out over good sense (reality principle).[2]

The same can be said for other varieties of masochism. In food, drug and alcohol abuse sado-masochism is a prevalent force. The masochist will go out of his way to satisfy his urge toward destruction. For example, the obese food addict will not delay gratification because delay causes pain. Instead of feeling what it is that the food represses, he puts off the greater satisfaction of regaining a lost part of himself and eradicating his addiction, and thereby, loses an opportunity to increase his self-esteem. The price that the sado-masochist pays for this immediate gratification is to become hooked on his displaced libido object. The repetition of this compulsion becomes the ingrained habit of self-destructiveness.

The patterns of sado-masochism are many and the Total Feeling Process aims to help people get in touch with how they "do themselves in." It is very difficult for any therapeutic program to completely control destructive behavior and it may be quite undesirable to do so. But we have found that certain behaviors have to be confronted and eliminated because, as resistances, they do hinder and slow down the Total Feeling Process and the search inward.

For example, we encourage people to give up smoking when they enter the program. Cigarettes are alienating to deep feeling and contribute to an already overloaded, armored body. The nicotine numbs the cilia in the trachea and makes it virtually imposssible to "breathe up" deep core feelings. We have found it necessary for some patients to spend hours coughing up mucous and phlegm accumulated from years of smoking before their bodies can be freed up to feel at even the lightest level. Most individuals who have come into the Center's program have given up cigarettes gladly once they have discovered them to be a deterrent to feelings.

Extreme overeating is not quite as simple a matter to eliminate, since eating patterns are usually established right after birth.[3] When a child is restless and nervous and showing obvious signs of emotional pain, a mother may intuitively notice this situation and

---

[2] Freud, Sigmund. *A General Introduction to Psychoanalysis*, (Washington Square Press, New York, 1960), pg. 363-365.
[3] Hannig, P.J., Ph. D., Hypnosis and Group Process in the Treatment of Obesity", *Hypnosis Quarterly*, 17 (1972), Nos. 1, 2, 3.

become concerned by the child's condition. She will then try to quell the child's symptoms with food. The child learns, eventually, that food relaxes pain and will come to the mother to feed more often than is necessary.

Obesity may be the price a child pays when the mother attempts to symbolically respond to an emotional pain. Later, because of our society's emotionally repressive orientation, he will focus his attention on the problem of obesity and away from the real need for a caring mother. This may result in a frantic search for "cures" for the overweight condition. A symbolic solution for a symbolic need may be why many overweight people, who try to lose weight through sheer will power, only gain it back again in a short time.

When the body is in a state of discomfort, an individual will usually take learned steps to subdue the hurt. If we turn this physical/emotional discomfort into an emotional release, the person won't need to overeat. Unfortunately, the obese individual has so much pain inside that he can't seem to get enough feeling out to get real relief. The fat itself serves as a hinderance to fully releasing the feelings.[4] The amount of fat that a person carries on his body is a measure of how much self-destructiveness he is enacting. Thus, we see the formation of obesity as a unique character structuring of body armor and destructiveness.

One female patient stated:

"I used to think I ate when I was bored, but since therapy I've come to realize I unconsciously eat to keep feelings down: a lot of Mommy hurt, buried so deep beneath my layers of fat and food."

Most early destructive influences are felt deeply and dramatically in the earlier stages of the Total Feeling Process and many major issues and problems in living are cleared up. Severe and noticeable neurotic traits are changed due to the power of erupting feeling connections.

---

[4] Hannig, P.J., Ph. D., *The Psychology and Treatment of Obesity"*, (Unpublished Ph. D. dissertation, Heed University, 1973), p. 108-172.

Eventually, as sickness diminishes, self-actualization proceeds and the individual comes to know who he really is, through a series of strong core identity feelings.

As time goes by and self-actualization proceeds on to transcendental realms, the client begins to discover even subtler hidden defenses that hold him back from greater realization. As he feels these subtle influences from the past, he begins to fully accept that continual feeling defines him to be, "always in *Process*, always *Becoming*." He is an unfolding creature that wrestles with small and large impasses. By doing this he comes to know his nature that has its foundations in the innocence and purity of childhood.

To draw a parable from the Bible, Jacob wrestled with God and prevailed. God thereafter changed his name to Israel, which means, "Man who wrestles with God."[5] People who wish to grow, in a sense, wrestle with the divinity inside of themselves. I believe that we were meant to do just that: struggle with our debilitating behavior in order to find and feel ourselves to the core!

DISTRACTIONS

There is a very difficult principle, rule or value for people to learn when they first enter therapy: self-destructive distractions from self will always take over if the person does not place his feeling self first. The cardinal rule for the elimination of emotional disease and the attainment of self-actualization and self-transcendance is that *feelings come first*. The top priority in life is feelings over distractions. Jobs, money, spouses, lovers, houses, degrees, etc., of necessity, must take a back seat to feelings if the self and its recovery and actualization are to be realized.

This way seems remarkable, but there can be no compromise or one's humanity will be reduced to the petty struggles of endless distractions. Feelings do not compliment life. Life *is* feeling. One cannot connect fully to life without fully experiencing what is occurring at any given moment, feeling in a deep core way all of the momentum of that moment and sharing that in a feeling significant way with others in one's life.

---

[5] Confraternity of Christian Doctrine, *The Holy Bible*, "Genesis" (Chap. 35, verse 10-12)

This is what always surprises me about feeling people. They know the value and power of deep core connected feeling. You don't have to convince them. They will not get into any so-called growth and therapy activity unless it has as its end result, the deep, full feeling, connective experience. If working with dreams, gestalt, meditation, movement, etc., does not ultimately lead to deep feeling, then they would rather not waste their time.

People who have experienced the benefits of deep core feeling are usually dissatisfied with light, unfinished feeling. They learn that there is a drive to finish a feeling gestalt. Anyone who has not felt deeply enough or completed a feeling experience may feel edgy or even weird. When the feeling is completed, they will be relaxed, happier and more in contact with themselves and others.

One female in the program was behaving very self-destructively on her job. She would push herself and her feelings way back in some dark corner and act out a role that she thought she should be doing. In some way she must have measured herself and found herself to be lacking in who she was. She would end the day with her head spinning and dreading to go to work the next day. She denied herself all day long and when she got home to her husband, she could not be herself with him either, because she was still in her head from the job.

Unfortunately, many people compare themselves to others and compromise themselves by trying to be what they think others would like them to be. It is as if there is some performance criteria for being human. I see these traits in Total Feeling patients and know that they are not relating to the world from their hearts, but from their heads. The head is always loaded with expectations and "shoulds." When a person finds out that he is really very valuable for being just himself, then he can become free to be just that, himself. The following are comments from members of the Total Feeling Community.

Robbi: "A fully feeling way of life is an emotionally 'no holds barred' way of life, wherein people can relate to each other without the contamination of the past. My own desire to be fully feeling is the main quest in my life. I am pushing myself to greater depths of feeling and honesty in all my relationships. I am constantly questioning my motives and listening to my own physical reactions."

Eve: "My life is centering everything around feelings. My feelings are first and of upmost importance. A feeling way of life is living and working in a feeling environment and spending time with feeling people in my leisure. At this point in my therapy, I have no outside distractions. That is really the only way if I want to grow. I remember a time when I had many outside distractions and when I look back now, I realize just how crazy it was."

Ernie: "Until I had come in contact and experienced these feeling forces inside myself, I had not known what it was to live in a feeling way, to feel someone or something fully or to be really alive! I could not experience real joy or sadness or a real sharing of myself, until I could feel and trust the heart and soul and spirit that was buried deep inside me."

Don: "The feeling way of life is sort of a complete lifestyle. Every second of everyday I try to be aware that my feelings are definitely operating, whether it be subtly or directly. When you lead a feeling life, your heart is open and can be easily touched."

In therapy, it is common to see individuals compulsively behave in ways that naturally precipitate crises after crises. These crises can lead to further tension, neurosis and chaos or they can be instrumental tools in furthering one's feeling growth. In most cases, these episodes serve the purpose of providing the internal tension that untimately leads to a full cathartic explosion and connection to the real sources of disaster. An unresolved feeling must be superimposed on the external environment in order to trigger off the full feeling. Therefore, external stimuli serve as important triggers of corresponding buried feelings and issues. Whatever is not fully felt will work its way to its external counterpart and create all the old conditions that will lead to feeling, either in a symbolic or a full and meaningful way.

DESTRUCTION—ITS ROOT CAUSES

Many destructive acts in everyday life are perpetrated blindly, out of ignorance and just plain stupidity. Their root causes can lie in gestational or violent birth experiences. If a neonate is subjected to cruel birth circumstances, he or she will develop masochistic tendencies later in life. The acting out of early pain will continue throughout life and assure habitual, repetitive characteristics if a feeling connection does not bring closure.

To test this, examine those things that occur in your life that seem to always happen regularly. Perhaps, it is a distasteful event that comes back, time and time again, to haunt you and always causes pain. Maybe you feel that there is nothing you can do about it, and that you are a victim of unforseen forces. Unconsciously, you may set up these instances of misfortune and not even know it. It's like being helpless in the face of adversity.

Yet, these circumstances of malevolent fortune can beset you simply because you were helpless as an infant in the face of excrutiating pain. In order to complete an old feeling, an old gestalt, you compulsively put yourself into situations where you have no control. I am not referring to those instances that are purely accidental or due to natural causes. But, if one examines repetitive, painful behavior closely, it becomes evident that some individuals receive an inordinate amount of bad luck. I do not believe that it is unreasonable to assume that people make their own luck and misfortune.

The following is an example of one young woman's relationship with a mother who practically destroyed her in the womb and made her early life miserable with paranoid religious fanaticism.

"My mother was afraid of men and considered sexual intimacy sinful. It was something to bear in guilt and pain to please men who were all evil. She was 'married' to God and made all my natural drives seem dirty and sinful. She made me feel as if I was the most horrible little girl in the world because I had a vagina. Her constant reminder to me was that she prayed every night that God would save my soul."

"In order to survive and get anything from her, I completely rejected myself. This eventually drove me to three nervous breakdowns and the escape route of existence as a drug addict. She made me feel guilty for just being alive."

"My father was unable to offer any support at all. He wanted a boy and treated me as one: throwing me up in the air, boxing me backside my head and using his 270 lb. body to pin me in wrestling matches. After he had inflicted enough torture to induce tears, he would pull me to him and try to be friendly. I never knew when I could trust him. As I delved deeper into myself in therapy, I discovered that my boyfriends, father and brother symbolically became the instrument of my mother's contractions on my frail body (she was in labor over 30 hours.) I would always get into situations where I would arouse physical anger toward myself, just to reenact that early life and death scene."

"All my life I had desperately needed a warm supporting 'mommy' to love me. Since I couldn't trust males due to the sado-masochistic relationship I would set up with them, I would try to get that love in subtle lesbian ways with other women. As my mother has ruined me with men, I had to symbolically turn to 'her' to try to get the love she never let me have. I found my life was a muddled mess and violence and unhappiness stalked me wherever I went . . . "

"Over the past couple of years, I have recovered a lot of the lost me by feeling the old pain and I am now free of drugs, holding a very responsible job and relating well to people. My mother still thinks that I am in the throes of hell and damnation, but in fact, she is the one who is really crazy. I see how she used to make me believe that she was really OK and that I was the nut. I felt crazy and acted it. She is crazy and doesn't even know it. I guess that is what saved me: the fact that I felt and knew my own insanity. My mother has had to build a crazy superior world in her head to flee from her own real painful feelings. I had to feel my insanity first, before I could connect to the horrible truth of what happened to me when I was small . . . "

"Yesterday, a horrible fear began to rise inside me. I began trembling in terror and found I couldn't go to group, because I was afraid that people there were going to poke and prod me. There was just no hope that I could ever make it. I couldn't even go home, I was so scared of someone prodding me to death. My head knew in reality, there was nothing to fear but the feeling wouldn't leave."

"At two o'clock in the morning, I went to the Center and before I knew it, I was writhing on the floor in extreme agony. It felt as if my chest was being crushed. I couldn't catch my breath. I kept gasping and choking, fighting for air. It seemed as if my screaming went on forever; I felt I was in the midst of my birth . . . When I came out of it, I felt a lot clearer and I was able to move closer to my boyfriend. But I knew that fear and mistrust were not all over. I would have to deal with that pain, again and again, before I could function as a full female. Even now, I can feel myself withdrawing a little bit again and not trusting those that I depend on for love."

"I was nearly crushed to death at birth and treated harshly as a young girl and I guess it's very hard to let myself ever be that vulnerable and dependent again. It's going to be a long road back to recover the me that was never allowed to be."

THE SADIST

Because every chronic suffering act must combine an element of collusion with a sadistic element, for every victim there must be a perpetrator of the crime of injustice against him. The sadist is the colluding partner who has earlier been violated and turns around and punishes his would-be violator. He gets great delight or satisfaction out of hurting his victim, although later, he may experience great remorse and guilt over his monstrous behavior. The sadist must have power over his victim to get some form of compromised, symbolic love and at the same time be able to control the victim's power to hurt him.

In cases where paranoia sets in, the sadistic behavior can take bizarre and extreme forms. One can speculate that Hitler's vendetta against the Jews and other non-Aryans was an attempt to rise above his own early pain and obscurity. By destroying other people, he could defend against his own early infant fear of being destroyed. If you are the destroyer, you eliminate that threat to your own existence and thus, become stronger by the act of persecution. All sadists have been brutally damaged emotionally as very little children and in their sickness, they must destroy others who are outside and separate from themselves. Thus, they externalize and project their pain onto their victims.

Sometimes we may consider a theory of opposites, whereas what is apparent on the outside has its diametric opposite on the inside.

Within every persecuted victim is a brutal introjected, persecutory opposite. It is the task of the Total Feeling Process to bring out the hidden opposite parts and let them be discharged on the right subjects and in the safe atmosphere of therapy. Here is a case in point:

Poor Robin always wanted a beautiful girlfriend and finally he met Dina. He was overjoyed. At last, all his hopes and dreams were coming true, or so he thought. He was very frightened, however, by women and felt very inadequate.

Dina wanted to be a good girl for him and, at the same time, take care of his needs. She tried very hard, but somehow would always send him into a rage and he would beat her up. For awhile, she would learn her lesson and try to be a good girl for him again. Things would go along smoothly and then another great eruption would occur and he would beat her once again.

Everyone would feel sorry for poor Dina and wonder why she would stay and live with such a bastard as Robin. No one could see how Dina would subtly antagonize Robin in a completely innocent, naive way. He would be seen as crazy and she would be regarded as stupid. Dina's friends would tell her to leave him and Robin's friends would sympathize and advise him to control his temper and not be manipulated into such anger. They vowed they both "loved" each other and did not wish to be parted. After all, everything was fine *most* of the time.

Dina did not consciously want to hurt Robin and he did not want to hurt her, even though, in the midst of their struggles, they acted as if they wanted to kill each other. One has to look at the hidden rage inside people like Robin and also at the subtle destructiveness in Dina. They are both frightened and feel inadequate and yet, at the same time, they must defend the fragile baby inside from further incursions and insults. They need each other desperately, because they cannot run the risk of being left alone. Being alone and abandoned is a dread for sado-masochistics. So they must become violent in an attempt to hold on tightly to their love objects. Control must be maintained at all costs. The root problem is that they were not loved in a full productive fashion by both parents when they were small. As a consequence, the feeling of love is a very difficult emotion to handle.

Sado-masochistic elements are present to some degree in many relationships and, although the masochist may win the moral battle, he usually loses much needed self-respect and respect from others. The victim role is never envied but it does elicit sympathy and guilt from others. The sadist or aggressor never really feels victorious, because somehow he is not quite sure how he has been manipulated and provoked into being crazy. He, too, is seeking intimacy but somehow never quite makes it because he can never fully trust the power of the victim. He loses the moral victory and never quite achieves his real goals because of his circuitous methods and attempts at control. It is only by each feeling the deep core elements of their respective pains that clear contact can be established and destructiveness eliminated.

Chapter 7   Paranoia and the Perinatal Influence

PARANOIA AND THE PERINATAL INFLUENCE

As this book unfolds, we can see how the Total Feeling Process examines the way people fail in life and live only partially. We are also demonstrating how deep feeling and the careful working through and releasing of symbols can change lives dramatically for the better. I am including a section on paranoia because of my own interest in this disorder and its importance to the reader. It continues the theme of destructiveness and, in some cases, shows a comparable resistance to treatment as does the sado-masochistic disorder.

The paranoid can manifest both masochistic and schizoid tendencies as part of his symptom picture. In most cases, he is disconnected from his true core feelings and behaves as if his mental constructs are, indeed, facts. Rogers[1] sees therapy as a continuing process where the client enters therapy at some point and changes in ways that move him through seven stages of growth. The paranoid personality may be viewed, according to Rogers' stage one, as being rigidly structured in the constructs he forms about himself and his world.

He is deeply removed from his own internal immediate experience and may be only faintly aware, if at all, that he has any deeply buried pain that is controlling and affecting his life. He has practically no awareness that he has any problems and yet, he can be keenly observant to spotting the problems of others. He will even act as a "therapist," under the guise of helping others, to avoid facing his own pain.

Most of his attempts to "cure" others are usually veiled behaviors to hide from his own truth. The "helpee" in this situation is vaguely aware that the "helper" is acting out his own defensive hidden agenda. The true tip off that one who "plays" therapist uses in order to avoid his own pain, is the quality of insensitivity that accompanies his quasi attempts to help others. Stylistically, he acts cold, unfeeling and may be inappropriately cruel when trying to help someone. Symbolically, he may be trying to control the "helpee" or imitate the power he envies in authority figures, in order to gain the approval of others.

---

[1] Carl Rogers, *Client Centered Therapy* (Boston: Houghton Miflin, 1971.)

When he escapes from his feelings, the paranoid retreats into his head and conjures up a mixed-up conceptual system that hides and denies his intense rage. This rage must then be re-routed through his head and displaced onto others. One patient had a particularly difficult time breaking into feelings and ended up "dumping" a lot of symbolic anger onto one of the therapists while adopting the role of "playing" therapist himself in order to avoid his own feelings. His own unresolved issues with his parents and his inability to feel deeply kept him locked into a mistrustful misperception in the here and now.

"When I spoke to you the other afternoon, I wasn't able to really express my feelings about you. But when I saw you carrying on with Carol during the group, I knew that my feelings were valid . . . You have a need to be a Big-Strong-Therapist Authority and you've set yourself up in a position where it is quite hard to reach you. You come across as the 'one' who has all the answers . . . I also feel that people in your group are afraid to see you and let you know how they feel about you because it would be too threatening."

Interestingly enough, most paranoids find it very difficult to confront and test reality in the here and now. They usually "share" their feedback behind one's back or via written letter (as in the above case.) They would rather live with their delusions than the validity of their projections.

Because a paranoid must concentrate energy onto an observable or imaginary target, he makes his deep baby pain defensively inaccessible while projecting this pain onto an external "them." He fears feeling the agony of being a baby when he could not know that a "them" existed; thus, when he is in the throes of his escapism, he usually believes that all the sources of his troubles are in the present. The person who recognizes that his hurt is buried and part of his past is usually in a much healthier place. The one who makes his historic pain inaccessible to himself has restricted himself to the realms of insanity.[2]

---

[2] In therapy, we advise clients of the feasibility of establishing a regular periodic pattern of feeling deep core emotions as a means of staving off the insanity of non-feeling. We have learned that those who take too many breaks from their early therapy will have more episodes of insanity. That is why patients who come back from family visits, where they weren't washing out the pain, are crazier than ever. Sometimes, the home visits are so overwhelming that individuals have retreated very far from themselves and it can be quite difficult to get them back to feeling. Others have so much feeling coming up that they cannot wait to hit the floor. The first type is the more problematic, because so much pain has been inflicted, that feeling becomes too frightening for them and they need to defend more.

By nature, the paranoid is supersensitively suspicious of the intentions of others and tends to misinterpret and impugn their motives over quite trivial matters. He imagines and manufactures danger when it does not exist and will manipulate a situation into being a hostile symbolic representation of his earlier prototypic deprived environment. The world becomes menacing to him (as it was when he was small and weak) and as feeling reality breaks down, he is dominated by what he is not in touch with. Projecting all unresolved issues and themes onto the outside world, the paranoid repeatedly shapes the external environment into situations that match completely the pain of his childhood.

At some level, the paranoid tries to create the safety and acceptance that he did not receive when he was small, helpless and unable to influence his destiny. Unfortunately, if acceptance is actually present, he contaminates it and turns it into present hostility, in order to recreate his earlier cold, unloving environment. Everything that is attempted, backfires on him. If he seeks love, he destroys it with his usual contemptuous, suspicious style of relating. "I can't trust your goodness. I can't trust you loving me."

Another characteristic of the paranoid personality is the suspicious way he handles feedback. He can't let too much data get to him because it would mean that he has to give up control. Encounters with a paranoid personality are usually distasteful and disagreeable because of this lack of receptivity. He tends to argue and disagree with everyone, because he can't have his own way. In effect, he is a walking temper tantrum that never fully explodes to relief and resolution. Although his interpersonal style is destructive, defiant and inappropriate to the given situation, he will rationalize his need to create a hostile environment over and over again.

The paranoid personality communicates with a subtle destructive message and, as a result, paranoids have difficulty in establishing close trusting relationships. Most clear people are sensitive to his manipulations and can either confront him on his behavior or withdraw and break contact. If the confrontations are successful, the paranoid may break into the feeling and connect it to its real source, thus, freeing himself to relate clearly in the here and now.

Unclear people usually can't help getting sucked into being a bad parent with the paranoid individual. It is necessary to be somewhat involved and genuinely supportive of the suspicious paranoid and yet, sufficiently detached and clear to see what he is doing. Because he clings tenaciously to his rigid ideas and sets up defenses that are hard to breach, the paranoid makes it relatively easy for people to reject him.

Perceptive people will see that the paranoid does have a chink in his armor and will recognize that the real person inside can be reached. But to care for him and provide some type of relief from his peculiar kind of suffering, people have to pay a very high price. They have to stick by him, no matter how much he projects his unreal "trips" onto them. And paranoids are always suffering even though they may not recognize it. Their denials and externalizations usually always catch up to them. A lie of the mind creates a boomerang effect with the truth usually coming home to roost in the midst of tragedy. Because he is preprogramed to fail, the paranoid cannot avoid disaster as the past returns in disguised forms to haunt him, time and time again.

Let me go into more depth as to what a "trip" is. Imagine that you are feeling warm and concerned for someone and your behavior and actions are consistent with and match completely what you are feeling. Now someone whose perceptions of reality are distorted by unfelt primary pain, misinterprets your behavior and intentions. He superimposes onto you a displaced, symbolic, painful past struggle. He claims that you are cold and disinterested in his welfare and it is your true intention to reject, neglect and hurt him. He accuses or blames you for callousness and other malevolent actions.

The point is that he lays a projection onto you that in no way matches you as a human being. The "trip laying" is an expression of extreme craziness and is a trap for the accused party and the trip layer alike. The heavier the trip, the more severe is the repression and the subsequent alienation. It is my contention that trip laying should never go unchallenged and unconfronted. If a neurotic is allowed to get away with his horrendous acting out onto others, he will be reinforced for his sickness rather than moved in the direction of the health-producing feeling that lies buried beneath the insult. Therapists who are weak and wishy-washy and need to be nice, loving people all the time, will never succeed in " crunching" the paranoid's malicious trip laying.

Part of neurosis is the inability or the unwillingness of the individual to take full responsibility for his actions. To be responsible is to recognize and admit that one has erred and perhaps even trespassed on someone else's self-respect, integrity and dignity. But a paranoid neurotic will justify and defend his behavior regardless of the disordering that he creates in other people's lives. If he really cares about others and possesses any degree of empathic social feeling, he would attempt to remedy the consequences of his destructiveness and go through a necessary redemption to make amends. But that is usually not the case, because trip laying is safe and completely nullifies any threat of intimacy.

One of the payoffs of the laying on of trips is the reversal quality of the projection. When someone lays a trip on another, they have shifted the responsibility of the resultant rejection and punishment. If you lay a trip on me, now I am the villian that rejects "poor little you" and you have found justification for defending yourself in an irrational way. You have guaranteed distance and the parties concerned enter a crisis stage of disruption. This all occurs because the paranoid is afraid of feeling some awful truth.

Perhaps the paranoid fears feeling more than anything else, but he defends vigorously against that feeling with crazy words. We have found that the paranoid may use words in a distinctively defensive, self-justifiable, non-feeling way. A fully feeling person can communicate very well without resorting to an excessive use of words because he has most of himself. The paranoid has lost hold of his true self and speaks disconnectedly in a vain attempt to gain acceptance for the self he can't find within. His unfelt pain is, "Love me, I'm desperate" or "I need you so badly, I might die."

To take away his words would leave the paranoid feeling tiny and alone because his present matrix of behavior has its primal roots in the trauma of the intrauterine environment. A small fetus that has been threatened with annihilation while struggling to survive inside the womb, may come to regard the entire world as potentially harmful. If he had to desperately fight his way out of his mother's womb and into the world without much help from her, then it can be no surprise that he is still manipulating his environment in order to stave off the threat of that earlier murderous memory.

A woman patient asked me to see her son who had been displaying severely paranoid behavior. She explained that he was afraid that there was a plot against his life and that he had made references to his food being poisoned and the communists plotting to kill him. He was sure that he was being spied on and that his conversations were being taped. I asked the mother about his birth and she replied that it was an unwanted pregnancy and that she planned to abort him.

107

My internal reply was, "No wonder he is paranoid. You'd be paranoid, too, if your parents were planning to abort you." We now know that mothers who wish to abort their offspring secrete certain substances that have an effect on the fetus and such an intrauterine trauma can be the precursor of later paranoid behavioral breakouts.[3]

Further, an expectant mother who does not really want her baby will defend against the reality of carrying and delivering her child. This will place the burden of the struggle to be born on the infant. Thus, a future pattern of paranoia is set in, by the interaction of the resisting mother and the struggling baby. The baby learns intrauterinally and organically that if he does not struggle and fight, he will die. Mamma will not lovingly and joyfully help him to be born. It will not be an orgasmically cosmic, beautiful, natural event. Instead, the mother will bear the infant begrudgingly, painfully and with incredible anxiety. At that moment the baby is a born "loser."

The following are excerpts from a young woman's session. She has discovered through deep feeling that she was unwanted as a baby and abandoned very early. Her deep rooted mistrust and paranoia with females is evident.

Polly: "I'm really feeling a need for my daddy . . . I've been thinking a lot about him lately. I'm feeling sexually needy too. I went out on a date and I really enjoyed myself . . . the following day I realized how much I wanted to have someone to play with . . . how much I depended on my daddy for that. I depended on him for everything . . . Even when I was sick, he took me to the doctors . . . I have trouble trusting females . . . I only want my daddy. I need him . . . Oh, I feel so crazy!!"

Ther: "Why do you feel crazy?"

Polly: "I feel so needy for him . . . the last time we talked, you mentioned how alone I always look. I've really been feeling that aloneness in my soul . . . I feel so alone and crazy!!" (crying)

---

[3] Williåm Swartley, *The Undivided Self* (London, England: Churchill Centre, 1978), pg. 33. A mother can attempt to abort implantation of sperm in the egg through internal secretion. The author of *Feeling People* has experienced this implantation or gestational threat in his own deep core pre-birth feelings.

Ther: "Polly, this sounds like it is very deep and very early."

Polly: (breaks into heavy crying) "I can't take this . . . Help me!! I don't trust you to help me! . . . Mommy, I don't trust you! . . . I don't trust you! (starts thrashing her whole body)

Ther: "She's not going to help you . . . and you want to trust her . . . you need to trust her . . . but you can't . . . "

Polly: "You're hurting me!! . . . (deep crying) . . . You're hurting me!!! . . . Why must I do this alone?! Why must I do this alone!!"

Ther: "You were born to be alone . . . alone . . . alone."

Polly: "The minute you said that word, I couldn't breathe."

Ther: "What word?"

Polly: "Alone . . . alone . . . alone . . . Momma . . . Momma . . . why don't you save me?!"

Ther: "You may die in there alone or go crazy . . . "

Polly: "I don't want to die . . . I don't want to die . . . I don't want to die!!!"

Ther: "You've got to get out of there . . . you've got to get out . . . you are going to have to fight . . . little babies can yell . . . they can yell . . . "

Polly: "Let me out! . . . Let me out!!! . . . I don't want to die!!! . . . I don't want to die!!! . . . I'm not your child anymore . . . I'm my father's child now . . . I've got to get out of here before you kill me . . . I'm not yours anymore . . . I Want My Father!!! . . . Daddy . . . Daddy . . . Daddy . . . (heavy crying) . . . I'm my father's child . . . I'm not her's . . . I'm not an orphan . . . Let me go home . . . Let me go home . . . I need my father . . . I want my father . . . I don't want you either, bitch!! . . . I don't want you!! . . . (angrily kicking and

109

thrashing) . . . I don't want you!!! . . . I've got to get out of here!! Why do you want to hurt me so much??? . . . What did I do??? . . . Why do you want to hurt me!!! . . . " (deep crying)

Ther: "Why does she want to hurt you?"

Polly: "I don't know why . . . (heavy crying) . . . Why do you hurt me all the time?? . . . Why is there so much pain?? . . . (thrashing and crying) . . . I don't belong inside of her . . . not inside her . . . This is beyond the realms of babies and consciousness . . . I'm a Jew inside a Gentile!!!! . . . (heavy crying) . . . My mother never accepted that part of my father . . . never accepted that part . . . that heritage from my daddy . . . never felt a part of her . . . always different from her . . . *I DON'T FEEL SAFE IN YOU!!!*"

When the paranoid individual begins to see that he was born a "loser" and that early gestation and the birth event has negatively influenced all of his later interpersonal contact, then he might begin to delve even deeper and ask himself how his parents felt and thought at the time of his conception.[4]

As the real picture begins to emerge and he connects to those old feelings, the paranoia that has destroyed his communication with people begins to disappear and real contact and trust emerges for the first time.

That is why it is important for those who are working with the Total Feeling Process, to understand this disorder and its roots in the gestation period. It can be very easy for anyone to be seduced by the paranoid into being the destroying parental symbol of the original birth sequence. Since the out of touch paranoid invariably projects and externalizes his unresolved pain onto those who come into his sphere of influence, he will repeatedly create traumatic episodes for himself and his intimates, including his therapist.

PARANOIA, FEAR AND GENERALIZED PROJECTION

Since paranoia is a distorted and symbolic expression of intense fear, we can examine the various overt manifestations of this fear.

---

[4] William Swartley, *The Undivided Self* (London, England: Churchill Centre, 1978), pg. 30-32.

First, it is an unfelt, unresolved, projected transference onto an object that may resemble the original perpetrator of the fear. Second, this projected transference is a defense or resistance against the source of the real, deep core, early pain. It usually leads to a fight/flight pattern which revolves around a system called ideas of reference and generalization.

The following is an example of an idea of reference and the resulting generalization. The individual refers to some person or object in the past. For example, "I've been to five doctors in the past and they didn't help me. You are a doctor and you are just like they are. So I may as well not trust you, either." "My father was as big as you are and he beat me up; you will do the same, so I better not come near you."

These ideas of reference and the generalizations that follow are usually highly *irrational*, in that they are a mixture of past and present. The paranoid *rationalizes* and justifies his fight/flight behavior and he can't be talked out of his thinking without great difficulty. In other words, his ego becomes involved and he clings rigidly to these ideas of reference, in order not to lose face.

Usually, there is some form of sexual malfunction or distortion with the paranoid individual. While there is an overabundance of pain, it is very difficult for the person to relate in a straight, productive and adequate way on the sexual level. Acting-out occurs organically and socially.

Finally, paranoid interaction displays malfunctioning in Schutz's three areas of inclusion, control and affection. Inclusion revolves around the pain of not getting enough attention or getting too much of the wrong kind of attention. Very early in life, an infant learns whether or not he can trust mommy and daddy to be there for him, physically and emotionally. If there is a painful interpersonal reality, then the infant must learn to bury or control his feelings. Since organic health depends on a vital exchange of nurturant emotions, then the withdrawal of feeling sets up the dynamics of paranoid distance.

Inclusion presents difficulty at two extremes. The child who was made to feel worthless and valueless tends to try to get his attention needs met in an obnoxious way as an adult. This is so alienating that he sets up one failure situation after another. The other extreme is the adult who was smothered by an over-bearing, manipulative, controlling parent. Defensively, he is taught that he is superior to everyone else. This child was never allowed to be little. Instead, he was led to falsely believe, that people are not to be trusted and that an exaggerated sense of self-sufficiency, control and pseudo-independence is the best interpersonal style for self-protection.

Based on a feeling of utter inadequacy, the patient moves away from his real "little" self and creates a pseudo self that is superior or better than the objects that he compares himself with. He is so threatened by his own inadequacies that he attributes them to others, especially those who would reject him. He will seek what he perceives as weaknesses in others and make himself grander than they are because he denies certain threatening impulses in himself. He never opens himself up to others, but instead observes other people intently and then deludes himself by degrading them and unrealistically upgrading himself.

Sometimes he compensates his inadequacies by symbolically formulating the belief that he has been divinely chosen to be a great prophet. His delusions deviate strongly from normal ambitious strivings, in that he secretly fears that he is a worthless nobody who has not lived up to his parents' unrealistic expectations and performance demands.

The vicious and angry side of the patient's passive-aggressive nature displays itself in a rigid insistence on his own compensatory superiority. The need to feel superior to other people does not usually match the way he views himself at a deeper level. He, too, grows up to relate obnoxiously, by pretending not to be helpless or dependent. He can't ask for help and yet, his life is a shambles because of deficiencies in his interpersonal repetoire.

Both types display their failure mechanisms in two distinct ways and their sytles are evident in the group situation. The first type is gushing with need and projects that need onto everyone else in the group. The second type remains distant and withdrawn and refuses to relate to anyone, while he hides his real needs behind pretentions. Since his early needs were never met, he will never allow himself to be vulnerable again. As a result, he sacrifices the benefits of affection and closeness for the safety of not feeling again the early hurts.

The first type always acts vulnerable and victimized because he compulsively manipulates rejection and anger from symbolic others. Neither type has resolved the inclusion issue, so they find it very difficult to attain partnership with groups of people. The "underdog"[5] keeps feeling rejected and thus, elicits concern and guilt from others. The "topdog" keeps rejecting first for fear of letting anyone get close enough to find out how horrible he feels inside. Both are fearing and feeling alone and cannot establish, maintain or sustain a meaningful, fulfilling adult relationship with anyone else until they clean up and resolve the early pain.

As the inclusion needs get worked through, interaction with people becomes a predominately pleasant, positive venture. The paranoia diminishes and the person develops a harmonious balance of being comfortable with or without people. He is no longer either solely seclusive or overentangled in destructive, symbolic, interpersonal relationships. He can commit and involve himself with real honest groups of people and withhold involvement, appropriately, in non-feeling neurotic situations. As the individual becomes more authentic, honest and open, he will feel more worthwhile, significant and successful as a human being.

Unfortunately, truth can be painful, but not to feel one's deep truth will usually result in more here and now symbolic pain. The old adage "History repeats itself" was never truer than when applied in this context.

THE PARANOID COMMUNITY

Many times paranoids will sympathize and identify with other paranoids. They may even ban together for mutual support against real or imagined authority. They share certain feelings in common that have their original targets in childhood.

The community of people that they "fix on" in the present is merely symbolic of something that they see as potentially causing them pain. Therefore, they must isolate the source of their pain and make them quite identifiable. Thus, the paranoid lives with two distinct pseudo communities. If his paranoia is laced with strong elements of masochism, he will identify with those that he sees as weak, victimized and hurt by more powerful people, such as authority figures. If his need and hunger is for power, then he will

---

[5] Fritz Perls, M.D., Ph. D., *Gestalt Therapy Verbatim* (Lafayette, California: Real People Press, 1969).

want to "shoot authority down" from their powerful positions and take on the role of the "all powerful" one himself.

The former always feels small and weak and finds some kind of secondary reward in remaining in a "one down" place. He fears being powerful because he can't trust his own rage and hate. He wants to kill but he can't survive without the support of those that he would kill. Every once in awhile this fear gets the best of him and he tries to cover it by lashing out at others.

While witnessing many people in the throes of deep core birth feelings, it is common to see them break into enormous rage after discovering that their mother may have wanted to destroy them in the womb. This rage is the natural reaction to a devastating threat to their very lives and may account for adult practices of genocide. Those that are convinced that their genocidal murderings are for a good and higher cause may be absolutely emotionally correct. It is the targets that are wrong. There is very little doubt in my mind that Manson and Hitler were the surviving victims of incredible fetal shocks. If fetal genocide is contemplated by the mothers of these individuals, then the intrauterine secretions will alert the baby to prepare itself for the supreme battle of its life. It is only in adulthood that the individual feels powerful enough to seek revenge on symbolic substitutes for earlier hurts.

The grandiose paranoid can't stand to be "one down" and weak, so he will look for every possible opportunity to elevate himself out of his inferiority to a much more superior position with other people. His pseudo community must be superior to the enemy pseudo community and at the same time, he needs to alienate, subjugate and destroy his hate objects. Upon questioning his motives, he will deny that he intends to hurt anyone but he repeatedly maneuvers evidence in his favor and against the other pseudo community. He is really trying to make himself look good by making someone else appear to be bad. In this way he gains a semblance of power based on external advantage, but inwardly he is frightened of feeling his own pain.

THE PARANOID NEED FOR ABSOLUTE AUTONOMY

Certain types of paranoids find it very difficult to trust authority. They fear power and yet need it desperately. Since paranoia is an expression and manifestation of unfelt fear, this person is usually in a continuous state of tension and total mobilization. His alertness to authority is intense and watchful as he focuses a disproportionate amount of mental energy on protecting himself from alleged control and "brainwashing." His body armor or musculature reflects this heightened sense of alertness and readiness. Certain expressions on his face and fixedness of staring, attentive eyes, combined with muscular and skeletal protective rigidity of the chest reflect his defensive mobilization against attack. His body is not relaxed and flowing, but tight and unspontaneous.

It may not be an oversimplification to assume that extremes of inappropriate passive quietness, in some instances, can be an expression of paranoia. The outward facade may be completely expressionless, placid and contemplative, while inwardly the "real" behavior is taking place. Such behavior may be furtive and under complete voluntary control while with normal people it would be spontaneous, expressive and with no desire to be hidden. This unexpressive, quiet, watchful furtiveness might very well leave others with uneasy feelings.

"I wonder what is really going on inside of him . . . I wonder what he is really thinking . . . I don't trust him fully . . . I get the sense that sooner or later he is going to attack . . . He's really in his head. . . He always seems to be *lining* me up in his sights. I don't want to be the target for his hostility . . . He seems so friendly, but that is not the real him."

This list is certainly incomplete but it reveals the general effect that paranoid interactions have on other people. It would seem that these reactions, themselves, contain elements of paranoia, but it must be remembered that projective, subjective suspiciousness does "set up" or create in the targeted others, the same self-fulfilling, confirming behavior that is the touchstone of the typical paranoid interactional dynamic.

We cannot overlook that besides the internal workings of paranoia, there is the unique paranoid interpersonal complex set of behaviors. One does not have to look far in order to find examples of disturbed paranoid interpersonal communication patterns. The paranoid is a master at messing things up. It would seem that his limited interpersonal success falls far short of his intellectual potential. But then again, the paranoid may have to be intelligent and perceptive for purely defensive reasons. If one's early childhood is dangerously threatening, it becomes absolutely necessary, for strictly survival reasons, to develop an acute cunning perceptiveness and intelligence, even at the expense of reality oriented, corrective emotional experience.

Defensively, the paranoid individual gives the impression of being extremely independent or overly autonomous. If he is the pseudo-autonomous type, he will appear to others as if he must "do it" by himself, with no help. He seeks professional help, in some cases, strictly to show the authority figure how well he can do it himself, thereby, letting the authority know that he really doesn't need him. His response is indirectly defensive and full of coded symbolism.

For example, if there was considerable disturbance in his relationship with one parent, he will defend against that parent's rejection and abandonment by denying his need for that parent and develop an autonomous style of life based on that buried hurt and need. He will later reflect, in his body armor and his interpersonal style, that need "not to need daddy."

When we begin to see and understand the devastation that was wrought on these individuals, we can begin to empathize with the kind of pain that drove them to defend in this pseudo-autonomous manner. Perhaps, it is within this realm of understanding that therapists can begin to look beyond the complexities of the paranoid's intricate defenses and subtly distorted perceptions and delusions. Then, we can begin to see the roots of his pain and with his reluctant assistance lead him to feel that pain fully, thereby ultimately freeing him from his alienating symptoms.

THE PARANOID RELATIONSHIP

In a paranoid relationship the paranoid partner is always forewarned that there is something drastically wrong with the relationship. But he pays no heed, because his hearing is intellectually impaired. He completely blots out all the obvious feedback signals that have told him that he better do something constructive and fast. He can't and won't hear the obvious truth that if he does not take the necessary steps, he will turn his partner against him and eventually suffer the loss of that partner. He is selectively inattentive to all obvious warning signals and overly attentive to non-existent messages of hope that feed him with the delusion that things are really alright, when in actuality they are not.

When there is a female love object involved, the paranoid may set up a competitive struggle for her love. If she is relatively free of excessive neurosis, she will find it very difficult to remain in a relationship with him and she may divert her attention elsewhere, away from him. This occurs in serious relationships and/or marriage where the paranoid's defensive rigidity and denial finally drive the partner out of the painful situation into a therapist's office.

Many individuals, as they gain back more of their real selves, find it very hard to live with someone else's craziness. We must remember that certain paranoid types deny that there is anything wrong with them. They usually always project and externalize their insanity. According to the paranoid, the real problem with his love relationship lies outside himself and resides in some external influence that is taking his partner away. He never blames himself for the craziness that has alienated and turned off his partner.

Realistic pairs fully understand that nothing outside of themselves can ruin their relationship—only they can. One partner told his lover:

> "I love you and no one or no thing can ever break us up. Only your craziness and mine can do that . . . If you are going to be crazy and do crazy, mean, rotten things to me, I want you to go. I can't live with that insanity."

His partner replied:

> "I don't want to be crazy and do those things to you. I know I set you up to reject me with my weirdness, but I really want to be with you. I love you. I, too, want to be rid of my craziness for me and our relationship."

Sexualized paranoia is a specific area of the paranoid relationship worth my comment. The individual, usually a woman, falls madly (insanely) in love with someone she sees as above her. The love object can be either real or imaginary, but he represents in her thinking the idealization of the perfect father. In reality, the early relationship with her father was probably rather ambiguous along the dimensions of affection and eroticism. This left the child to create a multitude of ideas concerning her hope and need for her father's exclusive love.

Erotic paranoia may occur in families where all or most of the siblings are of the same sex. An intense rivalry arises between the females which may only be allowed to exist on a nonverbal unacknowledged level. The young female grows up to be emotionally insecure and forever anticipating that she will be unfulfilled by a man, but yet hoping unrealistically that the next man to come along will be her long lost hero, come at last to love her.

She may go from one love affair to another hopelessly vulnerable, intensely unreal in her thinking and projecting all her disowned feelings onto each new "big daddy" that becomes her new love object. She suffers from unreturned love, but she never quite sees reality. She rationalizes that the loved one cannot make a full committment to loving her, so she distorts her perceptions of him by thinking that he does indicate his love in silent, indirect and circuitous ways. Even if her hero sets her straight as to his ultimate intentions, she cannot bear to hear any hint of rejection and so, she rigidly holds onto her hopes of subsequent daddy conquest. Eventually, reality comes barreling down on her with overwhelming force. At this point, the anticipation of feeling the original pain is so devastating that she must flee with all of her might.

Severe cases of paranoia are usually characterized by manipulating everyone in a symbolic family to be angry with him/her. The paranoid needs the anger from others to justify his flight from the here and now situation and the panic of his own feelings. The sexualized paranoid, like other paranoids, must make others angry so that she doesn't have to feel her own early rage at neglect and deprivations. Buried rage begets fear, distrust and anger in others and, of course, it is hard to detect this type of paranoia because it is usually buried behind a passive facade. The buried aggression, however, will eventually surface in subtle ways and will have a revenge-like quality to it for imagined hurts and insults.

Anyone who becomes deeply involved with a paranoid must inevitably reject them because they unwittingly cannot avoid becoming the symbolic ojbects of a very severe transference neurosis. Transference objects must themselves flee for fear of losing themselves in the unmanageable disruptive influences of the paranoid's "bullshit" logical and irrational ideation.

PARANOID JEALOUSY

As I stated earlier, paranoia usually requires a certain loss of reality. This loss of reality involves a suspicious comprehension of all situations and communications. The true facts of a situation are ignored and certain inferences and suppositions are manufactured to replace reality. The suspicious person loses the real world and substitutes a subjective, distorted, narrow view of it based on a specific symbolic base. He/she is pre-set to judge something, not on its real merits but on his pre-conceived notions about it. He needs to say, "Ah hah, I told you so . . . I looked for the evidence and I found it. Now I've got you, you sonofabitch!."

Jealousy can be a normal part of establishing limits, claims and boundaries on developing relationships. But when jealousy possesses a mixture of the past and the present, with the past predominating, then it is evident that a particular kind of paranoia exists.

Usually, there is some precipitating event that the patient misinterprets or reads as betrayal or desertion. The interpretation of the situation never matches the actuality of the event. Even if reality is revealed to the patient, he will eventually be triggered to imagined slights and go through the jealousy cycle over and over again. Since all paranoids are continually watching and believing that they are finding confirmatory evidence for delusions of persecution and rejection, they will distort all situations into potential jealous threats. They will use denial and projection mechanisms as defenses against the awful truth that they were damaged severly when they were very small. It is usually easier to stay caught up in here and now struggles and rejections than go back and feel the awful truth of an early primal scene. It is for this reason that they usually create strong delusions about what really happened to them in infancy.

Jealous paranoids who possess inadequate personalities and lack general social competence will feel utterly helpless to control their love-object's imaginary strayings with would-be competitors. The jealous paranoid wishes to possess, own and control the love object. He/she will feel crushed if the object of their affection pays the slightest attention to anyone but him. If full confirmation is lacking and the basic trust issue has not been worked through, the patient may reject first at the slightest hint of subsequent rejection by the love object.

The key factor here is that the paranoid sees betrayal where it does not exist. Because of extreme insecurity, he needs monumental amounts of reassurance that never fully allay his fears anyway. Another key factor in this jealousy is the threat of real or imagined competition. Normal competitive strivings are aimed toward helping a person reach his full potential and enhance the ego through expanded feelings of success. The paranoid sees everything as threatening to his ego and must develop malignant ego defenses to cope with the fantasized threat. (In any competitive situation where a person is threatened with loss of his ego, he will defend. If the loss spurs the ego to meet the challenge with appropriate and constructive striving, the ego can benefit and grow from the experience.) Children's egos that are destroyed in childhood can very rarely benefit from true challenging competition. The defenses to protect against that early annihilation are too deeply ingrained.

Chapter 8   Rage, Violence and Anger

RAGE, VIOLENCE AND ANGER

Anger does erupt in therapy and it is necessary to determine the level at which the anger is occurring. It might be a clear, integrated here and now anger at some individual for some transgression upon self or property. Or, on the other hand, it might be rage or anger loaded with historical, early pain and outrage being transferred onto someone in the here and now. This is usually the case, especially in the beginning stages of therapy. Anger also assumes varying proportions and we must allow each patient to vent his anger and rage in an appropriate, full blown way.

Violence also occurs in the Total Feeling Process. We have found that if a patient is pent up with incredible amounts of rage, he must have some means of discharging that emotion. Therapists who are afraid to deal with that level of violence are not going to be particularly helpful to their clients. Although we permit a wide range of emotional expression, we do have certain requirements and reservations about extremes of hostility. No patient is permitted to damage, in a physical way, another's face or body or communal property.

Patients do, however, wrestle, slap, throw each other across the room, have pillow fights, lash out at each other with encounterbats, scream, yell and spew out all kinds of venom, hate, and dislike. At times, it all seems like organized mayhem and it is. For the most part, if there is a feeling resolution, there are never any hard feelings left over. Patients who are subtly hostile before the discharge, are much clearer and relate much more honestly and openly after the discharge.

It took me a long time to come to grips with this problem because I was trained in a therapeutic tradition that therapists are to be open and honest and at the same time loving, warm, and supportive. It was considered counter-productive to get angry at a patient. I found myself in situations, however, where I would try everything to hold back my own here and now angry reactions, only to eventually let loose on a patient.

Many years ago, I found myself working with a particular young man. I tried everything possible, yet his resistance was at such a high level that nothing seemed to get through. During the course of one group that was being run by another therapist, I found myself reaching for an encounterbat. I picked it up and proceeded to beat him with it at which point, he immediately took off after me, ran me down and started wrestling. Neither of us got hurt. However, what followed was an incredible deep release of emotional pain for his own father. It is doubtful he could have ever gotten to the depths of that pain if he hadn't gone through that total combat with me. Since then, anger and violence have been a part of our therapy. Although there are bruises and scratches, rarely does anyone ever get hurt.

It is important to remember that this violence is done within the context of a protective, therapeutic setting. It may be totally inappropriate to express huge amounts of anger and rage outside of therapy. In fact, I have found it counter-productive for patients to spit out a lot of anger during an intellectual seminar where outside participants are present. In some cases, it does the outsiders good to see how others work their anger. But, I personally feel that it is more appropriate to express the extremes of anger and rage in the confines of the therapeutic setting.

Our society impresses upon us that only certain norms are allowed; we are supposed to be nice and polite and conform to a well ordered and controlled set of behaviors. This is all well and good, but many times individuals begin to pent up reactions to certain situations and they have no place for the safe discharge of these particularly disturbed emotions. It is at this point that the therapeutic setting becomes a viable outlet for release.

When I became more comfortable with expressing my anger and rage to whomever I was involved with, be it a friend, colleague, or a patient, I usually always found that there was some feeling resolution afterwards. There were times, however, when certain people could not handle or integrate my rage. If there was an inability to work that painful situation through, what usually set in was a form of alienation. I cannot be totally responsible for those particular situations. They happened. I'm sorry they happened, but that's the way it goes. I can only be responsible for honestly conveying my feelings, whatever they are, and being available to help another to integrate them. I have found that when I allow myself the full range of anger and rageful feelings, it is also possible for me to let other patients have their rage and their violence towards one another and myself. To me, this is a viable, workable relationship.

Now, as soon as I do express my rage and anger, it is often enough to move a patient into a feeling that they were blocking. At this point, I immediately melt and become soft, and I am with them while they're feeling that painful reality. Other patients have commented on how supportive I eventually become after I have expressed my anger and the patient has felt his early pain. In most cases, the patients are grateful that I did express those particularly painful feelings and free them up to experience a piece of their transferential reality.

Another problem arises when I do express my anger and rage and the person begins to defend and fight back. Then the situation escalates. Unless the feelings are eventually fully felt and accepted, we cannot go on to greater levels of understanding and intimacy.

What does this all mean? It means that not all rage, anger and violence is rooted in the fears and pain of childhood. Much anger has to do with here and now contact, and clients and patients must have the opportunity to express and act out that violence and rage in a "safe" therapeutic setting. If a therapist insists on always steering a patient back to the past to feel and express his anger, then it will mean that the patient may not feel free enough to express the full range of his emotions to the therapist and to other members of the feeling community. I have found this to be highly counter-productive. This can mean, that when a person is being "too nice," he may be hiding some very powerful, angry emotions which, when finally asserted and expressed in a direct and powerful manner, can result in some great insight and resolution.

Now, it is important to remember that certain norms are encouraged on the therapy floor which are not encouraged in an outside, non-therapeutic setting. I do expect clients to behave rationally and productively in the outside world. Their everyday work and school lives demand that they behave in a certain fashion, and the more appropriately that they behave in those particular situations without compromising themselves, the more success they are going to have in dealing with the outside realities. We do remember that therapy is therapy and it encourages certain norms within a therapy setting. The outside society has a different set of norms and each individual who enters into therapy must come to terms with his outside life.[1]

It is my opinion that patients should be allowed to negotiate contracts with one another where it is totally okay to be angry. At that time, they can spew out all of the feelings and perceptions that they

---

[1] I refer the reader to the following sources: Steve Simon, "Synanon: Towards Building a Humanistic Organization" *The Journal of Humanistic Psychology*, Summer 1978, Vol. 18, No. 3, pgs. 3-20. I also refer the reader to the book, *Creative Aggression*, by George R. Bach and Herb Goldberg, Avon books, 1974.

have been holding back with one another and their therapists. This norm is also to be established for the therapists as well. It is within the context of this kind of interaction that greater understanding is enhanced. Let me reiterate that not *all* rage and anger is buried in childhood pain and any therapy that encourages *totally* displacing here and now anger and rage and putting it into the regressive patterns of childhood, may be making a mistake. That is not to say that much of the pain of anger and rage is not historical. Of course, it is. But we must have the opportunity for full expression of all feelings in the here and now as well.

Patients in the Total Feeling Process are taught to communicate all of their feelings and emotions, whether it be past or present. Many people who get into deep core feelings strictly on their own at home, without benefit of having contact in the here and now with other people, will generally feel fine about lying down and screaming out their pain but they will not have the opportunity to work through the extremes of rage, violence, and anger that result in full emotional connection and integration with someone in the here and now. I cannot stress enough that although anger and rage has to be expressed, we do enforce the rule of no injuries to persons and property. Anything short of that particular norm is perfectly permissable. If I express a lot of anger towards someone and they feel punished, they have the option to express it back towards me. If I lash out at somebody with an encounterbat, they always have the option to come back and do the same, as well. In most cases, I will go back to them to find out how they feel about what I expressed and said, and most people tell me that they don't feel that there is any damage to our here and now relationship.

People who express their negative emotions through letters or telephone calls or long distance, are really short changing themselves in the full exploration of those feelings. I personally discourage myself from writing letters to people when I have negative emotions towards them. If I am experiencing negativity, it means that I didn't fully express myself in the group. All feelings, all perceptions, all behaviors belong in the group.

Many times, individuals operate under the mistaken assumption that anger is really a masking emotion. When we look very closely at infants, however, during the first days of life, we can sometimes observe them becoming very frantic, angry and raging; especially, when they are not fed according to the needs of their little bellies.

They do scream and cry when they are angry, and we can see that their bodies are full of rage and aggression. If this rageful aggression is not met with a satisfying response from adults, then eventually that baby will begin to withdraw and emotionally go dead.[2]

Infants are born with a very instinctive, aggressive drive within their little bodies which is absolutely necessary in order to guarantee their survival. They must get other people in the environment to get and do for them, because they cannot do for themselves. If they are continually frustrated, they will grow angrier and angrier. And if their angry responses are completely ignored, the baby will go into a state of lethargy and emotional death. As an adult, this will develop into all the behavioral symptoms of withdrawal and passivity. They may eventually learn that they must be nice and manipulative in order to get what they want. This is done at a great price to their natural, aggressive drives. Furthermore, it may be safe to assume that appropriate ambition and positive assertiveness also suffer .in the long run, because of the negative reinforcement of infantile aggression.

Babies who are allowed to be angrily aggressive are also more aggressive in their joy, their spontaneity, their laughter, and their joviality. After all, what is assertive aggression but the will and desire to go after what one wants. If an individual's natural drives to secure gratification and satisfaction for his desires and needs are thwarted, then he will enter a state of extreme frustration. His anger may build, and he may explode or turn it into psychosomatic diseases. It is easy to recognize that much of what passes for psychosomatic disorders may be the result of inhibited aggressive drives. I have seen many patients who are suffering from extreme passivity and emotional weakness, plus other psychosomatic distress symptoms. These symptoms completely clear up after the patient is given permission to ventilate all of his hostility, hatred and desires to destroy. It is no mistake for people to assume that when one successfully discharges a lot of negative emotion, he absolutely feels and functions better.

I think it is important to remember that every patient has an option of cutting off the action whenever he or she deems fit. Sometime ago I

---

[2] L.D. Young, S. S. Suomi, H.F. Harlow, and W.T. McKinney, "Early Stress and Later Response to Separation in Rhesus Monkeys," *American Journal of Psychiatry*, 130: 400, 1973.

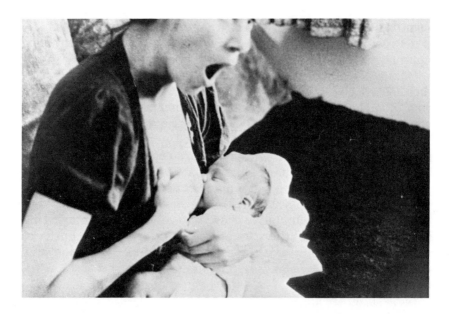

*"A baby responds with full force and strength . . . He uses his
body and his mouth in a very complete way in order to grasp his
environment. In this case, his mommy's breast . . ."*

learned from Jacqie Leichter and Mike Broder, therapists from the
Philadelphia Branch of the Center for the Whole Person, that
whenever I felt that I wanted to cut off the action all I had to do was to
use the cue words, "Stop it, I mean it." Anything that was being done
in my presence or to me, would be discontinued. I have passed this
stop-gap measure onto my patients and whenever a patient in our
program feels the need to slow down or stop the action, all he or she
has to do is repeat that phrase. I should probably add that this phrase
has been very rarely used in all the years that we have been doing deep
feeling therapy here at the Center.

It seems that those who become completely immersed and involved
in a full contactful, raging, violent encounter know that something
positive and helpful is happening. They seem to intuitively perceive
that they need to go completely through that experience to get to the
"other side." And I have never seen it fail, that when a person has any
degree of deep feeling, he can go into those rageful spaces with himself

and another human being and come out feeling fully resolved and much clearer than he did before he started.

When two people are involved in a total violent, angry exchange, whether there is any physical encounter or not, we have to be very careful that there are not any leftover unresolved feelings. I have seen in non-feeling contexts, when two people engage in an argument, that, although there may be some emotional contact, there are usually some leftover bad feelings. One party may withdraw and feel very disturbed and uncomfortable about the encounter. When someone walks away from a fight like that, feeling agitated and negative, we can assume that he is not getting to the bottom line of his feelings.

An individual who has been deeply into his or her own feelings, will not like staying with negative feelings. Negativity, like agitation, depression, and anger can be very disordering for a person. Our position is, if one is staying with these feelings, he is not getting down to his bottom line for it is always at the deepest realm of human emotion that cure and transformation takes place.

I have never seen it fail that if anyone goes through such an encounter and comes out feeling disturbed, when he or she gets to those deep, underlying feelings, all the negativity and disturbance vanishes. That person usually comes out feeling very positive. So, a general rule is, that if you are not coming out of an interaction feeling good about yourself and another person, that there are some very strong bottom line feelings operating. And, unless those feelings are fully recovered and felt, the participants are going to be left with a lot of residual negativity. Nobody likes to feel negative, even though they may be immersed in protecting and defending themselves. They may use all sorts of justifications for staying in that defensive space, but once they reach their very deep bottom line, they recognize that the full explosion of those underlying feelings clears away all the negativity.

Early in my training I was in a group that didn't provide for deep bottom line feelings. Of course, sooner or later, conflict arose and a confrontation took place between myself and a couple of other people. Following some arguing and fighting, we finally made some contact with one another. But, afterwards, for a few days, I felt disturbed. I realized that it was important for me to wash away and cleanse myself of my own negativity. So, I began to work with myself, deeper and deeper, into my real, true feelings. When the full explosion finally came, the curing sensation was felt as "Momma, I really need you; I need you to help me. You were really never there when I was being bombarded by life."

For me, the bottom line emotion was recognizing that there was some sort of deficiency in my relationship with my mother that had left me disturbed in some of my inter-personal relationships. In other words, I wasn't taught how to cope with certain situations, and my only response was to get angry and disturbed. After I felt that bottom line emotion, all of the negativity that I had felt towards the here and now protagonists practically vanished. That is not to say that I still don't have some feelings of caution towards certain types of people that I really don't wish to struggle with. I don't like being disturbed and I know that I have to get to the deepest levels of my self in order to transform those disordering emotions.

I have seen other Total Feeling patients in the same type of predicament. They'll be in a situation where they will experience some kind of attack, insult, or denial of their identity. They may either try to respond back, withdraw or perhaps even fight a little bit, but the pain still lingers on. When they finally come into a therapy session, we allow them to explode all their here and now verbiage and then slowly melt into the deep painful hurt of their very early years. It's important to remember that this type of ritual does exist and has to be gone through in that type of fashion. Any attempt to short cut or short circuit some of the here and now feelings by by-passing them will only show itself as a further disconnection between early deep pain and here and now disordering emotions and situations.

So, in the Total Feeling Process, it is necessary for us to allow individuals to have full explosive blowouts as long as they can eventually get to and immerse into a deep, curative, bottom line feeling. Many times, individuals don't do that and they take on all the attributes of avoidance. They may begin to withdraw with much of their negative ideation fully intact. It may be hard for them to realize that we, as therapists, offer them a chance and an opportunity to get to the deep underlying, curative feelings. If they choose not to melt into those deep emotions, then they run the risk of proceeding on with their life with certain systems of ideation and patterns of negative behavior still remaining intact. As I have said before, this limits their range of emotional contact and life space. If they were capable of delving deep into the bottom line of that core, disturbing issue then they, at least, would have the opportunity to learn and relate to all disturbing influences and stimuli in a much more appropriate and clear way. In other words, through deep core feeling, anxiety and pain can be eliminated with new insights implanted in the subconscious mind as well as the opportunity to relate more fully to all people in the here and now.

I have seen a few patients leave with negative feelings towards the therapists and other patients, as well. I have never been fully satisfied with that state of affairs. So, what we try to do is establish a norm that states, if you are feeling negative towards yourself or towards another, try to open up a channel to your deeper feelings, thereby opening up a better system of communication with other human beings. I cannot stress this enough. As an individual opens up more channels of communication with his deeper self, he, by and large, opens up more communication channels with other human beings.

Stated briefly, negative emotions can be instrumental in helping an individual to get to his deeper core self. The purpose of any feeling encounter or therapy is to help a person feel better about himself and the world in general. Deep feelings, fully completed and integrated, do allow people to feel very positively about themselves and this is what we aim for.

GESTATION AND ANGER

Babies who are carried around inside angry mothers will grow up to view the environment as being hostile and threatening.[3] Many clients in the Total Feeling Process, when troubled and disturbed in their interpersonal relationships, can trace back and relive the pain of being inside an angry intrauterine environment. It seems that a mother who is carrying insanity inside the tissues of her body will chemically transmit that insanity to her offspring. His/her later responses in life will reflect this struggle with that painful intrauterine environment.

If a mother works and lives her life in a crazy fashion, her infant will grow up thinking that he or she must work insanely hard in order to survive. That baby has had no time for real, clear beautiful feelings or the Golden Age,[4] as Frederick Leboyer so aptly describes it. Depression and anger may be the resultant outcome in later years.

---

[3] William Swartley, Ph. D., *The Undivided Self* (London, England: Churchill Centre, 1978), pg. 33-40.
[4] Frederick Leboyer, *Birth Without Violence* (New York: Alfred Knopf, 1975), pg. 22.

Many patients grew up in homes where there were enormous amounts of pent-up rage and hostility. Since we view the in-utero environment as that baby's first home for nine solid months, what occurs during that gestational period will have a dramatic effect on the new emerging human being, as a child and later as an adult. D.H. Stott,[5] in his follow-up study from birth of the effects of prenatal stress, concludes that:

> "Stresses involving severe, continuing personal tensions (in particular marital discord) were closely associated with child morbidity in the form of ill-health, neurological dysfunction, developmental lag and behavioral disturbance."

Many patients even after they leave their original parental home, carry around inside of them the exact replication of their earlier environment plus their in-utero living quarters. As I have tried to demonstrate time and time again in this book, gestation trauma carries with it an imprint and the programming for developing a painful life style as one grows older.

As one patient put it:

> "My mother was a very angry woman. I lived inside her crazy body for nine months". . . . and I've always wondered why at times I've lived within my own craziness. . . . . . It hurt me very deeply that my mother was such a human being . . . . She continually fought with my father, and eventually their marriage broke up . . . . . That broke me up . . . . . The way it was inside her stomach, that's the way it was inside our home . . . . There was no real home."
>
> "After going through much of my therapy, I was able to clear up a lot of that pain and formulate a new feeling environment inside myself, that has been transferred to my living environment . . . . . . There has been an incredible transformation."

The gestation environment also is the precursor for much of what passes as sibling rivalry later in life. An older sibling may have been

---

[5] D. H. Stott, "Follow-up Study from Birth of the Effects of Prenatal Stress", *Developmental Medicine and Child Neurology*, 15: 770-787, 1973.

carried by his/her mother in a very painful, traumatic fashion. A sibling that arrived later in the birth order may have had much more beneficial gestational circumstances. He or she will display different personality characteristics and will relate to the world in a less constricted and painful fashion. The older sibling may subconsciously act out and feel an incredible amount of hatred and envy toward the younger sibling. In reality, he or she might be hating that younger child because mommy was in a much more sensitive state of being when carrying his younger brother or sister. One fetal environment may have been more caring, nurturant and supportive than the other. This shows up in marked personality differences between two siblings. In fact, the two siblings may be fighting with each other over the differences in the way the mother carried each of them.

For example, an older female sibling was carried inside a mother who practically killed herself all during her pregnancy by overworking. The child grew up intensely depressed and always feeling as if she never got any rest. Here we see the transference of the mother's emotional state to the personality characteristics of the patient. A later sibling was carried in a much more sensitive environment. She found herself much happier in adult life with no chronic signs of depression. The oldest sister was very envious and jealous of the younger one and harbored enormous amounts of pent-up rage and hatred. They would fight with one another over the years because there was considerable animosity between them. The younger sister eventually got in touch with her rage towards her mother for carrying her older sister the way that she did. This in fact deprived her of the full emotional benefit of having an older sister.

Another case of sibling rivalry points to the circumstances surrounding the gestational period. Fred was always jealous and envious of his older brother and continually kept trying to push him away. Usually, people do this because they see the other sibling as getting something that they never had. Fred's older brother, Jack, was carried in a much different fashion than Fred was. The mother did not work at the time of her pregnancy with Jack. She was much more relaxed and did not have to put up with the pressures of having to take care of other children. Jack had all of his mother to himself; Fred did not. He was an unplanned pregnancy too soon after his brother Jack. The mother worked hard during the pregnancy and felt great anxiety and economic pressure over how to sustain her new and growing family. Inside of his mother, Fred experienced not getting all of her because her attention was split between holding down a job, caring for Jack and taking care of a failing relationship between herself and her husband.

Fred was certainly deprived and it is not difficult to see why he would be jealous and envious of his older brother, whether it be at a conscious or unconscious level. After all, Jack got so much more of his mother than Fred did. This excruciating realization helped to extricate Fred from here and now struggles with more powerful males. It also freed him from a debilitating form of passivity and withdrawal in the presence of more powerful brother figures. As he felt this pain, Fred became more spontaneous, open and sharing in group. He was also less threatened and intimidated by older, stronger males.

We can conclude that the very basis and roots of anger and depression lies within the different types of fetal environments in which people learn to grow and develop.

Social scientists have only recently begun to investigate the effects of disturbed intrauterine environments upon later personality development. This is decidedly a worthwhile course of investigation and as more knowledge begins to accumulate, we will begin to see and realize how very important it is to pay strict attention to the emotional condition of the mother while she is carrying her baby.

In other words, it is not the birth process alone that carries with it incredible amounts of trauma. It is also the gestation period, and the kind and degree of emotions that the mother has carried around locked in her tissues all of her life. She can't help but inadvertently act out her own pain and rage onto that little helpless infant lying within that soft womb. Consciously, she may deny it but her body cannot lie.

Another patient put it this way:

> I felt so little, soft and beautiful inside my mother. I couldn't stand knowing that she was all around me, angry and very uptight. I needed her warmth and her love to surround me. Instead, she was nervous, tense and very crazy. That insanity got transmitted to me."

I have seen many patients who have gotten in touch with this level of feeling and now feel that much of their anger, rage and internal insanity has cleared up. Once again, this points to the importance of the deep feeling process allowing individuals to get in touch with those very, very small parts of themselves. I cannot stress enough that the in utero environment eventually gets transferred to the entire household. "You are your house," and the earliest house that each of us lived in was our mother's belly.

PACIFISM

Pacifism is the other side of aggression. Many problems in history and in interpersonal relationships have been solved through anger, rage and violence. Political regimes have toppled, new social forms have come into being, archaic civilizations have died out, mass migrations of peoples overrunning other peoples have created newer and more complex forms of societies, and in most cases, these newer forms came about through some form of violence and aggression.

There can be no value judgement at this point in time, whether this is good or bad. Many individuals, however, have suffered from what we call social and psychological aggression. In interpersonal relationships most of the fighting that goes on between many individuals is very rarely ever resolved in a satisfactory way for all the participants.

In a deep feeling therapeutic context, however, it is quite possible for people to fight with no holds barred and to come out understanding, caring and loving of one another. Now the human psyche has other realms besides aggression and self-assertion. One of these spaces is universally found to be that of pacificism. Mahatma Gandhi was the chief proponent of pacificism in this century. He encouraged it to bring about profound social, political and psychological change within the minds of many political thinkers. Martin Luther King, Jr. was the American counterpart and used this approach to advance social and psychological change. The premise rests very firmly on non-violent foundations.

It is unfortunate that Martin Luther King, Jr. died in a violent way, for his calm, gentle, profound pacificism could move mountains. He stirred the hearts and thinking of most Americans. Many religious martyrs, saints and saviors have been noted to change the course of history by operating from a position of love, warmth and concern for all mankind. That is to say, that they had a quiet inner power that changed the course of human thinking and re-sculptured the concepts of the human mind to think in different terms. Most political movements have these forms of pacifism within their philosophies, while at the same time also having more aggressive components.

In psychotherapy, we encourage our patients to ventilate and express their rage and violence in order to cleanse themselves. It is quite common that after this cleansing process takes place, we can see these individuals operating from a very calm and grounded center. This calm centered place comes about with deep psychological and emotional working through of the distortions in human communication and fear. This kind of pacifism is not arrived at by philosophical or political means. It is something that comes about by working through one's state of being. This is not to say that if one gets enough psychotherapy, he will no longer have anger and rage. This would imply that there is a state of nirvana from which each one of us could exist and relate to the world.

On the contrary, I believe that all human beings have within them the propensity and the potential for anger, and that this emotion has its place in helping a person adapt and relate to his environment. A pacifistic side of man's nature also has the same function and role. By being calm and centered in our peacefulness, we can get things done and accomplished as well as explore many higher states of self and being.

Because a human being is a dynamic system of complex energies, no one ever stays in one place forever. Even Jesus, though filled with love, at times was saddened and on occasion was provoked to extreme anger and destructiveness.

Since human beings are part of and exist within nature, we represent or embody all the capabilities of nature. The weather, for example, isn't always calm and beautiful. At times it is harmful and turbulent. Seasons change from pleasant and mild, to harsh and cruel, and all the things that exist within nature need to function within those parameters of change.

It has been my experience while coming in contact with many different people, some of whom have been involved in various phases of the human potential movement and other types of religious growth experiences, that there is a need, an intense drive, to be loving and warm and to relate to the whole universe from a very loving place. I would agree that this is a very worthwhile goal, but I think at times it can be overdone. The end result is that a person who becomes totally immersed in only his goodness will suffer because of whatever forms of denial he uses on those other *negative* aspects of his personality.

If one is in a particularly good mood and feeling marvelous, elements that might disturb him if he were in a different psychological state of being, would tend not to bother him. What we call emotional and psychological health is probably a precarious balance of our various intellectual, physiological and emotional functions. I would say that if a person is feeling good most of the time, he is functioning at near optimum level. If he is feeling negative and miserable most of the time, he is going to need extensive psychotherapy to rid himself of those internal negative influences. Deep feeling therapy de-programs one's pain and allows the other sides of the personality to emerge. For many individuals feeling good is a rare and unfamiliar treat. In some disordered personalities feeling good is so rare that these individuals can't ever get used to that kind of energy.

Proponents of a total love ethic, if they pursue a blind pacifistic life as a defense against their own anger, rage and pain, create a unique form of neurosis. On the opposite side of the coin, one who would seem to seek out and only reinforce his/her own aggression, anger and violence, while rejecting and avoiding all gentler forms of contact, also creates a neurotic medium.

I mentioned before that deep core feelings can be used to explore all the realms and spaces of the human psyche. Whatever exists within the Universe also is reflected in a mirror image within the mind of man. Social and cultural conditions help program a man to formulate constructs of reality that may either approximate universal reality or deviate from it to a considerable degree. It is safe to say that there is an entire universe constantly unfolding around us but each one of us experiences it in a different way.[6] We form together into groups that will consensually validate our view of reality, thereby feeling comfortable within the majority.

It has been particularly amusing to me to see many different psychotherapists claim that their view of the nature of man is far superior to other world views. I would say that anything that is current will be revised within a short period of time by new concepts that tend to pull people together and form a vast consensus of opinion and judgment about that view of reality. The Nazi view of violence and destruction came about because of an incredible focus of attention by a large enough group of people on a particular psychological phenomena. The Christian view of the Universe was

---

[6] Joseph Chilton Pearce, *The Crack in the Cosmic Egg* (New York: Pocket Books, 1971), XIII.

formed in a somewhat similar vein, only the focus and the attention was different. It is all according to where you are and what you are drawn to at that particular point of time in history. At one point in one's life it would be perfectly reasonable to expect and assume that the pacifistic view would have the most survival and adaptive function for that human being. While at another point in time, aggression would be more in the service of the ego.

If a human being is a growing and emerging organism, we can expect that deep feeling will take him through many, many different realms of the vast Universe of the human mind. When I have reached a point where I can accept who I am totally as a human being, I can fight any inclination to put myself in a role or have someone else stereotype me within the constructs of their mind. Only I know the various parts of my personality. There is the angry and violent me; the soft, loving, gentle me; there is the calm and the powerful; the assertive and the aggressive; there is the clown, the hurt little boy, the pompous, confident, arrogant me; the depressed, failure-oriented me; there is the athletic and the lazy; the liberal and the conservative. There is little me and big me. All of the parts are constantly changing and merging and each will put me in touch with a different aspect of the Universe at a different time in my life.

Chapter 9   Gestation and Birth

GESTATION AND BIRTH

No therapy can begin or end without a full investigation of the ramifications of the deep core birth experience. Any therapy that does not delve deeply into the basic human importance of gestation and birth is not a full feeling, in-depth therapy. Likewise, human beings who have not deeply felt and explored the unlimited range of their implantation, gestation and birth processes will never be anchored to their full power and glory. They may have the potential for great power, but if they don't feel what has been denied, they can never be connected to it.

Those individuals who have been deeply involved with a deep core feeling process respond to life with greater spontaneity, depth and power simply because they have gone deeper and higher than most people. They recognize that there are no limits to the possibilities of feeling. They also learn that to go through life requires a consistent return to feeling spaces, in order to understand and experience the totality of one's existence. Feelings become a way of gauging where one is now, how one got there from the past, and where one can potentially go in the future.

Feeling awareness of one's gestation and birth provides a focal point to aim for in one's quest for freedom from neurosis. I suggest that this prenatal period holds significant core experiences that mold and influence a person's future destiny. For some, it is the single most influential life moving force. Gestation and birth is the prototype of all later happiness and/or unhappiness. Let me clarify. I don't mean the illusion of happiness, for many people pretend that they are happy having accumulated the trappings of happiness. But inside they are miserable.

I am postulating that humanity in general has no awareness or consciousness of what is really happening in the fetal and birth processes and only a few therapeutic investigators have touched upon it. Most people who have investigated the birth issue have not done so sufficiently. They have examined from the outside in, rather than from the inside out, and this occurs because most innovators have not experienced their own therapy. They remove themselves from the very therapy that they are giving to their patients. A therapist must be a part of his therapy and vice versa. It is only when the therapist can be open and vulnerable to his patients that he can get to and explore those very deep places, both in himself and in his clients. This is why the Total Feeling Process is a very effective system of personal growth, because the therapists are not limited by any system that locks up its people in only one single aspect of human experience.

As to the issue of birth, we must recognize that those who deeply feel their birth, develop an incredible empathy for children and the birth experience itself. Those who have never re-experienced their own births can only participate in and allow inhumane and violent births to continue. It is an unfeeling, out of touch society that continues to allow the outrages that are perpetrated against infants. When full birth consciousness occurs in society, then individuals will truly prepare themselves for childbearing and physicians will have to respond and learn the natural techniques as espoused and practiced by Frederick Leboyer.[1] I have no illusions that we will ever have a full feeling society. Most adults are very intimidated by the force of full feelings and the demands and rewards of a feeling lifestyle. But I do believe that we can launch a crusade for more aware and responsible pregnancies and better birth practices. People, in general, are somewhat sensitive about issues surrounding babies and even those who are out of touch with themselves could possibly support a more humane approach to birth. One further note, for those women who are aware of their deep core reality and who have worked extensively on freeing their bodies and themselves from neurotic tension and fear, the possibility of a painless childbearing experience is a definite reality.

CONCEPTION AND IMPLANTATION

The ovaries of a human female contain 500,000 egg cells. Of these, only about 400 will ever get the opportunity to create a new life. One by one, over a lifetime, these egg cells will develop into mature eggs with each egg protected by a jelly-like substance and surrounded by fluid. This egg, or ovum, is contained and nourished securely inside the ovary. Monthly, in a mature female, the egg will move against the ovarian wall and the tension will cause the ovary to swell and eventually erupt like a volcano. At this

---

[1] Frederick Leboyer, *Birth Without Violence* (New York, Alfred A. Knopf, Inc., 1976).

point, a mature ovum is ejected, protected by its jelly, and it is during this process, called ovulation, that the female is susceptible to being impregnated by a sperm cell from a mature male. If the egg is not fertilized within one to three days, it will die and be flushed out of the system by a process called the menstrual flow.

If impregnation or conception does occur, the fertilized egg approaches the opening of the fallopian tube and muscular contractions and paddle-like cells will propel it to its final destination, the wall of the female uterus.

Male sperm cells are among the smallest in the body as compared to the ovum which is perhaps the largest. The male produces about 200 million of these sperm cells a day and yet, it is only for a few days in the middle of the menstrual cycle that a woman is capable of being impregnated. So, timing is important as well as the emotional attitude of both partners. If both the man and woman are in good health, it is reasonable to assume that pregnancy can happen during this ovulation period. However, the physical act itself plays only one part in this awesome miracle of creation and life. The deep core emotional components of both partners and their respective historical antecedents play equally as important a role as the physical realities of sperm, egg, ejaculation and ovulation.

Research is just beginning to compile on the effects of early intrauterine life on the human psyche. William Swartley[2] divides major neonatal traumas into eight categories and for purposes of convenience and clarity, I will explore some of these same categories in the following sections of this chapter.

Prior to the conception trauma which is Swartley's first area of neonatal focus, we have found individuals feeling anticipatory conceptional experiences plus fears of ejaculation on the unicellular spermatazoan and ovular levels. This is consistent with our findings that patients can and do feel, on a deep core level, pre-conception and pre-birth trauma. This means that feelings can transcend what we would consider objective, physical life spaces as we understand them thus, leaving the path open to extend the range of human emotion beyond ordinary body and ego boundaries.

---

[2] William Swartley, *The Undivided Self* (London, The Churchill Centre, 1978), pgs. 30-41.

Thus, in a feeling sense it is possible to reconnect to realms of experience beyond existing planes of physical time and existence.[3] With these new extended ranges of feeling, we are justified in calling this therapy the TOTAL Feeling Process and I cannot overemphasize the "TOTAL" aspect of the deep feeling experience.

One young woman found herself experiencing a tremendous amount of guilt after she unintentionally hurt her son. She felt some of her guilt at a deep core level but was still left with the feeling that she was unlovable and didn't deserve to be forgiven. Her body was heavily defended and she felt that the pain she was blocking against was so devastating that her core self was in jeopardy.

> "If I let go, the feeling will rip me apart . . . I'll literally explode into a million pieces and die. I can't feel it—it's too deadly!!! . . . . . . I feel so far from my core self . . . . (crying) . . . . . In order to get me back I'll have to explode with such intensity that I just can't bear it . . . . . "

She stayed with her heavy physical and emotional blockage for quite some time until she, finally, was able to open up to a little feeling.

> "I feel so unlovable and unloved . . . . . like I don't even deserve to be alive . . . . What did I do that was so awful—awful to the very core of my soul??? God, what did I do??!! . . . I'm afraid . . . so afraid."

At this point in the session, the therapist started poking and prodding her until she reacted with some anger, exhibited by a strong, steady kicking motion of her feet and legs. She later explained it as a feeling that she had to swim for her life. The scene that finally emerged was that she was one of her father's sperm who was terrified of the imminent ejaculation because she was not supposed to live. Her awful crime was that she had survived. Corroboration by her parents confirmed the fact that she had been an

---

[3] I will go into greater depths along these lines in Chapter 14 on Transcendental Experiences.

unplanned pregnancy. In fact, the sperm (HER) was supposed to have died after sexual ejaculation.

The subtle ramifications of emotional and environmental influences on the conception phase of development are widespread. They can range from a receptive, supportive environment by two clear adults who are genuinely desirous of a child to hostile, murderous sensations and secretions by either a rejecting sperm or egg. The following woman experienced a great deal of ambivalence and craziness surrounding her own conception. The reality of immediate adoption following her birth confirms some of the conception trauma that she underwent.

"My conception was crazy . . . . I felt such anxiety from my dad's sperm and my mother's egg. There was a tremendous sense of sadness in my mother's egg and a fear of dying from my father's sperm leading to urgency (anger) to impregnate. I felt my father's pain of wanting his own child —that sperm had to impregnate immediately. I could feel the power in my legs as I swam up the canal—faster and faster—dodging in and out—almost as though I was looking for the right moment, the right spot. . . . . one more thrust of power and BAM—I'M IN!!! . . . . .

I could feel my dad's sperm overwhelm the egg as though he had to take over. My mother's egg was scared to death—I could feel her rejection at the moment of conception. She went crazy—the egg went crazy . . . . I knew from that moment on that my mother would give me away. I knew my dad wanted me. He needed his blood line—his transcendency to live through me . . . . His sperm did not give up—even faced with death—he tried harder. He had to make it and make it against all odds. He wouldn't quit until he did . . . . I never trusted that egg—it was the source of all my nourishment, yet it crippled me with its rejection. I feared that egg but I loved the warmth from my father's sperm . . . . I could feel the 'NO!' at the moment of conception from my mother—I could feel the egg screaming 'NO!' . . . . . that has always been my craziness.

She later experienced a heavy emotional rejection from her maternal grandparents which further contributed to her deep

141

rooted sense of unworthiness and rejection. The following are examples of non-supportive or negative sperm influences in the conception phase.

> Peggy: "I feel that I wasn't consciously conceived. I was
> received by a needy egg while the sperm didn't have a
> strong direction to really prosper and come forth. I didn't
> experience much of a life support system behind the sperm.
> There was, however, very much of a lifeline directly con-
> nected with the egg. It nourished me and gave me warmth
> . . . ."
>
> Julie: "I experience a sensation of falling fast in space I
> feel my father's sperm begging—I'm begging for life. My
> mother's egg is not accepting me. I have to beg and beg for
> entrance . . . . I feel pitiful in my efforts to enter my
> mother's egg . . . . cringing and begging . . . . I feel like
> I'm begging for life (The story of my life) . . . . The mo-
> ment of union is not a joyous explosion. It is painful. I feel
> enveloped but the union is not complete . . . . Like I still ex-
> ist as two separate parts . . . . I feel conceived in anger and
> hate."
>
> Cathy: "I felt as if my father forced himself to have relations
> with my mother. I felt both my father and my mother in
> me: my father's stubborn strength . . . the way he tried and
> tried and never gave up, his silent withdrawal, his
> aloneness, the way he shouldered burdens and responsibili-
> ty, the disappointment and emptiness of his life . . . .
>
> I also felt the weakness of my mother in me. The part of
> me that is sickening and weak is my mother . . . . My
> father's body was tall and strong. He was seldom ill and
> showed no signs of physical weakness. I feel that my body is
> like my father's body. I felt strangely closer to him—to his
> sperm—despite the angriness of his contact with my
> mother."

The law of natural selection and survival of the fittest also plays a
part in the conception drama. Personalities can be traced back to
the dynamics of cellular interaction with individuals indentifying
strongly with either mother or father, ethnic heritage, cultural influences, etc.

"I am my father's sperm. I identify myself as his sperm . . . The egg is also a part of me and I will become a part of it. I am trying to get into the egg . . . . Finally I am being chosen . . . . Why me? . . . All these other sperm cells . . . . my brothers and sister . . . Why are they letting me in? . . . They want me to live and survive. . . . I am the strongest . . . The most powerful and the most unique . . . I am selected because I am the one most likely to live and become a person . . . an extension of my father and mother."

To perpetuate the species and one's family lineage requires the mechanisms of nature to operate at optimum perfection and efficiency in order to guarantee survival. Thus, what will be created is a totally unique, new individual, giving birth to a magnificent ongoing history.

Following the union of sperm and egg during conception, cell division while traveling through the Fallopian tube can be either a smooth, flowing process or a disconnected, erratic one.

"I feel that the reproduction of my cells is erratic . . . like popcorn popping instead of a smooth, unified growth as a balloon being blown up."

Roughly seven days after conception we come upon the next category of neonatal trauma, the implantation trauma. There exists at this level a "threat of abortion" if the mother's body, at some level, rejects the fertilized egg and gives off internal secretions to destroy it. Thousands of white blood cells will attack this tiny being as though it were a foreign intruder, until the tide is turned and physical rejection turns to acceptance and nurturance. According to Swartley[4] the degree of trauma correlates negatively with the "will" of the fertilized egg to implant, the degree the mother desires the child (thus aiding in the implantation process) and the psychic and physical energy of the fertilized egg when it reaches the uterus.

---

[4] William Swartley, *The Undivided Self* (London: The Churchill Centre, 1978), pg. 35.

It is my contention that faulty or incomplete union at the conception and implantation phases can lead to schizoid tendencies or schizophrenia, depending upon the severity of the trauma. Negative energy, vibes or "demons" are so terrifying at this early embryonic stage that life energy gets turned off and a major split occurs. Such an individual may never feel whole or integrated.

One middle aged woman was experiencing a great deal of fear and powerlessness with her job trainer and was unable to feel clearly grounded with him. At one level she knew she didn't trust him and yet, she felt dependent on him for a career. She was in a transition period in her life and desperately wanted to move ahead in her chosen field rather than slip backward into her old profession which she had found stifling and neurotic. By remaining disconnected and powerless, she did not have to really risk her future by facing her true feelings about him.

Jane: I don't know where I am with you. I don't trust you
. . . . I'm scared of you . . . Don't know when you'll stab me in the back . . . .

Ther: You've given him the power of life or death over you. He can give you success—life. If you speak up, or confront him or even feel what your true gut reaction towards him is, he might cut you off, take away your hope of life.

Jane: Why am I so afraid of you??!! Why do I give you so much power??!!

Gradually, Jane regresses to a very early embryonic state where she is paralyzed with fear. She vascillates back and forth between defending herself from external demons and warding off the heavy vibes from her mother's body to die. The vibes (possibly white blood cells[5]) are threatening her very existence with annihilation. This woman was conceived during the Depression and her mother, in particular, was very emotionally resistant to having a child. So, it is not difficult to imagine the physical and emotional messages being relayed via the intrauterine environment.

Jane: I am an intruder . . . . an intruding sperm in my mother's body. I guess there is an egg somewhere but right now I only feel myself as a sperm . . . I feel myself uniting

---

[5]Ibid, p. 34.

physically with my mother's egg—but emotionally I stay split in two separate parts. There is a war going on within me . . . I feel as if the two parts of me—sperm and egg, male and female, body and heart—battle it out.

Ther: You must feel very torn inside, not whole.

Jane: I do feel torn. I feel so much like I don't belong . . . . like I'm an intruder. (crying) I always feel like an outsider, one who doesn't deserve to live. I keep feeling her lethal vibes attack me right to my core—until I am almost dead, until I am so very weak and only have a tiny spot of energy left right in my center. All that's left is a tiny pulse—weak and ebbing . . . . (deeply sobbing) I'm so grateful you let me live, momma . . . . . I feel so unworthy and so grateful . . . . That's why I can't demand or ask for anything or take a stand for myself . . . . I'm just so grateful that you let me live.

Jane was finally able to feel and integrate this deep core helplessness and terror and stand on her own two feet. The dependency she was experiencing with her trainer lessened to the point where she was able to stand up for her own beliefs and not be overcome by need, unworthiness and fear.

These early traumas that are inflicted upon the embryo during the first hours and days of existence can have a life altering effect upon the later adult. The degree and intensity of the insult determines the extent and type of physical and/or emotional damage. It is because of this incredible early vulnerability that I urge responsibility and awareness on the part of all sexually functioning adults. Casual lovemaking, whether it be in a back seat or a marriage bed, can have far reaching effects if either partner is not being responsible. Children should be conceived out of a genuine, deep-seated desire, on the part of both parents, for a newborn child. Anger, fear, rejection and neurosis have no place in the creation of an innocent new life.

GESTATION

The therapist merely has to watch the symbolic language of the patient in order to determine what early feeling is disconnected and unfelt. The patient will talk in here and now adult terms, but the language will give clues as to what stage of development the feeling is located. For example, one woman kept having trouble coming out of herself and making contact with the outside world. She kept reiterating an intense need to be safe and at the same time felt very contented, on some level, with being locked inside a secure shell. As her feelings began to unfold, it became quite obvious that she was wishing to return to an embryonic level where she was completely passive, taken care of and safe inside her mother's warm, soft womb.

As I have stated before, a patient will act out his life in direct correlation to the significant, unfinished, disconnected events of his own fetal development. It is not unreasonable to assume that one's defenses and ways of relating to the world are being formed during all stages of fetal development. What happens during the third or fourth month of pregnancy may have a significant influence on the remainder of one's life. If one needed softness and support during the twelfth week of pregnancy and didn't get it, but instead got something painful, then we can understand why he/she might be afraid of intense closeness and contact at 42 years of age.

When something painful occurs during any phase of fetal development, it is very hard to undo it by traditional therapeutic measures in adult life. There is only one way to lift life-crippling repression and that is to go back and feel that early pain, in the here and now, while one's adult ego is strong enough to integrate that early experience.

It is difficult to comprehend that a shattering fetal experience can be so threatening that a baby may have to close down a part of himself permanently or at least until he is strong enough as an adult and ready to feel that particular pain. We have witnessed children at the age of five years, who show absolutely no desire or proclivity for warm, close emotional and physical contact. Some of them crave attention but try to get this need met by flirtatiousness, coyness, and coquettishness. It is the beginning of the classic cat and mouse game that many adults have developed to a very sophisticated level. These children seem to be innately born with this fear of contact and actually withdraw from and reject intimacy. They try to get their contact needs met vicariously, by teasing from afar.

Retrogressively, we can witness many adults who require extreme safety in their intimate dealings with others. They fear closeness and when we trace their history back to early fetal stages, we can locate the root feeling experience that necessitated the development of a guarded, suspicious approach to intimacy. We have found much evidence that points to adaptive fetal environmental learning.

The following case is an example of a young woman whose early gestational environment caused her physical and emotional trauma which stayed with her into her adult life. It was only by deep core feeling that she was able to resolve some of the emotional insult, although the physical damage was permanent.

Ther: Just let that horrendous fright come over you . . . . the most horrifying fright you can think of . . . choking fear . . . . life stifling fear . . . Life threatening fear . . . .

Sarah: (crying) . . . She doesn't want me . . .

Ther: Who doesn't want you, Sarah . . . Who doesn't want you, your mother? . . . And yet she told you she planned for you, she wanted you . . .

Sarah: She didn't know that she didn't want me . . . She thinks she wants me . . . .

Ther: What is it doing to you?

Sarah: Ohh . . . . I'm floating . . . I'm floating . . . . (crying) . . Like I would go away if I could, but I'm already floating! . . (crying) . . I would go away if I could, but I'm already floating . . . (crying) . . . I almost did what she wanted . . . I knew what you wanted . . . I knew . . . . I always knew it, but I'm floating already! . . . . I'm floating already!

I don't want to feel this . . . . . (crying)

Ther: Say it again, "I don't want to feel this."

Sarah: I don't want to feel this . . . . (moaning) . . No, No . . . . I feel I knew that she didn't want me to live; it's like she changed her mind . . . I almost did what she said . . . I almost did what she wanted . . . When I was big . . . I was already big!! . . . I'm already floating! There's a part of me that wanted to die, just because she wanted me to . . . I was going to do it! . . . (crying) . . . I was going to do it!!! . . . (crying)

I'm not flowing with this . . . it's too terrible.

Ther: Say it, . . . "It's too terrible." How could you flow with dying?! How could it be anything but terrible?

Sarah: I'm pulling back . . . .

Ther: Pull back and notice what you do with your breathing.

That breathing is what is happening in that womb . . .
Sarah: NOT breathing!! . . . . You know what else? If I lay
next to you, momma . . . . for every two or three breaths
you take, I'll only take one . . . little ones . . . . little, little
ones . . . . (crying)
Ther: Hold your breath . .
Sarah: I'm scared to take what I need . . . happy just to be
alive . . . just to be . . . just to be alive . . .
Ther: (Role Playing) . . . You're lucky to be alive, and I don't
ever want you to forget it . . . You are lucky I let you live
. . . Be thankful that I let you live . . . I really didn't want
you; I changed my mind afterwards. I wasn't sure. I had a
lot of doubts whether I wanted you or not.
Sarah: You know I was going to die . . . I was going to do it
. . . I was going to do it . . . I was going to go along with
what you wanted. I was going to do it . . . I like floating
. . . I like floating . . . *I like floating!!!* . . . *I like it* . . . . .
(crying) . . . I won't be a bother to you . . . Oh, God, she
changed her mind . . . She said how good I was . . . She
always said, "You were so good when I brought you home
from the hospital . . . I didn't even know I had a baby . . .
You were so good."
Ther: She didn't even know she had a baby . . .
Sarah: I did it myself . .
Ther: When you came in here today, you had been floating
all afternoon long. You were in that blissful state of being inside mommy . . . very afraid of it changing into that horrible
truth. That is why you are so afraid to lose that blissful state,
why you are so afraid to lose that "feeling good." You don't
want to slip into that agony, that terrible truth, that she
wasn't sure she wanted you . . . she changed her mind. Imagine having your life in the hands of a woman who's bouncing back and forth, trying to make a decision as to whether
she's going to have you or not. Imagine being in that kind of
dependent situation. Totally dependent on her, whether she
gives you life or death.
Sarah: I do that with my husband, Steve. Sometimes I give
him total power over my life and happiness.
Ther: Absolutely, there you've got it! You are really set up.
You are set up to suffer. You were set up to struggle to get

acceptance, to get love . . . remember all the times you said, "Steve, I only want you to want me" . . . You were saying the same thing to your mother, "I only want you to want me . . . all the way, only me. I want you to fully want me. Because I really want you . . . . . I need you!"

Sarah: I know how early she must have changed her mind . . . the spine is the first thing, the first thing that develops . . . and mine is all fucked up. But you know what? Later I got the message that she changed her mind. My spine is fucked up and I always did what she wanted. But I liked floating too much . . . I didn't want to stop floating . . . You know, nothing else is the matter with me. I'm fucking perfect! I always did what she wanted . . . . just didn't want to stop floating! . . . The only problem was I just got so *big!*

That's why I'm so big. Both my parents are very little . . . I had to be *big!!* . . . I had to be big and healthy . . . (crying) . . . *I did it myself!* . . . . *I did it myself!!!* . . . Don't change your mind! . . . (crying) . . . Please, Mom, don't change your mind . . . .

(Patient cries heavier and experiences a lot of body sensation . . . originating during gestation . . . also a great deal of pain in her lower back)

Dr. Denis H. Stott[6] of Guelph University in Ontario demonstrates the relationship between marital discord during gestational phases and the subsequent risk of physical handicap to the newborn infant. According to his research, the great majority of mothers who had suffered from interpersonal tensions during their pregnancies had exceedingly unhealthy children. When the pregnant woman was subjected to continuous or recurring serious interpersonal tension, the children ran twice the usual risk of handicap in health development or behavior. "There is an indication," says Dr. Stott, "that an adverse environment sets off an alternative set of genetic instruction." If the mother was kept short of money during the pregnancy while the husband spent heavily, the

---

[6]D.H. Stott, "Physical and Mental Handicaps Following a Disturbed Pregnancy", *Lancet*, Vol. 1 (1957b), pg. 1006.

children were nearly two and a half times more damaged than the average child in this sample. Unwanted pregnancies yielded 44 percent more liability to handicap. If the mothers did not intend to have the children and did not accept them, there was a 24 percent greater risk. If the mothers were desperate at the knowledge of the pregnancy and perhaps tried to secure abortions, there was a 46 percent probability of a physically damaging handicap.

Thus, we have here a substantial study verifying the effects of physical and emotional damage being based on certain circumstances surrounding one's gestation and birth. In other words, we can hypothesize that the conditions of the mother, the milieu in which she lives, her relationship with her husband plus the attitudes of both partners toward the developing fetus have a profound effect on the subsequent health of that newborn infant. It is interesting to note that when stress is introduced in the early phases of gestation, what may occur is an alteration in the genetic makeup of that developing human being. Possible ramifications of this kind of finding are far reaching.

EFFECTS OF MATERNAL HATRED (NEGATIVITY)

What happens to us at the moment of fertilization through gestation/birth and the formative years molds our character for the remainder of our existence. The circumstances surrounding conception and implantation, as well as the external events during the entire gestational period, are the precursors for prenatal personality development. It is that in utero personality, with all its peculiar characteristics, that carries us all through infancy and into adult life.

A thirty-one year old male client of mine was screaming in intense agony because of his sudden immersion into the truth of his early gestational environment. His first statements were, "There is hate all around me." Here the client was describing the inutero experience of his mother's emotional/physical state of being. The hate that was inside of her created a psychic panorama for the way that this young man would view all women and life's circumstances. He learned, inutero, that his mother was hating him. It is hard to speculate that he would spend a lifetime burdened with the anticipatory anxiety of imminent female rejection and hatred. Thus, that early inutero communication system had imprinted on his personality an intense fear and sensitivity towards all female rage, anger and hatred.

Freud's scheme of the repetition compulsion bears out the truth that what occurs to us in early life is bound to repeat itself in a never ending circle of unconscious "set up" situations. To put it another way, what goes around once comes around again. An early unmet need keeps repeating itself in order to be completed. Every time this client would provoke certain responses from his wife and other women, he would be refiring that old unfinished feeling of "mommy hates me and wants to destroy me completely."

This client also started having intense amorous, needful feelings towards a female therapist. The old anxiety arose, but fortunately, he had enough ego insight to recognize its familiar origins in infancy. He started crying:

"My mother hated me as soon as I was born . . . As soon as I came out, I was despised and loathed . . . I was a boy . . . a cardinal sin, a crime against humanity and my mother . . . the third son.

My life has been full of attempts to get acceptance and love from females yet I always turn them into unfulfilling mothers."

This client always seemed to be walking around as if something or someone was totally missing from his existence.

"I'm always looking for another female who will be the one to fulfill me, but I'm always disillusioned because she never comes. That one woman, that perfect female, the mother that I never had. Sandy (the therapist) is like that, which is why I'm so attracted to her. She's so warm and open and accepting; she could give me everything that none of the other females could. I'm a better man than her husband and she should really care about me . . . . . . (crying).

Every woman is just like my mother . . . . never giving enough. All I want is a female who will take care of me . . . . My mother always resented taking care of me. I deserve better."

As Irv begins to tap into his own self value, he is filled with anger and rage toward his own mother who was not able to respond to him.

"Treat me like a decent human being . . . . If you treat me like a prick, I'll be a prick . . . . You resented me when you diapered and fed me. It was all hate . . . . there was no joy in your face for raising me. I was Irv, the burden . . .

I can see it now with all those other females (starts screaming and yelling loudly) . . . . *I am a joy!! . . . . . I have a lot to give!!* . . . (crying deeply) Why didn't you see that! . . . . . Why didn't you see that! . . . . God Damn You, why didn't you see that!!! . . . . . . "

Irv begins to realize the positive repressed part of himself; that part which reiterates that he is "a joy" with "a lot to give." His anger is directed towards his mother and all other women who did not "see that." As he comes out of the session, Irv experiences sadness at his own core truth; he is resigned to where he must go and what he must do. Eventually, his own feeling momentum will carry him to the ultimate triumph over his own blockages.

The following section further expands the concept of intrauterine memory and how trauma can be imprinted by separating a child from its natural mother through the process of adoption.

EFFECTS OF ADOPTION TRAUMA

Adults who were adopted at the moment of birth present a very particular kind of psychological trauma. It is not my intention to reiterate the importance of adequate bonding between a mother and her newborn infant. That has been covered elsewhere. The fact is that an adoptee spends a major part of his/her adult life wondering who are his/her real parents. There is a psychobiological memory imprinted on the sensory/emotional apparatus that cries out for a reuniting with one's natural parents.

During gestation an infant becomes completely familiar with the rhythm and flow of his mother's internal emotional/vegetative system. That child is bonded to its mother by a familiarity of in-utero communication and similar genetic physical typing. Skin to skin and viscera to viscera is bound together by a common biological inheritance. To yank a child away from that familiar universe is to inflict trauma and then the insult is compounded by thrusting the baby into a totally alien and foreign environment. This is why many adopted adults feel as if there is something very strong and powerful missing from their physical existences. That missing part is the true biological parent.

The need to reconnect and bond to the original parents remains an unfinished piece of business that cries out for closure. There is a pre-eminent drive to go backwards and cling and be held by one's natural mother and father. Many adoptees try to adjust to this basic primal trauma by covering it up and instituting the severest forms of repression. Survival dictates that they learn to "adjust to" and accept their new and somewhat alien environment. Those who have completely "adjusted" need to blank out any memory and desire to return to the original parental matrix.

But where repression is incomplete, or if one becomes aware that he/she is something of a stranger with his adoptive parents in his new home, then the drive to return grows stronger. Dissatisfaction or unmet need with the adopted parents may also stimulate the drive to return to the biological parents.

Clients in therapy who are adoptees manifest adult difficulties covering a broad spectrum of behaviors and those behaviors show a direct link to the separation trauma of adoption. Some have trouble forming any kind of close affectional bonds with any other human beings. These clients create a cerebral fortress that distances them from their own deeper realities and any human contacts that may re-trigger that old bonding trauma. Others who have formed bonds find those affiliations to be somewhat faulty and unsatisfying. Love object unfulfillment is the major symptom of traumatized adoptees; because it is difficult for the adoptee to be fully satisfied in a relationship when the roots of dissatisfaction are back in infancy. The adoptee will always find confirmatory evidence that a love partner is going to abandon and desert; and perhaps we can postulate that this individual may even set up a compulsive desertion ritual.

Those who overcome and work through much of that early trauma can become quite capable of being substantial and successful love partners and mates. The task is never easy, however, for there is much significant, related pain that needs to be worked through and connected to the bottom line desertion trauma. Many adoptees have felt strange in their adopted parent's arms and homes. Some clients have even connected to the ethnic origins of their real parents without obtaining any substantial data from their adopted parents. This would indicate that even one's ethnic and inherited culture may be transmitted inutero.

The question can be raised, of course, about how an adult can remember all that has happened to him inutero. The brain is not the only organ that remembers. The skin is one of the first sensory apparatuses to develop inutero and it retains a primitive sense of memory of its original, one-celled connection to mother and father. This memory later gets transmitted to the slowly developing extension of the nervous system, called the brain. I should not neglect to say that the viscera of the vegetative processes also develop shortly after the skin, and the organs remember the experience of the skin plus the major incidents of their own evolutions. Thus, the body stores and remembers everything.

The human cortex is a relative late comer in the evolution of the human animal. It is an adaptive mechanism that developed out of the necessity to expand survival potential in a wider range of environments. The one cell protoplasm, epitomized by sperm and egg cells, came first and has its own evolutionary, historical memory. The ever increasing complicated structures that grew from primitive one cell animals are all contained in a complex body that we call Human. Memory for all experience is implanted in every part of that organism. Repression, or forgetting, is a biological byproduct for developing newer and more complicated structures. This is the price we have had to pay for evolving from minute unicellular structures to that total being, that we call Humankind.

Consequently, there is much justification for the fact that a developing embryo and fetus can remember its precise, inherited environment. Permanently separate that full blown, nine month infant from its natural home inside mother and it will be traumatized. The brain may not remember the initial abandonment, but the body will. Let us never forget that a baby remembers at its primary levels, even though as an adult, it may take much emotional work to connect to that memory. We now know that sperm, egg and gestation experiences do get transmitted to the more primitive parts of the brain and that these memories become

revivified in dreams, LSD sessions, hallucinatory states, meditation, transpersonal experiences and deep feeling therapies.

BIRTH OR THE WILL TO LIVE

In the chapter on destructiveness we discussed the various
elements of sado-masochism in everyday life. We are now ready to
delve a little further into the etiology of this syndrome by examining the birth process itself. First, we need to look at and understand
the relationship between birth and adult growth motivation and
orientation. Second, we want to gain a better insight into the
various defensive expressions of birth-traumatized infants who
later develop weak growth motivation. This is manifested in an unconscious need to fail in life followed by attempts to prove that one
is absolutely worthless in every way. Third, we will also attempt to
locate the various escape routes that are later practiced by those
who have faced the possibility of death during the birth process.
And fourth, we will try to examine the role of both mother and
father in the birth process and subsequent growth motivation.

When I speak of the period of the birth process, I am referring not
only to the birth itself and the immediate circumstances that surround it, but also to those external influences that have direct bearing on the kind of gestational milieu and the post natal environment
that the infant will have to deal with. As I have already stated, this
includes the emotional and physical environment that the new family member must struggle and come to terms with: the socio-
economic level of the family, nutritional habits, general health of
the family members, the cultural and ethnic influences and the
parent's attitude in general toward children and childbearing.

Many researchers have explored the birth process, among the
more well known being Otto Rank, Alexander Mott[7] C.G. Jung, and
Arthur Janov. Janov[8] attempts to fuse observations of patients with
the latest developments in the neurological sciences. He explains
that there are three levels of consciousness that get laid down in
brain functioning and that these factors determine human behavior.
The first level of consciousness pertains to the earliest encounters

---

[7] J. Mott, *Nature of the Self*, (London: Alan Wingate Publ., 1959).
[8] Arthur Janov, *Primal Man*, (New York: Thomas Y. Crowell Co., 1975).

with the processing of pain and the birth primal is seen as the precursor or causative factor in all later consciousness development.

C.G. Jung[9] also, has greatly emphasized the experience of birth, but he functioned within a psychoanalytic framework which focused on psychological and spiritual elements, while ignoring biological phenomenon. He proposed that birth was the prototype of all feelings of separation. The real trauma for Jung was the painful experience of leaving the warm maternal womb and being thrown into a hostile, cold world.

Stanislav Grof has done extensive research on the birth experience itself and breaks it into four distinct clinical stages, which he terms Basic Perinatal Matrices (BPM).[10] He describes very vividly the phenomena discovered in each stage and goes on to explain the etiology of mental disorders as having roots in particular stages of perinatal development and expulsion. His findings are based on observations from LSD therapy.

Grof's Basic Perinatal Matrices describe patterns of experiences related to the various stages of birth. In BPM I the child experiences a primary union with mother before the onset of delivery. This intrauterine period is ideally marked by symbiotic unification, peace, security, protection, satisfaction, and the gratification of all needs. The environment is roomy and nurturant and feelings of oceanic bliss and ecstasy are common, provided that there is no noxious stimuli to interfere and disturb normal development. In Leboyer's terminology it is the Golden Age.[11] One individual describes it this way.

"I just experienced all the wonder of it . . . all the magnificence and the beauty of it . . . (long deep sobbing)

---

9 Carl Jung, *Man and his Symbols*, (New York: Doubleday and Co., 1964).
10 Stanislav Grof, *Realms of the Unconscious* (New York: E. P. Dutton Co., 1976). pg. 95-150.
11 Frederick Leboyer, *Birth Without Violence* (New York, Alfred A. Knopf, Inc., 1976), pg. 24.
Both Leboyer and Grof see this as lasting for fully one half of the pregnancy, soon to be followed by a second half of almost continual stress and pain.

. . . Oh, my God . . . . It's like I'm seeing all the beauty of being in the womb . . . (continued sobbing) . . . . all the beauty of it, all the magnificence . . . Suddenly, my hands are just reaching out to feel how big and wonderful this all is . . . me . . . OHHHH! . . . It's like I hear music of the universe . . . . It's total bliss . . . . Like nothing I've ever felt before . . .

. . . Somehow all that I've ever experienced as being beautiful and serene stems from this experience. Everything I've ever appreciated or felt . . . My love of little people, little children, my own little boy comes from this feeling, this moment in eternity . . . I'm in eternity . . . AHHHH . . . Like coming from the stars . . . It's like being in the universe . . . My whole body opens wide with this wonderful, marvelous experience. And I feel you here, my mother. I feel you here with me, next to me, as I experience this bliss . . . I feel all the beauty, all this magnificence . . . All my decency and kindness and gentleness . . . AHHHH . . . All the holiness and the sacredness comes from that core experience. That magnificent part of me, before I got all sick and crazy . . . A miracle, a wonder, a sacred treasure. I love that little me."

As the infant grows in the womb, he feels more and more confined and his limitless space converts into a prison. He refuses to accept this confinement and fights back, but in time he must give in, thus restricting himself even more by submission. During the ninth month, the mother's contractions are not strong and are experienced as gentle, playful caresses. The baby loves and welcomes this delightful sensual game and looks forward to each time it occurs. He joins in wholeheartedly in this temporary, pleasurable preparation for the actual struggle of birth, when the contractions will be much more intense.

Grof moves on to describe the next phase of the birth process that he calls BPM II. This stage is characterized by a closed uterine system and is related to the first stage of delivery. Here we witness an incredible life and death struggle with mother which is perhaps, the worst experience a human being can endure. There is total alienation from mother and no chance of immediate escape. Adults may experience this as being trapped, needing room, absolute hopelessness, and feeling completely overwhelmed.

Otto Rank claimed that "every opportunity which somehow 'reminds' the individual—mostly in a symbolic way—of the birth trauma is used again and again for the abreaction of the undisposed-of-affect."[12] He further claimed that the adults' "choice" of the form of neurosis is determined by the individual birth process, the specific point of attack of the trauma, and the individual's reaction to it. We have witnessed this, time and time again, as we trace back in therapy from the here and now behavior to specific gestational and birth antecedents. Claustrophobia, dread of elevators and tunnels, acute fear of flying or driving, a feeling of being trapped in certain life situations, as well as certain suicidal tendencies stemming from an "inhibited depression"[13] (no hope, a desire to not exist, very little energy) are all behavioral manifestations of a stressful BPM II birth phase. Grof does an excellent job of exploring these phenomenon so I will not go into much depth here. Instead, let me offer an example of one woman who was experiencing a great deal of here and now anxiety before regressing back to an intense birth experience focusing on the BPM II phase of labor.

"For over a week now I have been aware of the old dreaded birth symptoms. They have become a familiar sequence of physical and emotional forerunners to something big, something terrifying, something that on and off has haunted me throughout my deep feeling experiences over the past years."

"Like clockwork I can expect them to break out every few months and let me know that another terrifying piece of me is pushing its way up to be felt. I dread it because it is always so heavy and is usually preceded by days of craziness. And I welcome it because it always leaves me clearer and stronger and more Me . . .

The symptoms begin with a restless tossing at night and a feeling that I can't get enough room — too hot, sweaty, short of breath, panicky wrestling with the covers . . . A shooting pain behind my eyes . . . Grinding my teeth . . . A burning pain in

---

[12] Otto Rank, *The Trauma of Birth*, (New York, Harper and Row, Inc., 1923).

[13] Stanislav Grof, "Beyond Psychoanalysis III: Birth Trauma and Its Relation to Mental Illness, Suicide and Ecstasy", *Primal Community* Vol. 1, No. 3 (New York, Fall 1975), pg. 10-14.

my ears . . . Weakness . . . Inertia . . . A dread to really assert myself and feel or even try to feel . . . I find myself avoiding eye contact, or any contact for that matter, with my friends and group members . . . I am running from the very ones who could help me. But then, I haven't really decided I want to be helped through it yet. Maybe I can work it myself. Maybe it will go away . . . But it doesn't . . .

I begin group this evening by fantasizing a play script with me being in the womb. The spot-light is on me struggling inside a tight cocoon of little space, little air and echoing, terror-filled cries. I move from the fantasy to actualizing it by wrapping myself tight in a blanket and having a group member cover me with a heavy bean sack. As she slowly increases the pressure on me and partially covers my face, I break into frenzied screaming and sobs . . . Terror wracks my soul . . . I can only let it rise a little at a time. My rational mind won't/can't let go fully. It feels like if I do, if I let that terror over-take me, I will go completely berserk and break into a hundred pieces. I will die. 'My body can't breathe . . . I'm going to suffocate . . . God, I'm going to die . . . I can't bear this . . . It's too much for little me."

"As I become aware of body tension blocking my moving deeper into the feeling, I re-arrange my body so that one of the group members has easier access to it. The pain shifts from my back to my stomach to my jaw right near the ear, to my temples, to the instep of my feet and she deftly follows me and tracks me from one pain to the other, applying pressure to increase the sensations. Finally, I signal that I need an overload of physical pain in order to let myself in deeper. One of the trainees moves in to assist and they start a barrage of physical poking and shaking which helps to loosen up my defenses. Again, I feel a breaking up and a holding on . . .

In the here and now I can't let myself *explode* with love or sex or joy. I have to hold on even then. Exploding is so terrifying for me—whether in joy or pain. I feel more pain realizing I can't explode in sexual joy with my husband, the man I love most in the world, because I am still 'holding on.' I can't explode into the Universe and fully experience God and the cosmos because I am still 'holding on.' Will I ever be able to be fully alive and unafraid and free?! Or, will I always be scattered in pieces, not whole, until I'm finally able to let myself explode in terror—and live.

Sandra came out of this feeling experience very weak. She had not been able to sink into all the feelings of helplessness and devastation and as a result, she could hardly talk and was not able to make much contact with anyone. She felt lifeless. It was at this point that the group leader suggested she stand against the wall with her arms spread out. He then moved the group all around her and suggested they start responding toward her, however they felt. He began with, "Come out little baby . . . Come out little Sandy, you can do it."

"I am finally able to let their concern for me open me up again and each of their words and tears give me more and more energy to feel. They start throwing pillows at me and I am thrown deeper and deeper into a helpless, weak, little baby space, pinned to the wall and too little to defend myself or move. Finally, I let my body take over and my shoulders start grinding into the wall, I am sweating heavily and my crying is getting deeper and deeper. Frantically, I keep pushing to get out—out of this dead space, out of this crushing womb. 'Mommy, let me live . . . Help me get out.' My back starts aching and I begin to pound my whole back against the wall, letting my head and spinal column snap each time. 'God, the pain. I have to get out. I can't move these walls. So hard . . . Rigid . . . Have to keep on banging . . . I'm not getting anywhere . . . Where am I going? I can't make it . . .'
I continue for a while longer crying and banging and then sink down tired. I know I am not free yet. I can feel my body still holding me back. I can feel the tightness in my chest and lungs. But at least I have *moved* a little . . . I am no longer *stuck* . . .
Movement means life so maybe there is a chance. I feel now like there is. I feel calmer and stronger and more here. Not joyful yet . . . but here. And that feels good . . .

The release of pressure and the resultant anticipation of release from this closed uterine system exemplifies Grof's BPM III or propulsion through the birth canal. The intense life and death struggle is satiated and relief is in sight for the overwhelmed infant. In contrast to BPM II this phase of the birth process gives rise to an "agitated depression,"[14] a high level of anxiety and tension manifested by both inward and outward aggression. Suicidal tendencies involve bloody and violent acts, symbolic of a violent birth struggle followed by total release. Sexual deviations stemming from BPM III are of a sadomasochistic nature. The rage and aggression the infant needs to propel him/herself through the birth canal and out of the torturous environment of a lethal womb is symbolically acted out on an adult sexual level. Examples of physical symptomology, or "pregenital conversions"[15] which are mostly related to BPM III are psychogenic asthma, stammering, conversion hysteria, sexual neurosis (frigidity and impotence), ulcerative colitis, etc. Many of these manifestations of the early birth struggle have cleared up once an individual has gone back and felt the original traumatic circumstances surrounding his entry into the world.

If a baby is internally weakened by these early experiences, we can expect him to approach life and therapy with an extension of that deep weakness. Infants who have struggled desperately to live, may have become so washed out by that and subsequent experiences that they just don't have enough "heart" to push and breathe life. The following is speculation, but I believe that the old practice of slapping babies after delivery was an attempt to propel the energy into them that was dissipated during a painful, life threatening birth. They may literally have been slapped into life which may have set up an early pattern of masochistic and destructive tendencies later in life.

People who use the blunting of affect or depression of energy as a symptom or a defense usually set up conditions in the environment to get a symbolic slap or jolt to bring them to life. Perhaps the so-called therapeutic "busts" or "crunches" are the reactive external consequences to the blunting of feeling by depressed, withdrawn patients. These individuals can't supply the internal jolt that can get them moving out of their rut (womb).

---

[14] Stanislov Grof, "Beyond Psychoanalysis III: Birth Trauma and Its Relation to Mental Illness, Suicide and Ecstasy", *Primal Community* Vol. 1, No. 3 (New York, Fall 1975), pg. 12.

[15] Ibid, pg. 15.

Many depressed, withdrawn patients are stuck in the rut of birth (BPM II) and their initial response is to run away from the feeling. We must realize that they had to face this horrible experience all alone as a baby and we cannot blame them for not trusting the world. We, as therapists, can and do try to understand their pain, some of which they are not even aware of. They usually need strong support initially, before they feel safe enough to venture into those life and death birth spaces. Unfortunately, this can be difficult to accomplish if the patient sets it up so that he recapitulates his original birth alienation.

This is one of the traps of therapy. The patient will act in a defensive way to avoid the pain of birth. His best escape is to withdraw and make it virtually impossible for anyone to jolt him into his imminent bout with death. He may find excuses to discontinue his therapy, miss groups or be a marginal participant. He has learned to "stay away" from people and feelings. In the schizoid[16] and sado-masochistic personalities, deep personal contact with people or love-objects is intensely fearful because the mind remembers on a deep level what happened during that fateful birth period. The buried unconscious pain drives the person towards destructive life circumstances, all in an attempt to avoid feeling that near cataclysmic event of birth. It is at this point that therapy becomes exciting, challenging, creative and dangerous.

Eve was a masochistic schizoid personality who existed marginally. She was on the periphery with her family, her child, her lover, her job and life in general. This was how she escaped near death at birth. By emotionally moving to the margin of the experience, she was able to survive even at the cost of losing her intense energetic soul. She was close to death during her birth as was her mother, but both were saved after hours of labor by a Caesarian section. She could talk about the experience with no feeling whatsoever, because she continued to move away from it in order to survive. Her life reflects this influence. All of her major relationships have "died" for one reason or another: she never had a real contactful relationship with her father, her husband literally died and she had little emotional contact with her four year old daughter. Her current relationship with a man was on the verge of

---

[16]The schizoid personality is usually withdrawn, detached, emotionally uninvolved and biologically totally disassociated from his deeper feeling self. He may even exhibit a lack of emotional reaction in the face of disturbing situations and events. Lack of affect is a predominant symptom. Expressions and experiences usually emanate primarily from the cerebral level. This occurs as a defense, a disengagement and a fear of contacting his primary emotions.

deteriorating as a result of the insidious forces of her unfelt birth. Thus, a loser at birth became a loser at life.

It appears that if a child has had a near death struggle at birth with the mother, his later desire to live and grow will depend to a large extent on the role of the father. Although the father cannot undo a traumatic birth, he can certainly help and assist his child to face life with a secure unconscious motivation to succeed. If the father is there in all his glory and power, rooting for and supporting the baby, the child will develop a strong will to live and enjoy the juices of existence. If the father is absent, punitive, passive or weak during a life and death birth struggle, the baby will have the proverbial two strikes against him. He will not have the needed support to develop an optimistic winning attitude toward life and in many cases, such as the following, an anaclictic depression will form.

Beth: I'm feeling how disconnected the parts of my body are — in fragments, like I've been hit by some huge impact—a bomb or something and I've landed like a rag doll, all distorted and in pieces, in a corner. I'm aware of a great feeling of disappointment and depression because I expected my Daddy to be waiting for me and he's not here . . . I don't see him anywhere . . . Overwhelming hurt . . . What was the use of having gone through that ordeal? I did it just for him. I was born for him and he's not here . . . I worked and struggled so unbelievably hard, sustained only by the hope of that reward . . . Feeling so disappointed . . . abandoned.

Ther: Why isn't your Daddy here?

Beth: He's just not here.

Ther: Where is he?

Beth: (Suddenly like a bolt of lightening) . . . He's at work . . . He found work more important than *me!* . . . (loud crying) . . . He missed my *whole god damn life* because he was working!! . . . (angry beating of the punching bag) . . . I keep feeling rage at him deserting me . . . (my baby heart feels like he promised to love me if I'd be born) . . . And then heart breaking pain at the need and loss . . . Literally heartbreaking . . . my heart is hurting so bad . . . (Sobbing) . . . (Not my actual heart but the whole left rib cage that holds my heart feels like it's being blown apart from the inside.)

Ther: Go back and look at that birth scene again. Little you is

163

finally born after that devastating struggle. You had to do it alone. Now that you're finally born and you're taken from your mommy, no one is there for you . . .
Beth: I'm calling to you to come help me . . . Help me!!! . . . I feel like I'm calling out for my very life . . . My stomach is killing . . . I hurt . . . (patient is passing a lot of gas. She later confirmed that she had the colic constantly for 3 months) . . . Baby rage is tearing my insides apart . . . I'll never forgive my father for letting me down, for breaking his promise, for not helping me. (I haven't forgiven him yet) . . .

Contrast this case with a young woman who, although facing near death during the birth process, was able to overcome the debilitating emotional effects of that trauma and go on to become a successful human being. Her father had really been there for her at the time of her birth and provided her with role model support during her life to overcome difficulties and see her through to the end. She internalized her father's success drive and turned this energy toward her therapy, developing an internal strength that kept her from being a full blown masochistic neurotic.

Grof's final Basic Perinatal Matrix, BPM IV, terminates the symbiotic union between mother and child and forms a new relationship immediately following the actual delivery. Propulsion through the birth canal is completed and the maternal-infant bonding process begins. Maternal deprivation feelings, in particular, separation from bodily contact with mother at birth, are among the most frequent type of deep feeling experiences for most individuals.[17]

For example, one woman was born breech to a mother who was fully anesthetized. Following a difficult delivery, the infant was separated from her mother completely for ten days during which time she received no physical contact with her mother and a minimum of contact with the nursing staff. Is there any wonder that this child would have a life-long panic or dread of being abandoned! She learned to defend by using the reaction formation of

---

[17]William Swartley, *The Undivided Self* (London, The Churchill Centre, 1978), pg. 42.

pre-maturely marrying and having six babies in eight years so that she would never be abandoned again. Unfortunately, a defensive solution may work while one is young, but in adulthood the early disaster scene returns in a symbolic, disguised form to reap its destruction.

This particular woman could never make full emotional contact with her husband and children because she never had her own mother at birth. Her father further reaped havoc on her by being vicious and cruel, so that she had no one but herself to turn to. She eventually retreated deep inside herself, surviving only by sublimating her disastrous birth. She compensated by reversing her early need and became an excellent nurse for others. She physically took care of everyone else, although emotionally, she remained distant and withdrawn.

Another young woman experienced intense emotional trauma at separation from her natural mother immediately following birth. She was never to see her again as she was adopted minutes later by another woman. The effects of this early separation were still being felt years later in an emotionally stark and tumultuous marriage.

Polly: I can't believe I hurt myself like that, in that marriage!! . . . I can't believe it! . . . (heavy crying) . . . *You* set me up, Mommy!! You set me up! . . . You did it, you God Damn bitch!! . . . . You set me up to be hurt again and again and again!! . . . *Again* and *again* and *again!!!* . . . Over and Over!! . . . That's all it's been!! Why did you do that to me?! . . . You started it !!! . . . (beating bag) . . .

Ther: I hear you saying that from the beginning you were alone and hurting . . . It started right there at birth . . . right from the time you were born, you were alone and hurting. That keeps happening, time and time again, that old feeling . . . That old situation . . . keeps coming back.

Polly: Last night . . . all I kept hearing was Mommy, Mommy, Mommy . . . I just felt like there were more than 2 children coming at me . . . it was so overwhelming. I just wanted them to let me be for a minute . . . I wanted somebody to hold me . . . I wanted somebody to hold me . . . (crying) . . . I can't believe there's nobody to take care of me . . . I can't believe it, I really can't! . . . I can't believe that my mother did that to me . . . I don't want to

believe it, Mommy . . . if I believe it, I'll die . . . I'll die!!!
(crying) . . . How could you leave me!!! . . . How could
you leave *me!!* . . . (hitting the bag in anger) . . .

These feelings of abandonment were triggered by a precipitating
divorce between herself and her husband of 8 years. This primary
relationship brought up all the old feelings of her very first primary
relationship with another human being, her natural mother.

Polly: I don't want to be alone!! . . . *Hold me!!!* . . . (crying)
. . . Love me, Mommy, love me!! . . . I don't feel valued!!
. . . (crying deeper . . . yelling and crying) . . . I feel abandoned! . . . (beating bag) . . . *I feel abandoned!!!* . . .
Momma!!! . . . There's nothing left! . . . (crying) . . . You
fucked me over when you gave me away!! . . . You fucked
me over!! . . . (beating bag) . . . I went through incredible
pain to be born and *you didn't even touch me!!* . . . You
walked away like nothing happened!! . . . Like I never existed!! . . . *I exist!!* . . . (heavy crying starts) . . . I was
born, Momma . . . I was born . . . *I exist!!* . . . *I exist!!* . . .
(crying louder and deeper) . . . *You denied me!!!* . . . You
denied my very soul! . . . (angrily beating bag) . . . You
denied me!! . . .

Polly has a long period of crying and then stops as she realizes
that one of the reasons she's been triggering off of her children lately, is that one of them keeps saying to her, "You think you're so
great, don't you." Her need to see herself valued in their eyes con-
trasts sharply with her feeling so valueless inside. She wanted to be
valued by her husband and her children just to erase that old hurt
feeling of worthlessness and abandonment.

Polly: I'm nothing without you, Mommy . . . I'm nothing
. . . there's nowhere to go . . . no one to touch . . . Mommy!!! . . . I'm not special !! . . . I'm just like any other
baby! . . . I'm *less* than any other baby!! I'm the one here
that doesn't have a Mommy! . . . (crying) . . . I don't have
a Mommy here!! . . . I don't want anyone coming near me!!
. . . I don't want anyone touching me!! . . . I want *my*
Mommy!! I want my Mommy's touch!! . . . Somebody

touch me . . . Leave me alone!! . . . Leave me alone!!! . . .
I want my own Mommy!!!

Polly's early abandonment as a newborn infant was further aggravated by a violent, traumatic birth. It was as if every shred of human dignity had been brutally ripped from her and then she was deserted and left to deal with it alone.

Polly: I feel violated!! . . . Violated as a little person!! . . .
You let them pull me out like that!! . . . You didn't leave me
one shred of dignity!! . . . Nothing! . . . A fucking piece of
meat . . . That's all I was!! . . . a fucking piece of meat!!
. . . (beating bag . . . crying) . . . You took it all away!!
. . . My dignity, my value, my warmth . . . you stripped
me naked!! *Naked!!* . . . Inside and out!! . . . Damn you,
you bitch!! . . . You stripped me clean!! . . . (beating bag)
. . .

Ther: Polly, look at the monitor. (Video tape of a baby's birth
and the after birth treatment he received in the delivery
room)
Polly: Nobody holds him close either . . . Nobody holds me
close!! . . . Don't take me away!!! . . . (heavy crying) . . .
He can't believe it either. He can't take it all in . . . He can't
believe what is happening to him!! . . . Momma, don't let
them take me away!! . . . Don't let them take me away!!
. . . Why can't you hear me!!! . . . *Mommy!!!* . . . .

All of Polly's discoveries were her own. She had no record of her birth circumstances, so the only information she received was through her own feelings. One further example of the birth phenomenon might be valuable to look at. The case in point is a man who had been delving into his feelings for some time and wished to explore the roots of his own physical playfulness and aggression with women. He found himself sinking into a very tiny space which eventually led to his own birth and relationship with his mother.

"I'm small, so small and little and weak . . . Nobody wants to help me and I'm all alone. It's so frightening in here and I'm very, very precious . . . Momma, feed me . . . feed me

167

through the walls . . . I must fight to get out of here . . . It's so crowded . . . (crying becomes louder and with more sobbing) . . . There's this body all around me, like all the world's around me . . . *Ohhhh!* . . . I'm not coming out so easily! . . . I'm so frightened!! . . . I'm going to die!!! . . .

"I'm feeling the need to curl up into a very tight ball . . . I must get my feet up behind me . . . I'm trying to move on my own . . . I can't move! . . . She's holding me in tightly! . . . I contract and try to propel myself a little more . . . Nothing! . . . I can't budge her! . . . She won't give! . . . I push harder but still nothing . . . I am starting to get frantic, then angry! . . . I turn my entire body around and start to clench my jaw . . . tight . . . tighter. I am breathing very heavy and getting more and more frantic! I want to grab at her! . . . I want to clutch her but my hands are too weak and uncoordinated . . . I try to reach out and grab but nothing happens . . . I am getting very frustrated and angry . . . (Ron begins to make connections to here and now behavior) . . . I want to grab her! . . . Yes! . . . Yes! . . . I want to play . . . I'm playful and angry! . . . I'm rough! . . ."

The patient is stuck at this point and is afraid of going further. He will need time to integrate and understand what is happening. He senses the source of his anger and gains insight into the nature of his affection, anger, and playfulness with women. During this segment of the birth he is attempting to assert his own power over his mother's intransigence. This pattern has emerged with women many times in the past and led to conflict and pain.

In regard to my own experiences with BPM IV, I know that I was born "high" and that after being united with my mother there was a period of separation that left some emotional scars. I have subsequently felt and connected to those experiences and cleared them up. I know that being "born high" has left an indelible impact on my character. I am basically a high person and occasionally I slip into a low space. I know that whatever low feelings I have are not a real basic part of my personality. Witnessing other patients who exhibit strong depressive tendencies, it has become evident to me that they were not allowed to glean the full benefits from an appropriate BPM IV, of symbiotic, peaceful, contented unification with mother and father. Babies who are born fearful or

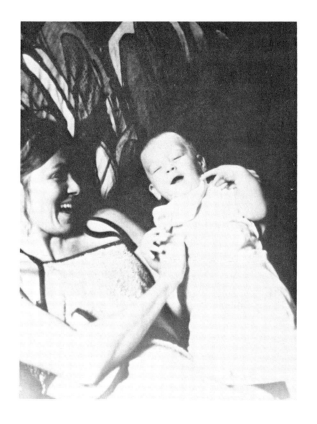

"The beauty and wonder of birth... Why is it that so many people have been given nothing but misery at the time of their entrance into this world?"

depressed stay that way throughout their lives, unless there is some interruption by a feeling process. Perhaps, Abraham Maslow's self-actualizers were those people who were not completely devastated and obliterated during the BPM IV stage of birth. Thus, we can see how utterly crucial it is to perfect the gestational and birthing experiences of the human infant. In so doing we may be able to interrupt the process of neurosis at its onset.

In conclusion, let me propose that the process of a true gentle birth is quite simple. It is neurotics who make it very difficult and complex for themselves and their children. A husband and wife who are fairly clear will conceive a child in true love and thus set up a uterine environment that is relatively pain free, thus minimizing all subsequent trauma to a growing infant. Parents who love each other and have eradicated major portions of their own historical pain will provide all the ingredients that create a sturdy infant in a tension free environment. He will be born free of a drugged mother with a chronically armoured, pelvic region and will be welcomed into the warm sensual environment of his parents' arms and bodies.

If he experiences any distress during the delivery phases of birth, it will not be enough to overwhelm him or set him up with debilitating life patterns. He will come out of a warm, supportive womb with a curious look on his face. He will breathe normally and possess good body tonus. There will be no need to cry in order to expel excess, in utero tension. His face will show no fear, his personality will be intact and his muscular, skeletal system will be strong and appropriately coordinated for his tender young age. He may not even need a warm Leboyer bath to soothe the remnants of his birth trauma. He will just be comfortable being with mother and father.

Most babies endure incredible agony, resulting in obliterated personalities. They, then, need to recuperate and reform their personality in the following months and years. A true gentle birth does not have this problem (provided, of course, that there are no physical abnormalities within the mother's system, that could cause undue stress on the infant). A mother giving birth in a gentle way ·will not have overloads of excessive pain that becomes evident during the birth process. She will show signs of deep concern and love for her baby and will perform her task for what it really is: hard labor, nothing more. But she will not be in excrutiating pain and agony. She will know, along with her husband, that the baby is going to be very strong and healthy, and this supportive contribution from the parents is a great gift to give a child starting out in life.

The Leboyer technique of giving birth is a great step forward for the medical profession, as well as for parents and children, but its main focus is the moment of delivery and immediately afterwards. As a birthing practice, it is an excellent joint procedure for doctor, child, mother and father but it doesn't take into account the pre-conception-implantation-gestation phases. Only parents who are willing to emotionally "clean themselves out" can provide a true gentle birth. Unfortunately, I know of only a few such births. It seems in my experience that most neurotics are still willing to hand themselves and the birth of their children over to the traditional medical model. This model has followed the Descarte view of the duality of mind and body, which, of course, can be disastrous. Thus, physicians, based on their own training, focus most of their attention on the physical aspects of birth.

The holistic health approach challenges this duality model by recognizing the inter-connectedness of mind, spirit, body and feelings. The result means taking the responsibility of one's body out of the hands of the physicians and placing some of it back on the patient. The Total Feeling view (true gentle birthing) goes one step further. We are responsible for our own beings and a physician is only there to assist but never to control or interfere with the natural flowing process of birth. That is why it is so vital that clear parents must be conscious of what is going on in the birthing room in order to step in and strongly interfere with any neurotic practices perpetrated by the medical profession upon the sacred family, birthing unit.

This is my solemn position and I stand rock hard on that unshakeable foundation. Gentle birthing will remain an infant movement on the desert sands of time.

Chapter 10   Sex

SEXUALITY, GESTATION AND BIRTH

There is a definite indication that gestation and the birth experience itself contribute significantly to whether one develops a secure sense of integrated sensuality and feelings. If one is not wanted during the intrauterine phases of fetal development, it would be easy to assume that this child would feel "unattractive" to its parents. This individual, thereafter, looks and often feels unwanted and unattractive.

Ugliness is not simply a function of genetic programming. Even the poorest combination of genes can flourish and grow in a full nurturant and feeling environment. The reverse is also true. If optimum genetic programming and engineering produce a physically attractive child, a rejecting intrauterine and post natal environment can bring about an emotionally unappealing one. The child would not be ugly in the physical sense but would lack the emotional qualities that make for a full feeling, sensuous, attractive human being.

Terry was such a case in point. She inherited all the positive physical attributes of her parents: a perfect body and a perfect face, and yet she was emotionally repulsive. She appeared less physically beautiful because she was emotionally twisted and distorted out of shape. A distressing intrauterine environment, followed by physical and emotional torture during and after birth, caused a recession of the emotional qualities that would have made her truly beautiful in an integrated, emotional, physical way. Though on the surface quite pretty, she could only attract males who were as neurotic as she was. Feeling males could respond to her sexually but would withdraw emotionally because of her unexpressed and unresolved rage towards her parents. She was a physical winner but an emotional loser.

Another young female experienced tremendous ambivalence and weakness when pursued by needy, out-of-touch males. Her own need for warm, loving contact with a male clouded her ability to relate in a straightforward, grounded fashion. Her resolution with this issue, in a primal sense, led her back to a feeling of littleness and vulnerability in the womb.

Peggy: I don't know how to handle my manager at work. He

172

has no feelings. I can't talk to him and now he wants to 'get it on' with me . . . I don't know what to do with him.

Ther: Wait a minute. Why is it that every time a man makes a sexual advance towards you, you don't know what to do and start to cry?

Peggy: I don't know. I don't attract any feeling men, only unfeeling men. (Patient is having a hard time humanizing her life)

Ther: Why is it that unfeeling men want to have sex with you? You come back to this place time and time again and your response is 'I don't know what to do' . . . Why do you get all upset when a man wants to get close to you sexually?

Peggy: Because I can't get what I want. (crying) I'm still too little . . . I'm still too crazy.

Ther: What does little have to do with not getting what you want?

Peggy: No power . . . I don't want to be a child

Ther: What is so bad about being a child?

Over the next two hours this young woman eventually regressed back to her own conception. The similarities between her here and now words, in a sexual contact situation, and her identification with her father's sperm in a primordial sense, are remarkable. Following this emotional release, she felt progressively stronger in relating to needy males.

"Such a thing to feel . . . The first really strong feeling was one of being pulled by this tremendous, horrendous need. I resisted that pull with a 'get away' feeling, a tremendous need to escape. These were my strongest feelings. To a lesser degree I felt a *ooh, ahh, yech*, of disgust."

(This ties up very directly with the emotional reality of her parents at the time of her conception. Her mother was disgusted with her father while at the same time, very needy for a child.)

"I felt a tremendous need for inclusion and a desire to be engulfed by warm loving contact."

The conception scene during this young woman's gestation period is being acted out over and over again in her here and now interactions with males. Her mother displaced her needs for warm loving contact from her own father onto a yet-to-be-born baby. As a consequence, she "tolerated" sex from a needy, unfeeling male (symbolized by the infant's father.) The young woman, in a similar fashion, also put up with sexual advances from needy males because of her own unfelt pain with her father. Thus, both mother and daughter failed in their attempts to make full loving contact with males (symbolic daddies). Until she fully feels this need and disgust for her father on a core feeling level, this young woman will remain passive, weak and needy with males.

Her situation was further aggravated postnatally by a rejecting father. She, thus, found herself desperately in need of a male to confirm her identity as a young attractive female.

"During the course of time my mother was pregnant with me, especially the latter six months, I experienced heavy rejection from my father. Ma really loved me but couldn't fully have her feelings for me or give me more than a minimum because my father, my brothers and sisters always needed so much from her.

Because of the heavy rejection by my father and my mother not ever really being there for me, I constantly *acted out* with males from a very young age. I've usually thrown myself at them and when I got their attention, the only way I knew how to relate to them was through my vagina (completely sexual.) I don't think that behavior would have ever happened if there wasn't that initial distance with my father.

I have a lot of need and hope for a man for myself. It's important to me to be devoted to a single man and be very special. I'm seeking to learn about life and about myself through a man's eyes . . . I was very deprived of my Daddy, as far as learning about myself and life, so I am looking for that in a man. I feel that the way for me to really understand or experience what a real woman is, would be through a man's point of view."

The birth experience itself has been the root cause of sexual problems for many individuals. These disturbances range from attitudinal contamination to specific dysfunctional problems. The chapter on Gestation and Birth explores this in more detail but let us take a look at a few examples of this sexuality—birth correlation in order to demonstrate its wide range of effect.

Eve: "My sexuality is definitely tied up with the circumstances surrounding my birth. I came into the program totally unaware of my own sexuality. I wasn't even quite sure I was a woman. I had many male characteristics—toughness, a non-feminine hard appearance, a heavy, lumbering walk, etc.—and it took many months to just feel what a woman was . . . I still can't let go sexually. When I'm closed down I can't even get pleasure from playing with myself. That seems to go in cycles. I'll go from being *somewhat* open to my sexuality to being totally closed down. There is a definite pattern. When I'm in my closed down space, I am dealing with birth. When I can *really* get down and feel the anger and rage from my birth, I can feel the difference in my whole body. My pelvis area loosens . . . I feel freed up and I can relax and enjoy myself."

Dan: "I have felt some deep spaces before birth where my sensory awareness was extremely sensitive. I feel my stage of development was about the fourth or fifth month of gestation. At this time I was totally sensitive to my environment—sort of a '2001 Space Odyssey' feeling of traveling through space. I don't know if I have ever felt this much sensation through my body since I was born . . .

My birth experience 'shut me down' on a physical level and has certainly blocked me from totally experiencing my sexuality. There is a point when I reach orgasm where my body feels totally open and this point is close to the totally sensitive spaces I felt before birth . . .

However, being born through conventional methods, along with the complications of having my umbilical cord wrapped around my neck, caused my body to kind of 'freak out' in a sense. Enduring so much pain at such an early vulnerable time caused a numbing of my senses that has taken years of feeling work to uncover. Through re-experiencing issues in and around my birth, my physical tightness and the damage to my central nervous system has disappeared almost entirely. . . . There still remain some blockages, although at the age of 28, I feel like I finally have my body back again."

Polly: "Sometimes I don't want to be touched, fondled or undressed. I feel too vulnerable, all naked and open. I'm afraid of sex—fucking and the close physical intimacy. My vagina gets tight and penetration is difficult. When that happens my vagina goes numb—I have trouble relaxing and enjoying sex. I want to curl up and stay away from people and yet, deep inside me, my body is craving for warmth and touch.

I have taken this back to my birth, but most of all, to the moments immediately after my birth, while I was being cleaned up and 'roughed' in the delivery room . . .

'. . . I am raw and battered . . . I'm shoved and poked and prodded until I can't stand it anymore. Everything about me and my body hurts—so sensitive to the environment—*Gently, Please!* Every fast touch is so overwhelming . . . I'm so naked, so vulnerable and the physical abuse never stops. Leave me alone! I can feel my cunt pull in from the external abuse . . . I can feel it to be the most sensitive part of my body. I want to keep my legs closed . . . I want to curl up tight and recoil away from all this abuse . . . noise, cold, lights, *rough*, rough hands. Where is the warmth . . . where is my mother's body? I was so warm, so safe—now such pain! Screaming and crying for warmth . . . crying for touch · . . . the right touch to end this pain . . . *Nothing!* Leave my body alone . . . leave me alone! . . . Touch me, touch me . . . no, no, no . . . no more painful touching! My skin is burning—on fire! Everything feels shocked . . . no end to this agony . . .' (The patient is sobbing heavily throughout this feeling release.)

This causes me pain in my relationships in the here and now. Sometimes I get so needy, all I want to do is fuck. Fucking seems to be the closest I can get to reliving the physical union I had with my mother. Sometimes I can't get enough—yet, the more I fuck, the more the emptiness grows inside."

"Other times I withdraw so far from people . . . I set up an imaginary 'force field' around me to protect little me. I can't have sex—don't want any—I don't want my body naked and vulnerable anymore. My vagina won't open—I feel terror in a man's arms and I avoid all eye and body contact with both sexes. Yet, it is then that I need all that contact — the physical touching — so much that I can't stand it. I feel so lost without it and yet, it feels so alien to me . . .

I have trouble even touching other people. I can't touch my own children when I'm like this . . . even they suffer from my pain. I feel so unwanted, abandoned, and physically abused . . . yet, so hungry . . ."

As I have indicated throughout this book, if we are to understand human behavior and its roots, it is necessary to be drawn back to the very beginning. And those beginnings include the moments of conception, implantation and subsequent gestational development proceeding up to the birth process itself. It becomes important to realize that birth is not the beginning but merely a transitional phase from one universe to another. Healthy infants who emerge from a minimal traumatic environment will usually display totally intact personalities that will prevail throughout life. These children are given a basic sense of sturdiness in mind and body and because of near perfect gestational environments will be able to withstand the vigors, demands and challenges of life.

Thriving, nurturing wombs will produce thriving, beautifully aggressive children who will be far ahead, physically and emotionally, of their less fortunate counterparts. Traumatic wombs will create the conditions that lead people to lives of mayhem. That is why a true gentle birth begins with a beautiful conception, a loving gestation period and a fulfilling, unified birth experience for mother, father and baby.

Mama, Mama
My little mouth searches
for your body, so frantically.
I want to bite, chew
and suck your warmth.

My mouth warms and waters
with ecstasy; you are my
first sexual conquest.

My body longs to
hold you so tight.
My chest, my stomach
and my genitals want
to be close in embrace
with you.

Love, Love, Love
I am to become
full man because
of you.

My head clicks to
the rhythm of my cries.
I am astounded and amazed.
It is all true . . . .

Oh, sweet sadistic aggression,
you found your roots
in my passion for mother.
The world today now makes
wonderful sense.

SEXUALITY, BONDING AND CONFIRMATION

Children, growing up, need very much to be confirmed by their parents for who they really are and not for what their parents want them to be. To reinforce a child for being something that is alien to his very nature will twist him out of his natural shape and he will then grow up into an unreal image of what his parents expected. He thus, becomes rewarded for being something other than himself. This is the core cause of neurosis.

Any kind of disconfirmation will reside in the deeper levels of pain, suffering under a heavy load of repression. The end product of such a situation is a sense of being alienated from one's core self and from other caring people. This split away from the authentic self further results in a kind of split away from a feeling existence with one's own parents and life in general. Though the child is being confirmed for becoming an image for and of the parents, he in a sense, suffers from a lack of deep confirmation for his own being.

Inclusion behaviors are those learned responses that an adult uses to gain acceptance, affiliation, and membership. If someone has the stamp of not really being wanted and desired during gestation, birth and early infancy, then he will display confusion, anxiety and ambivalence with all inclusion situations. Somewhere in early infancy, he will learn to adapt to this situation and deny and control his reactions and feelings. His coping behavior becomes an ingrained style of relating to others and the world in general.

For example, if a baby is not of a preferred sex, it will accommodate in some way. He or she will assume adaptive behavior and physical traits to control against an onslaught of painful deep feelings. If one or both parents and siblings maintain this attitudinal stance of rejection and denial of the baby's right to be wanted, treasured and held, then he will grow up feeling that nobody of any worth will ever want him. He may feel hopeless and rejected in all of his attempts to get anyone to really notice and love him for who he really is.

Walt: There's this girl that I used to live with. She's the one that was pregnant, had my kid . . . When I left town to go out on those business trips, she started fucking other guys. It made me feel like I'm not good enough, those other guys are better.

Ther: O.K. . . . You've made a conclusion. She's fucking other guys, therefore you're no good. Why isn't it possible that's just what she did, fucked around? O.K., so you've got a lot of pain to feel with that. But why was her fucking other males carried to the extent that you are no good as a male? That's what it comes down to 'I am no good as a male.' Women have all the power to hurt . . . You are very vulnerable in your balls, Walt . . . and in your penis.

Walt: My mom always wanted me to be a girl (crying) . . . She put me upon this stool and made me dance with this fucking dress on, like a puppet . . . I'm not a fucking puppet . . . (sob-cry). I felt so small, I didn't know what to do.

Ther: What do you want to do? Here you are on this stool. She's got the dress on you.

Walt: (Yelling and crying) I want to rip it off . . . Get this
fucking thing off me!

Ther: She has more power than you. You're going to have to
go through her. She's got you still on the stool.

Walt: I'm afraid (crying) . . . I'm afraid . . . I'm afraid to
take this fucking dress off!!

Ther: Why?

Walt: (crying) . . . Because Mom always wanted a little girl.

Ther: Talk to her now, directly.

Walt: What are you gonna do if I don't wanta play? What
are you gonna do if I want to take this fucking dress off?
(crying) . . . What are you gonna do?!

Ther: She's got you frightened. A woman, your mother, has
you frightened to death. She has you frightened to the death
of your manhood.

Walt: I don't know what she's gonna do to me if I don't wanta
play . . . I want you to love me, Mom (crying and yelling).
I want you to love me. I don't want to have to wear this
fucking dress. I wanta be a little boy. Why me? Why me?
Why me?!

Another case in point, a young female who is not fully wanted
by her mother will have to deny her vulnerability and softness. She
may adopt tough, masculine behavior that will keep others at a
safe distance. Her body still remembers the early neglect and lack
of warm, cuddling acceptance even though her mind may repress
the awful truth. Eventually, her body closes down and she is no
longer capable of eliciting warm responses from her environment.
Perhaps she will hide her softness and femininity behind a clutch-
ing, grabbing, devouring neediness and neutralize any potential
possibility of eliciting affectual responses from others. Her body,
her personality and her essence have become the adaptation of a
defensive style of relating.

"Mama, you said that you really wanted me . . . that's what
you said . . . you wanted a little girl . . . But you wanted me
for weird reasons. You didn't have a doll when you were a little girl . . . so when you had me, you had your little girl doll
. . . You wanted me, but you didn't know how to take care of
me . . . too much of yourself got in the way. You didn't know

how to hold me, touch me, or be soft. You were all discipline
. . . very bossy. You gave me things but you didn't give me
you . . . We are so cut off from each other . . . from the day I
was born."

Confirmation is a reciprocal form of communication. If parents
are sensitive to their children's real needs, these same children will
give confirmation to the parents' realness. This occurs because
children are born absolutely real and honest. One is never meant to
be born neurotic; one becomes neurotic due to traumatic insult. To
that extent, if a parent is truly listening, he or she will hear from
the child whether or not they are doing a good enough job. If a
child is twisted out of his normal natural flow, he will respond with
some expression of pain. If the parent is insensitive to his own pain
and that of the child, he will, unknowingly, continue to pressure
his offspring into becoming neurotic.

Instinctively, on a deeper level, every growing youngster knows
what is right for him. As an adult, when he enters therapy and
becomes subjected to the therapeutic influences, he feeds back information to the therapist as to the effectiveness of the treatment.
As in real life, where reciprocal confirmation hopefully exists between parent and child, so too, this reciprocity must exist between
therapist, patient, and other group members. If it does not, we
may assume that neurosis has entered the picture and disrupted the
natural forward flow of the participants.

Patients, just like children, need real guidance and direction.
The therapy provides this but only subject to the ultimate confirmation of the patient. As clients get well, their lives seem to take on
a natural, flowing progressive direction. It is as if they are finally
getting it together.

It is common in the group experience for relationships to develop.
Sometimes a male and a female may wish to establish some kind of
love relationship. This type of agenda must be explored by the entire
group in order to discover what constructive and destructive
elements are at work. Many times a couple will form a relationship
and act out all their unfelt past needs. It is important that the group
helps maintain the openness of those relationships in order to explore
the extent of mutual commitment, reciprocal confirmation, and
mutual direction seeking. In other words, is this a true love relation-

181

"Sometimes I want to get so close to him that we just become one. I want to kiss his lips, breathe the same breath, and take in the same air... It's marvelous! You and I breathe together...so soft, wonderful, marvelous..."

ship where the commitment is equal and where symbolic needs are not being acted out detrimentally?

It is relatively easy for neurotics to become entrenched in one another's craziness. As the web of sickness grows and grows, the ensuing dynamics can become incredibly confusing and interwoven and if left unchecked, become quite inaccessible to treatment. The therapist must get to these hidden agendas early enough in order to break up the neurotic inter-twine. If this is not done, disaster will result and "dead bodies" will be rolling.

For example, Jack was physically attracted to Myrna, who was quite seductive and definitely out to latch onto a man. Although Jack had no intention of committing himself to her, she was quite turned on to the challenge of making him select her as his "special" permanent love. She hoped that having sex with him and catering to his every wish would help to establish them as a permanent, serious, love relationship. Jack had other ideas. He needed to go through school and discover himself emotionally and intellectually. He considered Myrna merely a temporary interlude.

Like most males he eroticized his needs. He justified having sex with Myrna and monopolized most of her time as a way of satisfying those needs, although she did not figure extensively in his future plans. He failed to see Myrna's direction in life and his place in her future plans. They definitely were not in mutual agreement about their goals. Jack truly cared for Myrna but Myrna wanted him to love her, body and soul. The more that Jack held back from fulfilling this expectation, the more frantically Myrna would perform to win him over. They were headed for a collision course with disaster.

To totally sexualize a relationship is to become "hung up" on that particular aspect of contact. Jack was torn between continuing his strong sexual liason with Myrna and pulling back completely. He was concerned with how all these young attractive females kept "tripping off" their daddy needs with him. It was more difficult for him to realize how he had sexualized his mommy needs for physical confirmation with Myrna and his other previous love affairs. It is interesting to note that these two individuals had a continuous history of disruptive love affairs. Every one of their relationships became heavily sexualized, and through the medium of sleeping together, they would continually become heavily attached and completely entrenched in one another's neurosis.

As one begins to discover that closeness, warmth and intimacy is a product of communication, sensuality and playfulness, he or she learns to de-emphasize the over evaluation of adult sexual confirmation. As the neurotic attachment bonds between Jack and Myrna were broken, they were able to relate to one another with a firmer set of internal boundaries. Myrna learned that she didn't have to keep "fucking" in order to get and hold on to a boyfriend. She no longer felt that only by being a piece of ass would she stand a chance with a guy. Her therapy helped her to realize that by becoming a more feeling human being, she would be capable of developing and sustaining more meaningful and fulfilling relationships, without neurotic attachment. Jack, as well, discovered that his manhood did not rest on how often his girlfriends had sex with him. Real confirmation is of an emotional nature and not necessarily one of macho sexuality.

It is unfortunate that one of the prime ways that little boys receive confirmation of their manhood is through their penis, rather than through their humanity. The same is also true for little girls. This is not to say that we should underestimate the importance of sex gender confirmation. Most males and females feel very flattered when their sexuality is acknowledged. It gives them a sense of attractiveness and virility. But that should not obscure the fact that ultimately, it is on emotional grounds that feeling people make their choices for contact.

Another problem arises when a human being has all the emotional qualities for being a decent, authentic person but lacks the physical attributes and attractiveness resulting from early parental disconfirmation. Loving, hugging parents provide the warm, close skin contact and stimulation that creates an adult who is sensually and sexually attractive. If this type of confirmation is lacking in childhood, it will lead to a later physical deficiency on the sensual level.

Janet was a very beautiful person on the inside but due to inadequate physical parenting in childhood, she became a "plain Jane," devoid of the necessary physical attributes that would allow her to sufficiently compete with other more endowed females. Because she was never treated as a cute, warm, adorable little child, she grew up with an ambivalent sense of gender identity. Her sexuality was kept hidden for fear of rejection. She ventured nothing and gained nothing and as a result, she remained safe but didn't feel very happy or fulfilled. Her sensual and sexual experiences were very limited and she certainly deserved more than what she got from males.

"When I see the two of them kissing I can almost taste it myself. I feel the sensations and they stay with me all the time...fully real and delicious..."

While other females were gaining attention for their sensuality and seductiveness, she was able to establish more meaningful relationships on an emotional level. However, there still was the missing sexual element. To that extent, even with her apparent emotional qualities, she suffered emotional rejection by males on the physical level.

The more that she felt of herself, the more it could be observed that her denied sensuality and coquettishness emerged. As time went by, she actually became more physically attractive. Of interest in this particular case is that as more and more of her own pain was felt, she grew more capable of giving physical affection to her own child from an earlier marriage. At this point in her therapy she also met a man who showed considerable interest in her as a human being, as well as sporadic, sexual attention. She was afraid that he would eventually reject her because she didn't fit the image of the kind of physical woman he needed.

Sol really liked Janet and he entered therapy as a result of their contact. He had been in a relationship with another female who was incredibly sensual and seductive, but neurotically out of touch with her core feelings. Janet represented the emotional clarity and stability he was seeking, but she lacked the seductive attractiveness of the other female. In his head he was looking for a composite of the two women—that is a stable and emotionally clear female with the right physical chemistry.

It is my contention that when one is clear and mature enough, it then becomes possible to meet a fully appropriate and compatible soul mate. This usually comes in time. When such a situation occurs, an emerging couple becomes a new, unified entity that is capable of reaching new heights and depths of feeling consciousness. Compatibility becomes a comfortable blending of individuals who can reach the deepest and highest parts of themselves. Their emotional and sexual relationship is one of breadth and scope.

In those instances where true reciprocal confirmation is lacking in childhood, there is usually always a dysfunction in the way one relates in the sexual, emotional sphere. Of course, this implies that sexuality does not exist separately from emotional components and vice versa. Both are reciprocally inter-dependent. In other words, one may be sexually adequate in a functional sense but deficient in an emotional sense, thus cancelling out the full potential of total human encounter. The converse may not be true. If one is fully feeling and integrated on an emotional level, it would stand to reason that his body and sexuality would be integrated into his emotional life.

In other words, one is born a full feeling human being and gradually loses that as neurosis sets in. Because one does not become a fully sexual being until physical maturity, many adults function well sexually, but are split off from the feeling selves of childhood. This guarantees conflict and distrust in here and now relationships. Other human beings find that their early physical selves were denied by lack of confirmation and this manifests itself in later sexual dysfunctioning and disordered inter-personal relationships. These situations occur in direct proportion to the amount of early insult.

Early confirmation also involves the whole area of infant and childhood sensual contact and stimulation with both parents. Without proper stroking, fondling, caressing and holding, babies grow up with various internal and interpersonal disorders.[1]

Deprivation of these functions can lead to infant death as has occurred in institutional foundling homes where all the physical necessities are provided, but sensory stimulation is lacking. Dr. Rene Spitz[2] found that one out of three of these infants who had been breast and wet nursed for three months and then had their mothers give them up, died after one year. This occurred despite the fact that these infants were well fed and kept clean by the over-burdened personnel of these institutions.

It would seem that attitudes in the home environment get translated in action patterns that either give a child the sense that he is "making it" or not. If Mom and Dad can't "make it" with each other due to faulty and poor sexual communication, then the child may grow up feeling that the roots of his sexual conflicts lie in the fact that he needed more sensual contact with mother or father. Many females connect to present day sexual disorders as having roots in faulty sensual mothering. Their disorders do not have to

---

[1]Marshall Klaus and John Kennell, *Maternal Infant Bonding* (St. Louis, C.V. Mosby Co., 1976).
[2]W.L. Masters and V.E. Johnson, *The Pleasure Bond*, (New York, Bantam Books, Inc., 1976), pgs. 245-255.

manifest themselves in the orgasmic function, although much of faulty sensual parenting or lack of a sensual parent can and does lead to sexual dysfunction. In some instances orgastically functional people show disorders in sexual interpersonal relating.

One young man who appeared very adequate in terms of physical appearance, intelligence, sophistication and creativity, expressed a great deal of pain and inadequacy in relating to females. His parents divorced when he was a young child and he found himself in the midst of their mutual hostility and attacking. Their inability to "make it" with each other became a source of negative role modeling for him. This, coupled with the lack of a warm, nurturant, supportive mother, led to inadequacy, frustration and eventual depression.

"All kinds of girls show an interest in me and everyone says how easy it should be for me to get a girlfriend. I guess it's true but I just don't feel adequate enough to go up to a girl and ask her out . . .

I've gone out on dates before but I spent hours building up the courage to ask a female out. Each time I asked a girl out, she would go out with me, but the next time I had to ask her out again, it was just as hard as the time before . . ."

"I know I have a lot of Mommy rejection tied up in all of this. Her rejection causes such feelings of sexual inadequacy. I hate the way she keeps fucking me up! Every time I turn around, I can't enjoy myself because of an issue with my mother."

If parents feel self-confirmed, it will be easy for them to express warmth, love and affection toward their child, thus giving him a sense that he is very valued and loved. He will then internalize their positive feelings toward him and grow up feeling some sense of self-love and worth. He will feel confirmed as a worthwhile person and be able to relate to the world in an optimistic, cheerful, valued way. This, then, is the essence of parental confirmation. With it, a child will show a minimum amount of fear when reaching out and trying to make contact with his environment.

SEXUALITY AND ETHNIC / RELIGIOUS BACKGROUND

Freud, many years ago, conceptualized that sexuality was the root cause of all neurosis. Wilhelm Reich, amongst Freud's other followers, continued Freud's sexual theme while at the same time practicing therapy in a different fashion. Reich's Orgonomists and, to a lesser extent, the people who practice Bioenergetics, also see sexual dysfunction as being the root cause of neurosis. Freud believed that the sexual psychodynamic area was the main reservoir of human repression and illness. Therefore, in psychoanalysis, fantasy and impulse are given great attention, whereas in the body therapies character structure and body armoring are the main emphasis.

In psychoanalysis insight is important. In Reich's work the orgasmic reflex and the attainment of th_ status of genital character are the primary focal points. Psychoanalytic schools have done a splendid job of exploring human defenses and developing the therapeutic techniques that could undercut those defenses in order to create a healthier personality. Likewise, the body therapies have explored body armoring and done a great deal to loosen up chronic, rigid defenses in this way. However, very little attention has been paid to the underlying power of explosive deep core feelings.

In the feeling view, therapy cannot be reduced to the simple sexual cause. In a feeling sense, what we find is that when a patient regresses back to the sexual aspects of his personality disorders and neurotic behaviors, there is an enormous amount of human feeling and need surrounding these pertinent issues. We believe that it is those same feelings that are the central issue of human cure and transformation.

The feeling effects of gestational and birth influences, as well as the importance of early bonding and confirmation, have already been demonstrated. What we have not looked at yet is the environmental, ethnic and cultural determinants that strongly influences an individual's sexuality. The link between deep core feeling, ethnicity and human sexuality lies in the specific cultural determinants of individual ethnic groups. Each group has general and specific characteristic ways of expressing and manifesting human courtship and mating practices. Certain stereotypes and images, both positive and negative, have been imprinted along cultural lines in the psyche of each individual. These psychologically cultural characteristics are powerful determinants of human sexual choices, both in a constructive and pathological sense.

It becomes evident that sexual libidinal energies find their root motivation within specific cultural conditioning. Several individuals expressed a strong ethnic component to their sexual makeup.

> Don: "I feel a lot of 'Germanness' is deeply ingrained in my style and character. My sex appeal is certainly one of a German male."
>
> Martha: "I have felt some of my 'roots' in feelings that transcend way past my parents. It's like my genetic code has passed on certain, very real aspects of my sexuality."
>
> Sandy: "A great deal of my warmth and sensuality comes from my Irish roots . . . I feel that the lusty, earthy, sexual me has an Irish peasant girl as an ancestor."

Certain of our findings indicate that sexual mating choices are often based on individual attempts to secure something from someone else that was lacking or denied in the self. This displays itself by in-group ethnic choices and cross cultural mating practices. For example, a rigid Catholic or Calvinistic, sexually denied home environment may motivate a male or female to seek out a sexual partner from another ethnic or cultural group that would stimulate those deadened and denied parts of the self. Perhaps the trend in modern America for cross cultural marriages is an attempt to awaken those sexually denied parts of the self. The stereotype of the "Latin lover" may appeal to the Jewish princess who was not allowed to feel sensual or turned on to her own guilt-ridden, sexually acting-out father. The repressed, passive female may be very "turned on" to the aggressive, forceful, macho male who will "take" her body, thus eliminating any sense of decision or active acceptance on the part of the female. For example, there is the ongoing popularity of such obviously macho lovers as Clark Gable in "Gone With the Wind" and Sylvester Stallone in "Rocky." They may be polished up or dressed down but thousands of women still feel hot flashes when these aggressors "do their thing."

One woman traced her desire for a forceful male back to a conception trauma where she experienced the egg of her passive, repressed Catholic mother fighting to keep her father's sperm out.

"I experienced anger, feelings of aggression . . . Seemed as if my father's sperm forced its way in angrily. Felt physical illness, headache and vomiting. Felt my mother as sickening . . . weak and sickening."

A mixed trend seems to exist in the consciousness of certain white Americans towards mixed racial sexuality, with certain taboos exerting more censorship over some combinations than others. It is common in certain young white females coming from inhibited backgrounds to seek the excitement of clandestine sexual contact with previously forbidden ethnic groups. Amongst the females in a small survey, reactions to sexuality with a black male ranged all the way from pleasure and sweet titillation to revulsion. These reactions were firmly rooted in behavioral, cultural, sexual taboos, though motivated by many forces too extensive to pursue here. It was also interesting to investigate the emotional reactions of different white males at the prospect of the females, within their psychic territorial terrain, expressing a desire to stray away into alien ground. What we found was that some white males felt put down if certain white women hinted at preferring black lovers.

Sexual repression in some ethnic and religious groups is more widespread than in others. Some groups seem to do an across-the-board castration on all sexuality and sensuality while others are much more subtle and general in nature. For example, all of the Catholics I have worked with in this program experienced massive insult, deprivation and guilt in the sexual areas. They attribute this to repressive religious upbringing.

Tom: "Whenever sexuality is mentioned, I feel a need to be hush-hush about it. I tie this in, to a degree, with religion. During my few years in a Catholic school, it was as if everyone was asexual. I remember watching a movie in class and as a small kissing scene came on, the sister, running the projector, turned the light out until the scene was over."

Judy: "I was raised in an age and a time when most people were pretty up-tight about sex. I'm sure that a lot must have 'gone on' but I never knew a female who would admit to it. There was a lot of guilt and secretiveness. I did engage in premarital sex with the man I later married but I was filled

191

with a tremendous amount of guilt and fear—especially connected to my mother . . .

My background was Catholic and my mother was very old fashioned and strict in her views on morality. I recall the time she took me aside and explained the facts of life to me. Sex was O.K. and beautiful but only if two people were married to each other. Other than that, it was disastrous for a woman and would result in massive degradation and rejection . . .

I recall that as an adult I once mentioned something about masturbation to my mother (this was the first time the word was ever mentioned between us.) She said that the time to stop that was when the child was a baby in the crib—to slap the baby's hands. I guess that's what she did to me."

Sandra: "For so many years I had drilled into my soul that I was an unworthy sinner from the moment of my conception on: imperfect, born in sin, doomed to Limbo, even as a newborn. This was my religious heritage and I have carried these feelings of being a blemished, imperfect soul all my life . . .

How can I explode with life . . . with love, . . . with myself? How can I embrace my husband in my arms in one ecstatic moment of love and union, if my head is bowed with unworthiness, shame and withdrawal?"

One young male explored his Jewish roots and how they affected his sexuality and male identity.

"There seems to be a close relationship between my sexuality as a male and my ethnic background as a Jew. It is ironic that many of the connections and insights I've gained concerning my 'maleness' occurred, not by delving into my sexuality directly, but by plunging deeply into my feelings of being Jewish.

During a marathon one of the women in group began to get into feelings about her New York Jewish parents. My own parents are from New York and, until that moment, I had never really explored my feelings about this particular part of my family background. I was soon into very deep pain as I began expressing the oppression I was feeling. More and more I was connecting to the pain and suffering of my parents . . . how painful it is to be the children of Jewish immigrants living in New York.

The pain deepened in me as I connected to the rich and beautiful Jewishness that had been denied. My feelings put me in touch with the richness and beauty of myself, freeing me up to express movement, dancing and loving contact with other people. 'I was turned on!!'

The explosive energy that was released from the depths of my soul has had lasting effects on my sexuality and my male identity. I feel stronger, more confident, freer to express my needs for closeness and contact . . . plus, I've gained a groundedness and pride for my ethnic heritage . . . I'm more of who I really am!"

Exploring the roots of ethnic and religious sexual repression, whether it be male-female identification or specific areas of sexual dysfunction is an area we are just beginning to tap into. The affective components are endless as one looks into the myriad inner dynamic influences of one's ancestral background.

We must also remember to pay particular attention to the powerful social forces that tend to shape and mold people's sexual behavior. There are individual differences within each cultural group. However, we cannot ignore the fact that there are some very strong trends that seem to reflect the ways that certain ethnic groups express themselves sexually.

Calvinism has had a very powerful influence on repressive sexuality in our society. The American psyche is quite complex because there are many splits that occur within different sexual influences across our culture. There is a fear in Western culture that human sexuality is some sort of unbridled animal that, if left uncontrolled, will tear down the very structure of our industrialized society.

Television, for the most part, is geared to protecting this repressive fear, so as not to allow certain impulses to be rocketed into awareness. The media symbolizes our own attempts at control of those same impulses. However, a truly intelligent viewing public is insulted by programming that is geared to an imaginary, middle of the road character. No human being is only a middle of the road person although a neurotic may act as if he is. We are all a complex system of inter-related, connected and disconnected sub-personalities. That means that we are many sided and to exist within the realm of a one sided personality is, in fact, to be in neurotic pain. All sides of a person need to be expressed and allowed to be. This is what true integration is all about.

The splits in our own culture reflect the split in our national character and our own individual psychic lives. If there is anything wrong with America, it is because we, as its citizens, deprive ourselves of who we are. As I have implied before, every saint has his gross side and behind every virgin is a secret whore. No one is only just a coward. There is also the side that was not allowed to feel strong and brave. Nor is one just an urban dweller without having his roots in the earthy fields and farms of the country. Those who would swim the deepest seas need merely to turn the coin to find themselves soaring through the Universe. Likewise, behind every laborer is an artist and even great championship fighters have been known to be poets. All these many different sides of ourselves tend to make up a total personality that becomes sexually expressed in a given characteristic way. And that way is greatly governed by the long train of history of each ethnic group.

It is the blending of these opposite sides of the personality that creates a specific way of relating sexually. If someone is sexually relating in a strange way, we can assume that he is acting-out an unfelt part of himself which when fully felt, will result in some kind of modification of his behavior. He will become more centered in the here and now, relating from the straight core of his very being.

Richard came from an Irish background of high cultural and academic demands, while at the same time being influenced by the alcoholic other side of the family. Booze, women, and status make for all kinds of conflict. Richard had been very repressed sexually as a child as well as having a difficult time getting his affectional needs met. Later on in life, as a mature adult, he achieved considerable professional status while reveling in his sexual conquests. He became dismayed when all of his ventures failed to impress the Feeling Community. He could not understand why these people would not bow down and worship this male who had achieved so much. Although it was true that he had achieved much in the professional world and wanted to be seen as a great lover, these values could not make up for the fact that as a child, he was not allowed to be a feeling human being. His deficient emotional qualities detracted from all of his other acquisitions. Because feeling people tend to judge others on their emotional attractiveness and not on their would-be sexual prowess and professional acquisitions, Richard found himself floundering and on the fringe of the Feeling Community.

It is not so much what one achieves or what one can do that counts, although that is important. Rather, the emphasis is on how one has done it and *who* one is. One can develop great sexual prowess and professional excellence and still be an emotional dud. Lift the repressions, allow the feelings to come through, transform the person and what is achieved is mastery in the personal and sexual sphere.

SEXUAL LIBERATION—TABOOS

Neurotic people grow up being anything other than themselves in order to avoid parental and super-ego condemnation and punishment. The process is usually acquired slowly and insidiously. In the area of sexuality one explanation for its development could be parental reactions when the young child first begins to display sexual curiosity.

A little girl of five may exhibit a certain degree of excitement viewing her father's and brother's genitals. She has fun trying to reach and grab those "peculiar-to-her" organs. The male members of the family, coming from their own repressive backgrounds, become uncomfortable, embarassed and mixed-up at the precocious child's playful aggressiveness towards their sexual parts. Should they push her away and discourage such behavior or should they sit and talk to her in a nonevaluative fashion and find out how she is feeling? After all, most grown men and boys are not accustomed to sexually uninhibited little girls.

If she is pushed away, she may then learn to satisfy that curiosity outside of the home with little boys of her own age. Little Johnny displays his penis to little Mary and she reciprocates by showing herself to him. This all takes place in secret and in most cases the child never reveals this event to her parents, for fear of disapproval. Does the small child know what is happening? How will she integrate such an experience without being able to discuss such matters with her parents? Will her real sexual education take place outside of the home or will her feelings be integrated into the communication patterns of the household?

This raised the question of how honest one can be, sexually or otherwise, in a repressive society that reflects the inhibitions of its citizens. We, as therapists and feeling people, are helping our

195

clients to open themselves up to a more fully feeling life and that means that patients will come face to face with the everyday reality of their own repressions and fears.

Little Seymour is about two or three years old and is finding great delight in fondling his genitals, much to the discomfort of his parents. After all, this little person must be taught how to behave in an adult world that locks up grown men for playing with themselves in public. Little Seymour is not doing anything wrong according to his own standards. He is merely exercising his youthful pleasurable proclivity for curiosity. It feels good to him and he can't understand why daddy and mommy want him to stop such a wonderful activity. They also made a fuss about his thumb sucking and diaper messing. He is discovering, over and over again, that mom and dad want him to curtail some of his physical pleasurable pursuits. In an adult sense, this youngster may well ask, "Why is everyone so concerned with what I am doing with my orifices? Maybe I am doing something bad! Am I evil? Before, when I wet myself, mom and dad would change me and touch and powder me all over. They used to hug and kiss me all the time. Now I have to learn how to do a lot of things for myself."

As a child grows older he must take steps away from those early primary experiences of his senses. He no longer messes in his diapers. Instead, he messes up his room, his school work and maybe later on, his life. Where once his mother's body had always been available for warmth, love and food, now he must substitute a host of other activities. Instead of getting physically stroked by dad as in infancy, he must now learn what accomplishments will earn his father's praise and stroking.

Infants receive great pleasure through their mouths and tummy while sucking on mother's breast. They learn to smell and inhale her aroma and thereby, enhance their own pleasurable breathing. Their eyes gaze wondrously into the face of mother and watch her movements within their limited visual range. Mother and child fall marvelously and sensually in love because of the deliciousness of their physical contact. This emotional exchange can also be shared and experienced with the father and if all goes well, the threesome, plus other siblings, will bathe in each other's sensual delights. It is a wonderful experience in true emotional/tactile bonding and in the cases where it is life enhancing, the affectional bonds can last a lifetime and serve to nurture the emerging adult in all of his endeavors.

But what goes wrong? Babies are born naked and have no shame or disgust with their bodies. They soon learn that what was once permissive nakedness and touching must now be controlled and relegated to certain private places like bathrooms and bedrooms. Nakedness and toilet activities are relegated to the world of privacy and isolated from the view of others. Where once he was viewed without shame for these activities, now Mom and Dad begin to look away. He is slowly being conditioned to heterosexual development and contact outside of the immediate family. As he grows older he will discover that even though his parents have been preparing him for sensual/sexual independence, they and he will have deep conflicts of really letting go of one another.

Before long, the taboos set in. Parents and society begin to inculcate the child with a set of mores, rules and norms of behavior. He slowly begins to develop an unconscious super-ego. What were once pure, innocent physical drives now become subject to moral evaluation and control. His early, primary, core needs become the victim of repression and are relegated to the unconscious energy system called the Id.[3] He learns to internalize the prohibitions of his family and culture while struggling to keep the lid on to prevent an outbreak of forbidden impulses. He lives in two worlds. One is fantasy and desire. The other is conformity. Somewhere along the line, he must come to terms with these conflicting energies and deal with the pain that he has accumulated along the way.

One young woman was raised in a very strict, puritanical home. Nudity, especially between members of the opposite sex, was unheard of. Although she was raised with four brothers, she never saw any of them naked past diaper age. Her growth over a few years involvement with a feeling therapy led to a number of early repressions being lifted, among them a relaxation of the taboo surrounding the area of nudity.

It was not long until this area was tested and a whole new set of feelings and repressions emerged. A young pubescent male cousin

---

[3] Sigmund Freud, *Three Essays on the Theory of Sexuality*, ed. by James Strachey (New York, Avon Books, 1962).

visited her home where nude swimming was in progress. Immediately, he removed his clothes and dove in the pool. The following is her account of what occured.

"I found myself feeling very uncomfortable with Jamie in the water. Before long I was beginning to withdraw heavily from him, although previous to this, our relationship had been fairly close and open . . .

In order to get to the bottom of what was going on, I asked Jamie if he would work with me in our soundproofed feeling room. As he was very familiar with feeling integration, he readily agreed. What came out surprised me and bound both of us closer together . . .

'Get away from me . . . I'm feeling very small and I don't know what to do. You don't have a baby pecker or a grown man's prick. I know what to do with both of those. But I've never seen a young boy's penis! What do I do if it bumps me in the pool?! How do I react? I've never seen one before and it scares me . . . You scare me. Don't hurt me . . . My parents always told us to cover up and be modest . . . My father was very modest . . . I didn't know whether to be afraid or not . . ."

Following this feeling release, she was able to make clear contact with the young boy and not withdraw or reject him because of his genitals.

Masters and Johnson[4] refer to parental prohibitive injunctions thusly:

"Such parents cannot permit the spontaneous physical expression of feeling—the stroking, snuggling and enfolding movements with which almost all living creatures seek the warmth and reassurance that, particularly for the very young, is virtually indistinguishable from life itself."

This need for sensual contact never ceases, it only gets further

---

[4] W. L. Masters and V. E. Johnson *The Pleasure Bond* (New York, Bantam Books, Inc., 1976), pg. 245.

removed from its original sources. Give an infant enough loving contact and he or she will not be neurotically driven to seek the sensuality that was denied at birth, whether it be from a parent of the same sex or opposite sex.

THE DOUBLE STANDARD

As children grow older they are subtly taught that the sexes should be separated. Certain games are for boys and certain games are for girls. Conquest, mastery, superiority and aggressiveness are highly rewarded in boys. Daddy goes to work, watches football games and is the adventurous hero in war, while women and children are helpless victims. Females play with dolls and tea cups and are prepared for the role of housewife. A woman needs to "get" a man in order to fulfill her predestined role. She must adopt coyish seductiveness while the male must seduce and enslave. A little girl is trained to seduce and say "no" while keeping a male's interest alive and full of the promise of eventual physical reward. A male must sustain his ego by charming the female into eventually saying "yes" to his needs and desires. They both need each other to feel warm and close but the ritual of game-playing gets in the way of their coming back together and re-discovering what they once had in childhood.

The male is encouraged to seduce and play around while the female is urged to remain virginal and non-promiscuous. A male who "conquers" many females is considered a "lover" while his female counterpart who has extensive contacts with several males is considered a whore. Males are told to experience many women and then refrain from all but one at marriage. Girls are told to have none or very few, but be a "liberated whore" for their husbands. Boys go out on dates and if they "score," they report on their accomplishments to their buddies. There is a sense of pride, prestige and status in how much one scores. In fact, some adolescent males have been known to keep score sheets and diaries of their sexual prowess. "Tonight, I got bare tit off of Sally . . . Janet spread her legs for me . . . Sarah wacked me off."

In other words, a young adolescent's self-esteem may rest on the fact that his female love-objects "let" him have liberties with their bodies. The girls become the new mommies who reward the young males' persistent aggressive attempts to seduce them. These females very rarely feel a heightened sense of self-esteem for giving in to the boy. Usually they feel just the opposite. They don't have the option to go back and brag to their girl friends for fear of damage to their reputation. And reputation is no light matter for young females. The double standard claims that the harder it is to "make" a girl, the better is her reputation. While the more conquests that a male has, the better is his standing with his peers.

This conditioning operates well into adult life when a grown man believes that a woman who wants to have sex with different males is placing less value on him. If she desires to have sex with others besides him, then he is no longer special and he must then consider her to be not so special.

The conflicts that arise interpersonally as a result of this kind of double standard are numerous. As much as an individual might want to break this kind of stereotypic upbringing, its insidious influences are pervasive and subtle. One young man readily admitted to the double standard operating in his marriage. For years it had caused him and his wife untold conflict and pain.

"I have carried on a double standard in my marriage starting shortly after the first year and I had affairs with many girls. In many respects it was a way of getting even with my mother (via my wife) and at the same time try to fill my needs. I frequently would come home after an affair feeling a lot of guilt and remorse. I never really got my needs met on the outside, just a temporary relief from my pain. Although I messed around, there was no way I would tolerate my wife even having a guy kiss her. I was overly possessive and jealous . . .

Another aspect of my relationship with my wife was that I totally dominated her and belittled everything she did. I would cut her off in the middle of a sentence or ignore her when she talked to me. I know this was Mommy transference and it brought up a lot of early rage and contempt. My view of women was that they were subordinates, unimportant and "low lifes." They had little or nothing to offer me. I still carry some of these crazy ideas around with me. Unfortunately, they surface mostly in my relationship with my wife.

The women's movement has done much over the past few years to bring this issue to public awareness and concern. But until men and women feel the root causes of this kind of prejudice, time and time again, little can be done to eradicate the effects of this social and moral repression.

FRIGIDITY, IMPOTENCE AND PROMISCUITY

Let us take a look at sexual contamination surrounding inclusion and exclusion needs. A woman who has been burned in a sexual relationship, may have an historical issue triggered off without connection and resolution. If she harbors any elements of paranoia, she may be compelled to exclude and reject penetration and pleasure by the male penis. Her vagina may be tight and dry and she may be impaired in her climax capability. The common term is *frigidity*. She won't allow herself to warm up sexually to a man. She excludes the male member from getting inside of her where she fears deep vulnerability. In some cases, she may reject all male penises while in other situations, she will allow herself to feel sexual only when all her pain and inhibitions have been anesthetized by drugs or alcohol. The end result in either case is alienation, frustration and loneliness.

"I came into my session today concerned that my sexuality is not showing signs of health as I keep hoping it will. Instead I find myself deader than ever in my sexual areas.

I was able to take my tremendous need for orgasm back to my tremendous need for my father to love me, stroke me, hold me, talk to me and protect me. Not getting those needs met, I felt very unloved, neglected, hungry—as if something was wrong with me. Going back with these feelings took me to a sensation of falling into a black pit of depression and death. I didn't want to die, and held on for dear life but I was unable to live without my needs being met. Since I did not go to the bottom and die I am left in the depression of the pit. I have a feeling many of my depressed spaces come from this need.

The male counterpart is evident by not allowing himself to feel sexual towards a female for fear of rejection. "If mommy didn't accept or want me, then current females won't want me either. I am

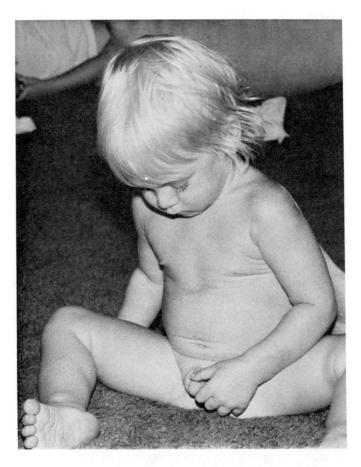

"Adam Discovering Himself"

not adequate enough or didn't perform well enough to please my parents, therefore, I will fail here also." The chronically limp or impotent penis and the tight, constricted, immobile, uncoordinated vagina are defensive symptoms that reflect the continual rejection of childhood.

At the other extreme of the inclusion spectrum is the desperate, extremely needy person who will have sex with anyone. Penises will penetrate and vaginas will open indiscriminately. Receiving only crumbs and exclusion as children, these individuals are always hungry for love. When the pain begins to surface, rather than feel it fully, they may act it out by having sex with just about anything that walks. As I have already stated, inclusion sexual contamination always results in a painful, unfulfilling pay-off.

A woman who acts out her daddy need by being sexually indiscriminate or by solely using her sexuality to gain attention, probably has no other parts of herself to pull from in order to get her real needs met. She may compulsively put herself into a stereotypic role of a "broad," "cunt,""playgirl," "goodtime Sally," etc. The male counterpart is the "stud," "barfly," "locker room Johnny," or "party boy." These roles, when acted out to the extreme, become prisons of shallowness, to the exclusion of other parts of the individual. These roles can be fun and quite productive when they are ultimately integrated into the total personality. They can be then called upon, by choice, to enhance one's life and awareness by being a form of expression and living by a total organism that has integrated, developed and felt all the parts of himself. If one part of the personality, however, dominates the entire personality while the other parts are buried, undeveloped and unfelt we have limited and neurotic personality expression.

"The times that I've fucked guys I've usually gone totally unconscious. When I see a guy that I'm attracted to, even if I was clear, I'll immediately start going weird. Whenever I do fuck guys, as a one night thing, the outcome is always bad feelings. I guess I make them out to be my daddy . . . I act out my feelings towards daddy. It's really hard for me to be up front and real with the guys. I always find myself stuttering or being shy when I'm trying to say exactly what I want or feel. Then I go unconscious and dead."

Another young woman found herself falling into bed with just about every person she met, male or female. Her need for stroking and affection seemed endless. Finally, through deep core feeling, she was able to tie up that endless acting out need with intense physical deprivation as a young infant and child. The following is an excerpt from her diary after she had been involved with the Total Feeling Process for a couple of years.

"Saturday night I was half aware of 'acting out' some craving for attention. My early need for my mother was pushing up again and rather than feel it, I slipped back into an old defense of flirting with males for attention. Unconsciously, I was saying, 'Notice me, pay attention to me, touch me.'

My acting out brought some later rejection from my husband, at which point, I finally acknowledged my need and hit the floor to feel. At first, I thought the need was for my father but, before long, I was thrashing on the mat in pain for my mother again. 'God, what have you done to me?! It never ends . . . you're killing me . . .' I felt my whole body awake with need for her, wretching for her, reaching out with every nerve cell for her touch. And she never came . . . I was choking and gagging on phlegm, sweating profusely and crying, 'Oh God, Momma, where are you?!! Will I ever be free of this need for you??!!'. . .

I came out of this space fairly subdued. It hit me deeply how much I had been emotionally neglected by her and how, time and time again, I found myself returning to that early need for my mommy. I was also a little disappointed in myself for having acted out the need, rather than feeling it. I have worked hard over the past few years to get rid of my 'games' and here one of them had crept in again.

Later, after I helped another female work through a very similar issue, I was able to laugh with her, as we realized how ridiculously we had been behaving. Our understanding of our mutual deep core need and how we had tried to defend against it, brought us closer together. We promised to help each other with this issue if it came up again, and to care for each other in the here and now in a way that our respective mothers had not been able to . . ."

Males, too, are victims of early emotional and physical deprivation and this can lead to the Don Juan syndromė and heavy acting out. At times it is difficult to ascertain where emancipation begins and permissiveness takes over in a symbolic compensatory act. For to define who is sexually liberated cannot be discovered in the actions of a person, but only in the feelings of that individual. For example, Richard viewed himself as very sexually liberated, honest and open. He had accumulated enormous amounts of physical evidence to that conclusion. It was an incredible boon to his ego to mildly boast that he had had sex with males and females of every known ethnic group. He professed his bi-sexuality and "availability" quite proudly. I would suggest that these outward evidences of sexual liberation are in no way convincing to others that he is indeed emotionally liberated. Quite the contrary, for these behaviors do not match his inward inability to establish deep, firm, total emotional contact with at least one other person. Therefore, I don't see him on a deep core level as being emotionally free. In fact, he is firmly attached in a defensive fashion to his superficial image of himself. Paradoxically, in a projective sense, he sees others who are not like unto himself, as being more conservative and less liberated than he.

Swingers may have the facade of being sexually liberated but upon deeper investigation, one finds a driving internal conservative nature in many aspects of human relations. To be promiscuous with one's genitalia does not necessarily eradicate one's emotional rigidity.

For purposes of description and further understanding, I refer to Bennis and Shepherd's[4] categories of over-personal and counterpersonal orientations to inclusion, exclusion and intimacy. The overpersonal or the overly needy individual tries desperately to feel included or close to others. But his behavior alienates and distances those that he would be close to. So he ends up distant, needy and unfulfilled. The counter-personal or counter-needy individual rejects, excludes or denies any desire to be included or to include others. He rejects first so as to avoid the deep involvement and commitment that is required for successful therapy and relation-

---

Benis and Shepherd, "Theory of Group Development", *Human Relations*, 1956, 9, pg. 415-437.

ships. He fears being small and overwhelmed by the demands of an adult relationship.

Both types eventually end up manipulating others into being bad, rejecting parents. The over-personal makes others attack and reject him because he "comes on" with sexually confusing messages. He may make pathetic pleas for love and acceptance and yet, he can't relate emotionally because he has no love feeling to give. Because mommy and daddy weren't open to him, he couldn't give them love so he buried himself from the whole world. He hides behind a wall of unfelt need and mistrust. Others feel uneasy when the over-personal makes his need-saturated, sexual or non-sexual move. They will often get angry because he makes them feel guilty for rejecting him. The counter-personal rejects everyone as if they had the same kind of plague that his parents had. His parents weren't fit to get close to, so he projects a mistrustful trip onto everyone else. Yet both types are excrutiatingly alone, since they both relate to others as if they were bad parents. By their projections, they ultimately deny their targets of their true identities.

The equation here is quite simple. "If you relate to me as if I were somebody other than who I am, then I will be hurt and in pain." The equation can go a little further. "I would like you to be who you really are, so that I can be fully who I am. Then maybe we can both make it together as fellow human beings."

The preceding formula is what I believe to be the essence of a conflict-free harmonious relationship with oneself and others. If all people were allowed to be themselves and would allow others to be themselves, then perhaps a new consciousness would be realized.

Chapter 11   Homosexuality

HOMOSEXUALITY

Over many years of clinical practice I have had the opportunity to work with many varieties and manifestations of homosexuality. In its simplest diagnostic form homosexuality can be defined as those practices and modes of behavior that reflect sexual interest in persons of the same sex. Homosexuality does not necessarily constitute a pathological disorder per se and it can be considered one of many forms of sexual behavior. However, as a behavioral scientist, I am naturally interested in the underlying dynamics and motivations of all behavior, and homosexuality, in clinical practice, does present itself.

The general public's attitude toward homosexuality varies from extreme phobic repugnancy to tolerant supportive acceptance. Those individuals who display marked effeminate characteristics seem to arouse the strongest response from a predominantly heterosexual society. However, the majority of homosexuals do not exhibit any of the affectations or overt signs of the stereotyped effeminate character. Conversely, many effeminate individuals are not necessarily homosexual.

Homosexuality, on the symptomatic level, is viewed as a psychosexual deviancy or an alternate life style and not as a form of severe psychopathology. Conversely, there is the natural adversary of the practicing homosexual and he is the dogmatic fundamentalist or rigid personality structure. These two classes of deviancies are natural antagonists and are bound to clash on personal, social and political levels. We view certain forms of homosexuality and rigid fundamentalism as disturbances in early feeling development, and prefer to focus on the underlying feeling dysfunctions. This is consistent with our belief that there is only one disease and that is the repression or the denial and blocking of real feeling. To try to change someone's surface behavior (i.e., sexual preference) is useless and will only lead to substituting another facade, while leaving the buried feeling expressions intact.

It is unfortunate that moral evaluations have been thrown at the whole controversy of homosexuality vs. heterosexuality. There may be moral elements involved but they are minor compared to psychological abnormalities that threaten life and property and other basic human values. Homosexuality does not threaten the structure of our civilization nor will it bring down the nation as its opponents declare. Slightly paranoid rigids have cited that the fall of Rome was due to homosexuality, thus there is a basic fear or phobic reaction in some sections of the population that homosexuality will spread and decay the moral fiber of our family lives. This is a delusion . . .

Another fear is that if homosexuals are allowed to freely permeate every sector of society, especially schools, they will engage in solicitous acts against heterosexual children and win them over to homosexuality. Children simply don't make sexual preferences the same way that they choose an ice cream flavor.

One common, very powerful underlying factor in the development of homosexuality is parental role modeling and attitudes in the child's emotional development prior to, during, and after birth plus the first few years of life. I contend that very early familial experiences are the foundation of everyone's sexual preferences. A boy who is born into a home where the father is not fully there for him as a warm, caring, close male, will develop an intense life long internal craving to recapture the good loving father he never had. This has to be compounded with certain machinations by a mother who subtly emasculates and seduces the child and fosters a very heavy female identification. If a father is not around to display a role model of full feeling manhood in a loving, close, strong way and the mother treats him like a little girl, you will have an adult male who has been completely "zapped" of his full masculinity. He will have to internalize the femininity that has been imposed on him by his mother. These children were never treated as highly valued males by either parent.

Take the case of a young adult who is struggling with his homosexual tendencies in the framework of a heterosexual relationship.

Walt: I don't think I really explained what was going on sexually between me and Liz. There was an effort at first to really fulfill that male role and it was easier at first, too. But the longer I was involved with her, the harder it was to do anything sexually. I don't know why it got harder and harder . . . she was asking for more and more. I don't know where that led to . . . a lot of frustrated attempts. It just seems that I couldn't make Liz happy. I would listen to what she had to say about what she was expecting from me sexually; how she perceived me while I was trying to have sex with her. When I really tried to listen to her and really tried to give her what I thought she wanted . . . it just didn't seem to be enough. It just made it all the harder to even try the next time around (sigh. . .)

It's like I want to share something with somebody. I just want to be relaxed. I guess with this guy this weekend . . . it was just being with somebody, being naked and sharing. It just felt really good to have someone beside me that was warm. There weren't any demands placed on either one of us . . . It's just a totally different feeling than when I'm with Liz.

Ther: I'm having difficulty understanding this . . . O.K., you didn't make it with Liz and there was no real sexual enjoyment. Why didn't you seek out another woman? Why did you seek out a male? Why would you suddenly go from mommy to daddy? When people don't make it with someone, they usually go on to someone else. You chose someone from a different sex . . . I have heard you express some amount of turn-on to certain females. I have heard you be quite expressive about Lorraine and some other females but I don't hear you that expressive about males, unless you keep that part hidden . . . The fact is you didn't seek out another female when you 'failed' with Liz . . . and I don't know whether it's even a failure.

Walt: I kind of judged it as a failure . . . I just couldn't satisfy her. I didn't know if it was me or her or a combination of both. I'm just afraid to start something with someone else.

Ther: So, do I understand this right? You have a lot of anxiety and fear about satisfying a female and less anxiety about pleasing and satisfying a male.

Walt: I don't feel the demand from a male as much as a female. I feel that a male I can understand . . . with a female it's like 'What do you want?!'

The patient is experiencing an incredible performance expectation for him, as a male, and he never quite measures up to it. He never fulfills his own performance expectations. The typical male (in a macho sense) would go in there, be really out to satisfy his own needs, and then respond to his female's needs. In this young man's case, there's always this anxiety "Am I going to be able to please and satisfy her?" Pleasing her really comes before his own pleasure, before his own needs.

As a fellow group member put it:

> "I know as a man, that I want to get screwed. I want to get all the goodies. I also like to please a woman, too—in that order. I want to be known as a good lover, a good stud, a good fuck."

But Walt has put himself down already. "Oh my God, I'm going to be a terrible, terrible lover." He's already got that evaluation laid out. He explores his confusion with males and females a little further and starts to sink back into some early feelings about his mother. It will become obvious the effect that her emasculation has had upon her son. This coupled with a distant, authoritarian father who was rarely at home, drove Walt to a confusion in sexual gender identity and a struggle with homosexuality.

Ther: O.K. stay with what you're into . . . now snap into the present. You're with a male. How does that connect with what's going on between you and your mom? You say, 'Mom, I want you to love me.' Are you still trying to please Mommy? Liz was making a demand on you in other ways. Was she making a demand on you to be female?

Walt: No, she was wanting me to fuck her, to fuck her good.

Ther: Liz wanted you to fuck her good. Did Mommy want you to fuck her good?

Walt: (crying) I don't think so.

Ther: What was Mommy doing? What was going on?

Walt: It's like my Mom was trying to turn me into a girl and Liz was trying to turn me into a man.

Ther: You don't really know what you are, do you?

Walt: (crying) I don't know . . . I don't know what she wants from me. (crying) . . . She wants me to be a little girl.

Ther: Liz, sit in front of him and make gestures like you are going to take his prick off.

Walt: Don't, Mom . . . (yelling, crying) . . . Don't Mom! What am I?! What am I, Mom? . . . I don't know, I don't know . . . (crying) . . . I don't want a pussy, Mom.

Ther: You're a soft little boy/girl, soft and gentle.

Walt: I don't want a little pussy, Mom, I don't want it! (yelling)...I don't want it,Mom!...Get away!!...Get Away!! . . . Leave my little pee pee alone, leave it alone . . . don't touch it! (Yelling while at the same time starting to feel smaller and smaller)

Ther: Give your pee pee to Mommy, Walt . . . Give your pee pee to Mommy. Mommy wants it now, give it to Mommy!

Walt: Get outa here, leave me alone! No . . . no . . . (yelling and crying) . . . Get Away! . . . (beating floor with feet, yelling and crying) Ahhh . . . I want my fucking pee pee back! . . . Ahhh . . . I want my pee pee back! . . . (hitting punching bag) . . . I want it back! . . . That was me . . . That was mine . . . That was my pee pee! I want it back . . . I'm gonna fucking beat you with my pee pee!

Ther: You're beating her with your penis. Now, let me know when it goes from a pee pee to a prick, when it goes from a little pee pee to a big prick, when there's power in your penis.

Walt: Someday it's gonna get fucking big! . . . I'm fucking gonna beat you! . . . (yelling and hitting the punching bag) . . . I want to fucking kill you with it!!

Ther: Someday you're going to get big behind that penis. Right now though, you're feeling very little, . . . a little pee pee . . .

Walt: Ahhh . . . Ahhh . . . Ahhh . . . I'm gonna fucking beat you with it! Ahhh...I'm gonna fucking trip you with it... (hitting) . . . Ahhh . . . I'm gonna fucking beat you with it! Ahhh. . .Good Fucking Night, Bitch!! (jumping up and down on punching bag) . . . I killed her with my fucking dick! . . . Ahhh . . . I got it back . . . Ahhh!!

Ther: . . . Not only are you getting back your penis but you're getting back to you, your feelings. You have to bury her time and again. You don't know fully what you are yet.

Walt: I just feel like a very strong prick.

Ther: That's good, a very strong prick . . . She won, Walt, a long time ago. You lost your penis, lost you, lost your feelings for a long time. But you're bringing them back. You've got to symbolically kill her so you can come alive. She can't stand to live with your big penis. She can't survive as long as you have a big rod. It's either you or her . . .

Someday you're going to have a choice. You got kicks from doing the homosexual thing. You also had pain from wanting to be a straight, powerful male, too. You got shit for your efforts. The shit came from her. Someday you'll say, 'I'm not gonna take your shit anymore. I'm gonna be me.'

Walt: I'm gonna be me. Someday I'm gonna be fucking all me . . ."

Many heterosexuals as well as bisexuals and homosexuals are confused about their identity. The problem does not lie in one's sexual preferences but rather in who one is. It is not an issue of where, how, and with whom one seeks gratification, for these are merely manifestations of early love object choices. The question of who and what one really is reflects and is determined by early primordial truths.

It is very hard for me to accept the fact that individuals who are homosexual and have other confusions about their gender identity can be full feeling, self-actualizing human beings. It is theoretically possible that certain bisexuals and homosexuals can reach a state of maturity where they totally accept their own sexual preferences and as such, are leading fully integrated, highly defined lives in spite of societies' ambivalent attitudes towards their life style. However, I do not believe that full sexual and emotional gratification can occur between members of the same sex. Because the liaison is symbolic and not sexual at its deepest core, it negates the possibility that the participants can relate to each other for who they really are. Proper *sensual* parental bonding and identification is the cornerstone of realistic gender role adaptation.

If a child is totally loved and cared for in a full emotional, physical sense by both parents, he will not manifest disturbances in gender identity or sexual preference. Rigid character types and many homosexuals create a delusion that their home and family lives were perfectly normal and average. Then, again, they have had no other frame of reference with which to compare. As soon as these so-called "normal," unyielding character types and homosexuals begin to feel their buried feelings, they start to come in contact with the painful disordering of their childhood and after a time, begin to realize how crazy it all was.

One young woman found herself running from one bi-sexual affair to another, acting out a tremendous need for love, affection and confirmation. Her symbolic cry was, "Love me, Mommy and Daddy. I'll die without your love." In time, her relationship with her husband began to falter as she turned more and more to females for sexual and emotional gratification. The emotional tenderness and physical *"letting go"* she was able to experience with those of her same sex surpassed that which she was able to have with males. Her initial attraction was toward weaker females whom she seduced and eventually *"mothered."* As her confidence grew, she felt herself attracted to strong, powerful females who she could possibly seduce, but eventually be mothered by.

This young woman, however, was torn by her sexual preferences. Her life style made it fairly easy to experiment and explore different modes of behavior but her core self was really a heterosexual female. Around this time she was introduced to the Total Feeling Process and began, what was to become, a long painful search for who and what she really was.

Many times it is quite helpful for clients to pay particular attention to recurring dream themes. If an individual has a kind of dream that happens over and over again, then we can assume that feeling material is operating at a subconscious level that may reflect periods of great pain and conflict. Such was the case with this young woman. As she began to delve deeper and deeper into her core self, her true feelings about her homosexuality emerged. The following is a dream she experienced on a number of occasions which eventually led her to some very strong historical feelings about her mother.

"I am sitting on a bus and a very fat, bloated girl sits down next to me. She keeps leaning on my breast and body . . . . . Soon she reaches over to my crotch and starts fondling me . . . . I reject her a couple of times and then finally, let her turn me on."

As Sandra worked with this dream in therapy, it became obvious to her that the girl was her mother whom she desperately needed and yet, was repulsed by at the same time. Her mother's deadness and lack of feeling made her grotesque in Sandra's eyes and yet the little girl in Sandra was starving for physical affection and touching. She had grown up in a home where all of her material

213

needs had been met but her emotional and physical needs were ignored. Physical touching was at a minimum.

It took a couple of years before Sandra really felt resolved about
who and what she was. Hours and hours of old pain and need for
her mother were at the root of her sexual identification problem.
This had been further compounded by her identifying strongly with
her father who had been able to supply her with a minimum of
warmth and affection. When she finally was able to let go of her
mother in a feeling way and realize that she was never going to have
her, she was also able to finally de-sexualize her hunger and craving
for a female lover.

"I finally broke open with incredible need . . . . Very
young infant space—heavy crying and body convulsing . . .
At that point, Gloria's (her female lover who was working with
her primally) sensual kissing of my face started to turn me off
and I felt I wanted to be alone with the pain. The realization
hit very heavy that I could *never* have my mother I
could *never* get that need met . . . . Incredible pain!!!" (Upon
coming out of the heavy feelings) . . . . "Feel like I'm below
the sexual need level . . . . I've come out of it sweeter and
quiet, grounded and peacefully alone. The hunger is no longer
in me."

Some homosexual liasons form out of a desire to rebel, out of
curiosity or out of a need to passively submit to sex. It is also possible
to slide into homosexuality because heterosexual love/sex objects are
unobtainable (prisons, etc.). In many cases individuals get ego
enhancement from the sexual attentions of members of the same sex
and often, it is much easier for these individuals to achieve emotional and sexual satisfaction from a partner of the same sex, rather
than someone of the opposite sex.

Roger was just such a case. His inability to make strong emotional
and sexual contact with a female led him to ego gratification with a
male. What he eventually had to face, however, was that he also
had great difficulty making full emotional contact with a male. He
didn't have to face his adequacy/performance issue with someone of
the same sex but he did run head-on into his devastating need for a
warm, loving father figure. There was no way he could get this early need met in a here and now relationship. Either he met males

who became a *"good daddy"* to him but he had to remain distant
with his sexual need for fear of alienating them or he established a
sexual relationship but was unable to develop a strong emotional
bond. Either way, he lost out.
The following is an excerpt from a letter we received from Roger
prior to the start of his therapy.

"I am a homosexual. All of my friends are straight and most
of them think I am too . . . . . I've never been able to completely overcome my feelings of quiet and shame although I
thought the gay liberation movement would be able to help. I
tried to make myself proud of what I was but it didn't help
. . . . As it is now, I'm unable to maintain a close relationship
with either a male or a female . . . . . "

As Roger delved deeper and deeper into his early childhood
memories, he realized how distant he and his father had been. Their
relationship was still shallow and superficial and triggered him into
a great deal of pain.

"It hit me what an empty conversation I had with my Dad
. . . It brought back all the things I had wanted to say to him
as a kid. It also brought back how many times he had made fun
of me and my feelings. Whenever I was scared, he would ask
when I was going to stop being a baby and grow up I
was never supposed to be scared . . . . 'I feel angry that I can't
go to you and talk to you. Why can't I go to you?! . . . Where
the fuck are you?! . . . . (yelling and crying) . . . . What the
fuck are parents for if you can't go to them?!! . . . . . "

Roger experienced much of the deep core pain stemming from his
parents' emotional distance and lack of support. However, as he
drew closer to the threat of here and now committment and intimacy with individuals in the therapy group, he chose to discontinue feeling altogether and withdrew to his escape routes of
solitude, superficial contact and distance. Real, straight emotional
contact was too threatening for him.
The homosexuality issue displays itself in particular transference
phenomena. As a homosexual enters therapy, he either seeks total and
complete confirmation and acceptance for his homosexuality or he

215

wishes to eradicate it and become a full functioning heterosexual. Whatever direction he chooses to pursue, he will come head-on into conflict with what he perceives to be group norms and structures.

One type of homosexual will attempt to become like everybody else in the group, thinking that if he conforms to full fledged heterosexuality, he will gain acceptance by being like everyone else. Another type will rigidly defend and protect his homosexuality and may even try to inflict it on other group members.

Some arrogant homosexuals will act out an insatiable need for human contact by attempting to have sex with every person in the program. He may flaunt himself at the group and even chide or punish them for not engaging in sexual behavior with him. To his chagrin, he will probably be met with much resistance and rejection for his overt sexual drives and advances. Many group members will feel placed in a double bind because he treats them as sex objects rather than relating to them as full human beings in a feeling way.

The more timid homosexual will refrain completely from sexualizing his needs with other group members and attempt to get his sexual needs met outside of the group. This meek type lives in two worlds. One is that of his outside homosexual contacts and the other is the realm of straight people with whom he does not feel fully comfortable.

The homosexual often finds great difficulty in a therapy situation, since his sexual need is his foremost ploy at attempting to get people to confirm him. Because he has trouble relating on a deeper more emotional level, he is stuck with his sexuality. When that does not work for him, he either rejects the group, withdraws or, if he is particularly courageous, he will fall into the deepest throes of a very horrendous historical pain.

There are some homosexuals who would claim that they have and are quite capable of forming a deep feeling emotional relationship with another homosexual. I would agree with this claim—to a point. It is my belief that there would come a time in that relationship when both partners would reach that deep point of painful transference that reflects the earlier primary pre and post natal insult. The pain would be so great that it would take incredible motivation, fortitude and patience to feel it and risk moving out of the gratifying homosexual lifestyle. In other words, when each partner reaches a point of symbolic conflict with the other, they would either have to stop the movement of the relationship, at that crunching point, or feel the horrendous pain that would pull them away from the symbolic acting out with the parent of the same sex.

This has got to be one of the most difficult, classical, doublebind, conflict situations. The pain that would burst forth might appear to totally obliterate the individual. It is my contention that this obliteration is a near total cellular disintegration at the primary conceptual level and lies as the root cause and fear of the homosexual's adjustment pattern. It is this threat of total cellular destruction that the homosexual defends and keeps intact and repressed. The pain would be agonizing and very few therapies are equipped to deal with it at this level.

This point of disintegration cannot be taken too lightly. A heterosexual may feel disintegration also, but his greatest fear is a disintegration of the emotional relationship between himself and his parents. His very life and physical being is not being threatened by total cellular destruction by an intensely hostile, castrating egg. The homosexual's pain is far deeper and more devastating because it is his very physical, as well as emotinal being, that is being threatened with total annihilation and the disintegration of all of his parts.

This point is crucial so let me reiterate and emphasize the degree of trauma for the individual. A heterosexual is emotionally threatened postnatally. The bisexual is threatened at birth and gestationally, but the homosexual is threatened at the unicellular level. This could happen at the moment of conception itself or even before while still having his genetic material locked up inside each parents' reproductive organs and glands. At this unicellular level, at least one parent is emotionally impotent and filled with a fear of castration. The sperm or egg *"makes it"* but never forgets that fear of near annihilation. This genetically transmits a homosexual pattern of deep rooted fear that will last a lifetime and can only be released through deep core feeling.

There seems to be one further primary similarity in the family backgrounds of most homosexual behaviors. Most of these individuals never received emotional confirmation as children. At best, they might have gotten a little bit of something from one parent. But, for the most part, their early affectional bonds with both parents are characterized by extreme desolation, distance, lack of warmth and contact. Even those individuals who would appear to have at least a neurotically close relationship with one parent are, in fact, hiding from the symbiotic, overbearing manipulations of a desperately needy mother or father.

I understand that some contemporary homosexual pain comes about because of societal pressures. I also know that human beings can be really happy if they are fully in touch with themselves and fulfill the highest positive standards of their culture and history. This requires a transcending of the negative effects of that culture and history, and becoming all that is beautiful and profound.

This subtlety is important for I am not speaking of a mere psychological adjustment to one's environment and society. I am referring to a transcendence from that culture to a sublime relationship with it. One must feel comfortable being *"at one"* with one's culture and yet beyond it. Therefore, we must be concerned with the subtle interplay of one's sex and the sexual mores of one's background and society. Because homosexuality and bisexuality does stand in variance with certain cultural ethics, it is imperative that we come to terms with this phenomenon.

It is a moot question whether one's sexuality has anything to do with his innate happiness, occupational interactions or contributions to society. The real question is how much of a contribution would that person bring if he were totally and completely in touch with his deep core self and his buried feelings. This is a question which can be addressed to all individuals, regardless of whether they are homosexuals, bisexuals, or heterosexuals.

Sometimes I feel tight and pressed and I go to my head . . . . .
That is when I know that I must withdraw and get deep into my
feelings . . . . feel my need and how only human that I am. When
all the feelings come pouring out I feel good again . . . . alive and
vibrant. I will spare no cost to feel more of me . . . . . "

Chapter 12 Tolerance

TOLERANCE

As individuals grow and are bombarded with insensitivity, harshness and repression, tolerance becomes one more response that loses its realness and spontaneity. Individuals become tolerant of a closed-down, mechanistic, alienating culture and forget how to respond to the emotional real self behind the facade. They tolerate pollution, neurosis, war, boredom, superficiality, crime, inhumanity and yet, they squirm in discomfort at an infant's crying, an old man's pathetic loneliness and real feeling of any sort.

As one slowly reowns his feeling core, however, he develops a sense of general human empathy and toleration for the plight of all mankind. He learns to love and respond favorably to authenticity, honesty and straightness and abhors and refuses to tolerate the sick, destructive acts of the neurotic. He loves justice and will not tolerate or put up with crazy behavior. He learns to draw the line and say "no," emphatically, to the acts of a crazy person and a sick society.

The more that one feels, the less one will tolerate clearly perceived, unjust, malevolent acts between people. An unfeeling person will take an inordinate amount of "shit" and not respond appropriately or in a matched way. He seems to be able to tolerate very difficult and painful situations by somehow effectively closing them out of his consciousness. This kind of tolerance is by no means a virtue. There can be no virtue in a tolerance that permits someone to do something that is destructively counter-productive. In fact, it probably has become an integral part of a pathological defense system.

Most of us feel impotent and powerless in dealing with a sick society, but sooner or later sanity demands that we see the craziness of the whole world and that each of us has our own particular kind of insanity. The beginning of clarity brings with it the realization that our collective insanity has created and tolerated a sick world filled with unfeeling, mixed-up, defended people. The number of real, feeling, grounded individuals will remain small unless people decide, en masse, to go back to the basics of the deep core, integrative feeling experience.

Much of destructive tolerance is nothing more than passive weakness. Those who remain forever quiet see much of the injustices of others but choose not to react. They, thereby, stifle their own feelings towards the precise craziness that needs to be confronted.

In most cases, we can trace this passivity back to early gestation and childhood roots. Many children cannot confront the craziness of their parents because they are trained to be obedient and passively submissive. They either sit idly by and become swallowed up in the insanity of their families or struggle in the midst of the craziness and go crazy themselves. Either way, they lose. If they choose the latter route and get caught up in the struggle, they frequently find it impossible to tolerate anything or anyone. They are doomed to complete an old gestalt of struggling in an impossible situation. If they choose the former, they eventually learn how to be insanely passive and powerless. Their ability to tolerate "shit" is incredible.

It is difficult for this kind of person to get fully involved in anything productive because he fears getting all swallowed up in craziness again. As a result, he rarely ever confronts anyone or anything. Thus, his passivity keeps him safe yet withdrawn and unfulfilled. Eventually, reality has to break out and if it can't come out straight, then it becomes a detoured, physical expression of intense pain, hurt, rage, etc. In time, this individual may even develop a serious somatic disease due to years of holding back his true self.

PHYSICAL INTOLERANCE

Many physical symptoms begin to appear as deep feelings rise. The autonomic nervous system reactivates symptoms that have emotional and historical meaning. Therapists learn to recognize that a feeling is being blocked and fighting for expression, when a familiar physical symptom begins to surface.

We can argue that each individual possesses certain organ deficiencies[1] and that these symptoms represent a detoured feeling that needs expression. When a defense or a form of insanity is operating, there may be an accompanying physical symptom. For example, as one slips into the throes of his neurosis, he may experience earaches, rashes, muscular aches and pains, fatigue, headaches and other maladies. Of course, if the repression is very debilitating, then more serious physical diseases may develop. Such diseases, previously believed to be primarily physical in origin, are now being viewed as

---

[1] Alfred Adler, *Social Interest: A Challenge to Mankind* (New York: Capricorn Books, 1964).

having possible psychogenic roots.[2] Once these feelings are decoded by a reality-creating, core feeling experience, the symptom appears less and less.

Have you ever noticed what happens when your body needs and wants to do something and your mind says, "No?" In this disconnected condition the truth of the body is denied by the inhibitions, repressions, and conditioning of the head. The body never lies, but in the neurotic, the mind continually deceives and denies the needs of the body.

The relative degree of neurosis present in the organism depends upon how many early real needs were denied in deference to the needs of parents. Early mind/body disconnecting can set the groundwork for a lifetime of continuous neurotic symptoms without the victim ever knowing the real cause for his discomfort.

The needs of a newborn child through the first couple of years of life are tremendous—much greater than the average adult realizes. An infant who needs to be with his parents, but can't because they may be tired, away somewhere or preoccupied with their own symbolic needs, has to find something else to take their place. He may throw tantrums, withdraw, bang his head, develop asthma, tics or stuttering in order to deny the pain that they will not be there with him when he needs them. He creates a symbolic sideshow of bodily symptoms to pull away from the real emotional pain.

Long term chronic bodily symptoms are a statement as to how much the person had to depart from his real natural expressive self. The severity of the symptom is an indication of how hopeless it was for him to be himself. At least with the symptom he might be able to get some secondary need met through symbolic pampering of himself by those who are involved in his struggle. Attention to a symptom, however, can never replace the gratification of receiving love for being oneself. At best, symptom relief through secondary ameliorative devices, such as drugs, diverts the attention to the bodily ache, thus relieving anxiety and tension, but it never fully eradicates the causes. Only by relieving the early pain and resolving it, by ripping out the insidious causes, does one become free of the bodily symptom. If the reservoir is drained of its neurotic repres-

---

[2] O. Carl Simonton, M.D. and Stephanie Mathews-Simonton, "Belief Systems and Management of the Emotional Aspects of Malignancy", *The Holistic Health Handbook* ed. by Bauman, Brint, Piper and Wright (California: And/Or Press, 1978) p. 212.

sions, then the fuel that drives the neurotic symptom will fail to operate destructively on the body's tissues.

Let us explore this phenomenon a little further. One man felt anger toward his lady friend because she refused to go somewhere with him. She had been acting strange and withdrawn and couldn't be with him when he wanted her to be. He immediately went into a dissociative reaction. He was angry and yet he felt guilty expressing anger toward her, because she was so weak and helpless. So, he withdrew and ended up with a headache. A few moments later, he expressed his anger and predictably, she dumped it back on him, leaving him unresolved.

He decided to pursue the issue a little further with her, even though he knew that he was in for a difficult struggle. The woman finally broke into a rage toward her own mother connected to the original feeling that she was blocking and "acting out." Contact between the couple was re-established and the man revealed that his headache had disappeared.

Later that evening, he developed more of the same symptoms. His headache returned, although not as severe. He overate at dinner and wanted his ladyfriend to masturbate him. He then laid down and fell into the feeling of being alone and needing mommy and daddy. The historical feeling was not completed and although he came out with no desire to eat, his headache practically vanished and the desire to be masturbated gone, he reported a slight wringing of the hands.

Thus, we can observe that if the underlying tension is not released and connected *fully*, then the neurotic energy keeps the body behaving symbolically by re-channeling the energy to different sites of illness.

Psychosomatic symptoms are not usually owned as such by an individual during a particular struggle. Some symptoms are similar to infectious diseases, because they transmit neurotic energy between people, through sub-conscious communication channels. This may sound mystical, but it is nevertheless true. If you have ever been around a tense person, you may notice that you become a little nervous yourself. It seems that our bodies are capable of picking up non-verbal bodily messages from others. If the vibrations are good, then we may feel good. If they are negative, then we may feel bad.

Reich believed that we live in and interact, influence and are influenced by internal and external energy fields that contain positive and negative qualities.[3] I believe this to be true. It is quite common in the therapy situation that when there is blocked energy present, it can be felt quite strongly between several participants, even to the point of similar ailments occurring simultaneously between group members, far beyond coincidence. When the energy block is freed, the vibrations spread throughout the room and a clear, high energy charge is evident.

One woman was blocked and claimed to be acting out by urinating frequently. When the group unconsciously picked up on her blockages, everyone had to go to the bathroom at the same time. Epidemics like headaches, low energy and the "munchies" are instructive. They can indicate and signal that a painful reality is being denied and that the neurotic energy transfer is just as contagious as any infectious ailment. Perhaps this is why family members are prone to similar diseases. If they are born with a constitutional predisposition to certain ailments, then the acquisition of familial repressive defenses may fix particular bodily symptoms into the overall system.

Certain families are cancer, heart attack, ulcer or obesity prone. Many neurotic families show several different combinations of diseases such as diabetes and colitis, heart attack and stomach trouble, ulcers and psoriasis.

The unreal facade holds psychosomatic illnesses in check, but the surface armor holds back the body breakdown for just so long. Buried pain works its insidious damage on the body in subtle unfelt ways. When the armor can no longer hold back the destructive influence of unfelt hurt, then the disturbed body processes destroy vital organs and full blown disease ensues.

This is why early in Total Feeling therapy, when the false front starts to collapse, the body may begin to develop all kinds of temporary ailments. These symptoms are possible predictors of the types of diseases that brew internally and can break out at any time. Feeling that deep core pain in therapy may prevent the occurence of these diseases, by emptying out the well of hurt.

One young patient claimed that feeling his long term hurt probably saved his life. He believed that eventually he would die of lung cancer from smoking too much. Smoking had been a part of his unreal front

---

[3] W. Edward Mann, *Orgone, Reich and Eros* (N.Y.: Simon and Schuster, 1973).

and as long as he continued to postpone feeling his real self, then he was guaranteeing his eventual death.

Another woman, a young therapist, contracted diabetes at the age of 20, a few months after she had broken up with her boyfriend. She was very depressed for sometime and then the symptoms of the disease broke out. The loss of her boyfriend was symbolic of earlier unfelt pain and she had no way of releasing or reaching it. She was not aware of Total Feeling therapy at the time. Had she been able to release and integrate the early pain during that period, possibly she could have eradicated the causes of the body breakdown.

Medical authorities believe that diabetes is an inherited trait that is caused by not enough insulin or an interference with the action of insulin in the body. No one can give a very satisfactory explanation for the root causes of this ailment. The same is true for many other diseases. Unfortunately, most treatment is aimed at control and halting further deterioration. It is clear that when a doctor gets to see an ailing patient, he is really seeing the end result of the course of the patient's history. In most cases we can't expect too much at that stage. What we really need are parents who are clear enough of their own pain to allow their children to be fully themselves. Then many of today's diseases will have been prevented at their roots before destructive bodily defenses are erected. When physicians begin to treat the whole person, including the emotions, in a preventative, rather than merely a controlling fashion, then maybe we will be able to eliminate much useless suffering.

We may never be able to cure diseases that are too far advanced. Once an organ is fully destroyed there is not much that can be done. But a core feeling type of therapy can certainly be a major step in the prevention of many diseases. A real world where people are encouraged and free to feel themselves fully is the best preventative medicine.

In Total Feeling therapy somatic ailments are very important and both the staff and clients learn to observe and work with these very valuable bodily clues to the emotions. Whatever is not felt fully in the guts, will show up later in the craziness of a partial body breakdown or weird acting out behavior.

I have witnessed clients "feeling" their way through cysts, colitus, mono-nucleosis, colds, fatigue, obesity, skin rashes and breakouts, psoriasis, impotence and frigidity, backaches, headaches, spastic conditions, bloatedness, urinary problems, coordination problems, allergies, etc. There are many more that are too numerous to enumerate here.

I have mentioned the relationship between acting out behaviorally and acting in somatically. Feeling people observe the significant signals of their behavior and bodies and most would agree that practically everything we do is symbolic to some degree.

One man spent quite a considerable amount of time and energy struggling to find a place where he could work and live. Commercial properties in the city were too expensive and they lacked the room and natural atmosphere that he wanted. He feared that a farm might be too far away from his customers and might affect his business income adversely. He was torn between the two choices. During a group therapy session, he noticed a headache developing. This signalled to him that a feeling was pushing its way up to be felt.

He laid down while someone touched his head gently and he began to cry deeply. When he was little, his family had been very, very poor and lived in an upstairs tenement slum. Strangers lived underneath and alongside of him. He had to climb down three flights of stairs to go outside to play in a busy narrow city street that had no trees or fields. His father never made enough money and they could barely afford second rate food. The atmosphere had been impoverished and repressive and during this core feeling experience, he felt the pain of being poor and not getting enough to eat.

After 39 years, he realized that he was still living in the city with hardly any room to move and be free. It felt right for him to live in the country, breathe clean air, be able to cry when he wanted to and be his own man rather than always wondering what the neighbors would think.

One further example can demonstrate the effects of deep core repression on bodily functioning. During the second year of her therapy a young woman began experiencing periodic colitis attacks on a somewhat regular basis. She was no stranger to the ailment as her mother and grandmother had been victims of colitis for years. She began to trace a pattern between here and now anger which she was not fully expressing, birth trauma (Basic Perinatal Matric II)[4] , her

---

[4] Stanislav Grof, "Beyond Psychoanalysis III: Birth Trauma and Its Relation to Mental Illness, Suicide and Ecstasy", *Primal Community* (Vol. 1, No. 3, Fall 1975), pgs. 8-19.
Also, refer to chapter on gestation and birth in *Feeling People*.

menstrual period and colitus attacks. The four seemed to coincide within a few days of each other for a period of five months. Eventually, she was able to work through the intense rage that she was feeling toward her mother at the BPM II level of birth. Afterwards, the colitus disappeared. This was three years ago and she has never experienced any problems with her colon or urinary tract since.

FEELING AND CONFRONTING THE CRAZINESS

Most "normal" people are crazy and their craziness works for them by protecting them from the reality of their feelings. In place of deep emotional groundedness, there exists only ideas, fantasies, words, acting out and physical symptoms.

When a client first begins the Total Feeling Process, he is anywhere between ninety and ninety-nine per cent crazy. As his insanity is confronted by the therapy and his own feeling reality, the elements of insanity are gradually stripped away. In other words, feelings are the powerful force that rips away the vestiges of craziness. As time goes by and the cumulative effects of curative feeling take effect, insanity decreases and health begins to prevail. Eventually, the individual is more real than unreal. His day is full of challenge, growth and change. But we must not be seduced into being complacent or overconfident.

Insanity is not gone. It remains at a very deep core level protecting very painful, hard to reach feelings. As those feelings slowly emerge from their deep, submerged slumber, they tend to activate the crazy, defensive system. At this stage the acting out presents itself in an ever more resistant manner, defying all would-be good intentioned attempts to crack the last bastion of supressed feeling.

The potential pain is so threatening, that an incredible effort is needed to break this last stronghold of repression. But not all attempts to reach the buried feelings are successful. Consequently, we give all clients the option to either feel the pain or stay with the partial benefits of their insanity. Clients will either fight or run away from the potential "crunch" of their craziness. Those who successfully "work through" their deep core neurosis become free of the oppression of their own craziness. As the major issue clears up, the client is left with "little" insanities, small problems that generally reflect the normal problematic issues of life as a human being.

The following is an example of how a young woman is beginning to wrestle with the insanity of her symptoms. She will have to feel it time and time again until she has all the pieces of herself back again.

Marge: It's too much, too overwhelming. . . . I have to cloud or fog it out . . . that's my craziness. My craziness protects me from something terrible, terrifying . . . I don't want to be alone.

Ther: When were you left alone? When did you feel that you were not connected to a family or a group? Why are you so sure that nobody cares?

Marge: There are no people to belong to . . . They are away somewhere. I want to be part of a family . . . I want a family . . . They are crazy . . . They are far away from themselves . . . If they were living near by I still wouldn't want to be near them . . . They are so crazy . . . You all make me feel alone. I can't be a part of you . . . I don't have a family. I hurt . . . I hurt . . . I'm in pain . . . I need to feel included. I don't want to be alone . . . I don't want to be alone . . . (crying deeper) . . . Don't leave me by myself . . . I'm running out of hope . . . (She walks around the room crying deeply and dragging her feet). All I got from you was craziness . . . always leaving me alone (saliva dripping profusely from her mouth) You left me crazy! . . . That's all you gave me.

To feel this is painful and there is so much of it for her to feel that her craziness (fogging out and going dumb) will return again and again.

Marge: "I don't have any hope for a family . . . When I hope, I get more crazy . . . (Still pacing around room, crying more desperately and deeply) . . . I'm feeling this deeper and deeper . . . There's a chance for me not to be insane, if I cry deeper . . I still feel weak . . . I hurt all over. My body takes over and makes me sick." (Crying gets stronger with a deep rasping sound as her power starts to emerge. She indicates some lower back pain that the co-therapist manipulates into deeper feeling).

"I go out with my sister and start acting goofy and simple, I feel weird . . . It's not me . . . I get dippy . . ." (Therapist role plays a rejector of the dippiness as the client cries deeper and deeper)

"You make me weak and crazy! (Addressing her unwanted dippiness) . . . I want to be the center of attraction! . . . I want attention . . . I go dippy because I don't want to be alone . . . I can't take being out with other people . . . I don't like being hurt."

Because of her difficulties in dealing with life, this young woman possesses elements of depression, manifested by depletion of energy, weakness and feelings of impotency. These symptoms exist as a direct result of her self proclaimed, insane, defensive behavior of fogging out or going dumb to avoid feeling her deep inner alienation. It's easy to see why insanity is resistant to change. The behavior was adapted in the first place, because it helped the client to survive a difficult, if not intolerable, childhood. Her insane defense was a successful, self-protective device that proved to be difficult to eradicate as an adult. Fogging out has become an integral, highly-ingrained, habitual part of her character structure.

This particular client began to develop a very strong positive transference onto the therapist after a considerable period of resistance to commitment to her feelings. She finally broke off from an insane love relationship that had served to distract her from getting into her feelings. After the dissolution she became more involved in therapy as she had nothing left but herself and her feelings. She began to look upon the therapist as an ideal type of male with whom she could learn to relate. Many times a therapist or group member can become a prototypic example for future possible relationships.

Many neurotics possess certain images of families, friends, and lovers. In most cases these images are subconsciously fixed and pre-determine one's choice of peers and spouse. Most clients are not very aware that they have other choices beside the ones that they have been programmed to make. By getting in touch with deep feeling and the process of role modeling, one learns to re-program themselves to perhaps have more options and alternatives in making life, mate, job and friendship choices.

CONFRONTATION AND DEFINING THE SELF

When people are confronted with an insane situation, there are several responses that can be made. Usually a clear individual will wish to avoid a crazy scene, but sometimes a confrontation is unavoidable. In the Total Feeling Process, psychosis itself is not a difficult problem to deal with because the sickness is blatant and easily recognizable, at least to the observer. It is my belief that the most difficult person, according to feeling philosophy, is the schizoid individual with highly entrenched, paranoid ideation. In Transactional Analysis terms, he sees himself as O.K. and everyone else as not O.K. He defines himself this way in order to protect himself from the horrendous early pain of "not O.K." parents.[5] Since he will not feel his own craziness, he reverses everything and chooses to perceive insanity as existing outside of himself and in other people.

By the very nature of his unreality and persistent projections, he creates an imaginary cerebral environment that perpetuates his schizoid mythology about himself and other people. This wall of "I'm O.K. and you're not" is a self-sustaining feedback system that rejects all outside data that would contradict this manufactured unreal self-image. The wall is impenetrable, because of the need to keep the pain at bay and out of reach, both from self and from the intrusion of others.

Trust, of course, is the first issue that has to be worked before the walled off pain is made accessible to therapeutic interventions. This is difficult to establish because this type of individual is imprisoned in an unreal, misplaced world. We are referring here to the manufactured symbolic realm of the defensive sub-conscious. It is unreal because the feelings are correct, but the objects are displaced. In other words, the feelings are accurate representations of reactions to a different time and place and it is the people, plus the situations, that are the newly perceived targets and recipients of the old reactions. Thus, a given

---

[5] Thomas A. Harris, M.D., *I'm Okay, You're Okay* (New York: Avon Publishers, 1978).
[6] J. Andrews, "Personal Change and Intervention Style", *Journal of Humanistic Psychology*, Vol. 17, No. 3 Summer 1977, pgs. 41-63.

here and now scene is an exact symbolic replication of an earlier very crazy, painful reality.

To define something as crazy requires consensual validation of an experience by several integrated people who are subjectively and objectively reacting in similar fashion to a scene. This does not imply that there is any tyranny involved, but rather it indicates that enough social deviancy is present to render some sort of applied corrective measures. No organized group can function well and proceed towards common goals if one of the cogs in the wheel is behaving eractically and disturbing the smooth flow of the other cogs.

If a deviant defines his craziness as sanity, he will run head on into the reality testing of more feeling people. An integrated individual will show relative degrees of clarity and sufficient coping mechanisms in various areas of psychological functioning. A person who defines himself as sane while exhibiting consistent and chronic disturbances in thought, action, affect and somatization will be adjudged by a feeling community to be insane. And this does not imply psychosis as defined in the traditional psychiatric sense. Insanity, in a total feeling context, is anything that is not consistent with a purely connected and integrated grounding in reality.

As I indicated before, a group is like a wheel made up of cogs and if a cog breaks down, the whole wheel becomes weakened and possibly even breaks. Fortunately, a Total Feeling group can recognize craziness where it exists because the members have experienced much of their own insanity and can perceive the insanity of others quite easily. However, what may be crazy for one person may be sanity for another. It all depends at what end of the spectrum of feeling that repression exists. For example, if one person acts out too much aggression, he may be fighting the opposite tendency in himself to be weak and helpless. If another individual never gets angry, we may assume that he masks his anger behind a wall of passivity.

To define oneself it may become necessary to submit one's concern about his sanity to the scrutiny and feedback of others who can communicate reasonably well. This creation of a feedback loop between an individual and trusted, concerned others may be one of the best systems of consensual validation of reality. For example, if I see myself as having a problem in expressing anger, my self-image will be effected by this perception. Suppose I take this self perception to the group and submit myself to their scrutiny and feedback. They can help me to facilitate a feeling change in myself that may bring about a better synthesis of my self-image. Perhaps, I will begin to see myself differently because of whatever potential breakthrough that takes place.

This example can be carried further as we investigate the symptoms and specific areas of disturbance. First, there is the sphere of thought and cognition. Suppose I am angry at someone who has supposedly attacked me. I could fantasize punching him in the mouth. If he continues to antagonize me. I might act on this angry impulse and perhaps assault him with a light slap, thus, warning him not to continue with his disturbing tactics. My thoughts have now extended to the action sphere. Since I also displayed and acted on the feeling of anger I am also in the affective sphere. If I later lose sleep over this incident, I will be showing a disturbance in somatization. This conflict that permeates these four spheres can eventually result in a disturbance of self-image.

Professional norms of certain organizations imply that their constituents should never act out any forms of violence or sexuality on their clients. Thus, the self-image of a therapist must operate within these limitations. However, what if the professional self-image conflicts with one's personal inclinations and reactions? The answer is simple. There will be some form of disturbance or disordering.

It may be that different degrees of violence and sexuality actually take place in various forms of therapy. Martin Shepard[6] does a creditable analysis of sexual intimacy that exists between certain psychotherapists and their patients. But no one, to my knowledge, has written anything about the use of violence in treatment settings. We have known for a long time that Freud's own neurosis caused him to set up his own self-protective taboos in the science of psychoanalysis. These taboos have infiltrated the entire field of psychotherapy and only the most daring and rebellious of therapists have risked a great deal to extend the boundaries of treatment procedures.

The Total Feeling Process is no exception to this problem in the field. We must define ourselves and our process in accordance with established procedure and theory and then risk breaking existing taboos, if we wish to penetrate into newer realms of possible cure. Thus, we must continually redefine ourselves with each new situation.

When someone defines himself within the confines of a highly

---

[6] Martin Shepard, *The Love Treatment* (New York: Paperback Library, 1972).

fortified defense system, we must remember that as an infant he was very vulnerable to seemingly brutal, bestial psychological acts. His misplaced projections and rigidness are unfelt statements that he will not allow those acts to be perpetrated upon him again. The craziness of this situation is that other people, perhaps quite innocent, are made to feel the brunt of the defended person's attacks. If he insists that his projections and attacks are accurate, then there only exists the insanity of the people in that situation who cannot connect with one another. Perhaps insanity itself may be simply defined as one person's inability to connect to anything or anyone real. A neurotic person is alone and can only relate to the phantom, disguised figures of his fantasy life. If his fantasy life becomes too bizarre, he enters the realms of total alienating psychosis.

John Andrews[8] states:

Our self-image is the touchstone of personal orientation, and from the concept of self each person generates a network of expectations, behaviors, perceptions of others, and interpretations of events which are consistent with it. By doing so we form a personal environment which, through its feedback, confirms us in a given identity and sense of continuity. In Norbert Weiner's (1950) words, 'We are not stuff that abides, but patterns that perpetuate themselves.' By selectively setting aside actions and experiences incongruent with the self, we establish a negative feedback loop that keeps change at a manageable level.

I would urge the reader to study this quotation intently and perhaps underline it for future reference. There may be many situations in your life where you will find this material to be personally applicable. Let me give you two examples from my own background.

During my tenure as a teacher of therapy and a therapist at a state mental hospital, I found many of the patients to be quite resistent to therapy and any attempts to move them out of the hospital and back into the community. It seemed as if being in a mental hospital helped to sustain them in an identity that was perfectly acceptable and even provided enough supportive feedback from the

---

[8] John Andrews, "Personal Change and Intervention Style", *Journal of Humanistic Psychology*, Vol. 17, No. 3, Summer 1977, pg. 41.

patient environment to keep them entrenched in a backward style of life. Why should they leave when all their needs are being met: three square meals a day, a place to sleep, a roof over their heads, clothes and the security of knowing that their future will be assured as long as they maintain and display an appropriate amount of insanity. Thus, craziness has its tangible rewards as long as the patient suppresses his appetite for change, growth and novelty.

Most healthy people will welcome and perhaps even seek out new, exciting and challenging situations so that they can be in a manageable state of getting to know themselves and redefining who they are and who they will become. A sick person may say that he really wishes to change and grow but his fear may be so great that he can hardly cope with the necessary intensity of the change process. The psychotic has practically lost all his drive for the novel and sometimes painful stimuli of a transforming experience. A neurotic can only tolerate small and slow changes because some change may involve negative feedback and the subsequent pain that overloads an already overloaded system.

As a result, the growth rate of severe neurotics appears to be much slower than the less disturbed because the latter has less to overcome. Their progress is usually more dramatic, thus enhancing their egos and supporting them in the idea that therapy is wonderful and useful after all. But the more serious the illness the more trying it is to those who would care enough to invest the required energy in rehabilitating the sick personality. Let us never forget that along the road toward transformation there is always the constant threat that sickness will break out again and again in its myriad forms. So with the very disturbed, it is necessary to guard against unrealistic hope and content ourselves with the knowledge that progress is slow and prognosis is poor to fair. If the client goes beyond fair to a good outcome, we can be pleased with such a pleasant result.

Many severe neurotics and, of course, psychotics can only stand a certain amount of therapy, especially such an intense therapy as the Total Feeling Process. The ability to integrate an experience into the self depends on the degree of pain overload. Very severely disordered individuals need intensive therapy, but it must be spread out and induced in manageable qualities. That is why the Total Feeling Process has a basic structure which can be modified to fit the client's capability for managing and integrating the incoming data feedback. If the data is too much to handle, he will defend himself with his usual craziness because he does not have the necessary feeling capacity to take in the full impact of the therapy.

For those who find their self-image being ultimately nurtured and in consonance with the Total Feeling Community, there is a flowering, confirmation and expansion of the self within the personal, psychological and social environment of the Feeling Community. Those who can sustain themselves with the Feeling Community, grow according to their own manageable paces.

Most people define and let themselves be controlled by the programming of the family. The values, belief systems and the way one is supposed to live his life is greatly influenced by the images of one's early childhood. Many times these early images compel one to live within a certain narrow framework. He barely dreams that there might possibly be another more existentially rewarding way to exist. He adopts the patterns of thinking and relating of his parents and when he finds that others cannot conform to be his mommy and daddy, he goes into emotional shock.

One female, like many women, was told by her mother that, *"you're nothing, unless you have a man."* Here, the mother was defining who the growing child would be. Heavy clinging need and dependency was drilled in before the child could test the mother's distorted view of reality. Statements like this can almost be considered a form of cruel child abuse, even though it was not the mother's intention to be brutal and to inadvertently set the daughter up to be hurt time and time again.

An intricate and complicated dynamic gets played out in this example. The girl grows into young womanhood searching for the perfect man to ensnare, in order to fulfill her mother's expectations and prophecies. Since she is seeking the god-like father, she must fall in love with a man that she can never fully have. She puts him on a pedestal so that she can worship him from afar and hopes desperately that someday he will really love her the same way and with the same intensity that she loves him. But, of course, this will be the proverbial, unequal, unreciprocated love relationship that has a built-in disaster. She cannot have a man who is a something, while she is a nothing. It becomes vitally important that she pursue herself with the same fervor that she pursues her hero, because he cannot love her if there is no self to love. Through deep feeling she can have all of herself and ultimately be capable of having a relationship with a man who has all of himself. They can meet and relate as full equals. No one can live their life through and for someone else. They can only live for themselves and learn to define themselves for who they are.

This young woman used her mother's illusions to sustain her unreal goals. As soon as her delusions of Prince Charming and the vine-covered cottage were shattered, all that she had left were herself and her feelings. At this "crunching point," she began to grow up from being just a little baby with her teddy bears to being a woman who wanted more of herself for herself.

When a person lets an unreal, programmed illusion be shattered, he is faced with an on-rush of sudden and strong feeling. This feeling has many components and each component needs to be felt and integrated. Sometimes it may take a few weeks for such a feeling to be fully experienced and synthesized. This can be a very painful period for some people since they cannot feel it all at once, but only in bits and pieces. When the entire issue is finally felt and connected, the individual may feel very good and resolved and go on and live differently without the built-in disastrous hurt of the illusion. When all that pain comes bursting forth, the client may need support from very caring people and this will help to sustain him while he is going through this trying, but necessary time.

Chapter 13   Group Roles, Norms and Deviancy

GROUP FUNCTIONAL ROLES AND NORMS

Every individual is born into a series of groups: the immediate and extended family; age and sex group peers; community, financial and clan groupings; political, religious, educational, ethnic and racial groupings; plus, many more that are too numerous to mention here. It is within the framework of a particular set of groups that an emerging individual grows and finds out who he is. Hence, it is only reasonable to assume that if groups help to form and influence a personality, then it is within a group setting that a person can correct the debilitating effects of previous painful group affiliations.

I have already indicated that a group can be a powerful force in bringing about positive, growthful changes in an individual through the facilitation of deep core feeling and integration. An entire book could be written on the unique dynamics of Total Feeling groups. It is my intention here, however, to pinpoint only a few facets of this dynamic phenomena.

It has been incredibly exciting for me to take part in feeling groups for well over a decade and find that they grow and become more dynamic as the years go by. There is no such thing as a bad group. Some are more exciting than others, and no two groups are exactly alike but there is always something to be gleaned from every group interaction. I have found that we have had to stretch the boundaries of our imagination in order to allow for a wider creative capacity for the expression of feelings. Ten years ago I thought that groups were exciting. I never dreamed then that the sky was the limit.

Groups today are many times more powerful than they were years ago. In fact, for some people, they may be even too powerful. Not all individuals desire to experience the intensity and interaction of Total Feeling groups.

Our ideas about therapy have changed drastically as well. We used to believe that there was something called therapy that existed within a given period of time. All that a person had to do was a year or two of therapy and that was it. Now we realize that growing and feeling is a life time process.

Evolution has provided us with a series of built-in problems that each one of us must come to terms with, feel, integrate and then move on. Every person faces periods of critical transition and passageway in their lives. These include the pains, ecstasies and agonies of gestation, birth, adolescence, young adulthood, the mid-life crises, emergence into old age and the inevitability of death. If each one of these transitory phases is not negotiated in a full feeling sense, then what will remain will be the vestigial leftovers of previous unfinished life cycles.

We see clients seeking therapy at some point along these critical cycles, hoping to find some feeling resolution for their problems. These phases are an accepted part of being human and the therapy group is one of the most powerful tools for helping someone deal with these life cycle situations. It offers an opportunity for the individual to go back over his particular life phase crisis in order to rework the problems that were involved. If the pain is not resolved at each one of these points, it will show up later at a different life phase.

A person of twenty may be working on similar issues to that of a 50 year old, but each phase has its own distinct characteristics. And these characteristics emerge in the group process. For example, Jane at the age of 45, upon re-examining her entire life, felt that she no longer had anything to live for. Death would be a welcome relief. After going through an intense emotional working through, Jane is now living a happy fulfilled life and is eagerly looking forward to establishing herself in a new profession with an appropriate love relationship as part of her second maturity.

Don, at 26 years of age, is searching around for some kind of profession or occupation that will fit his emerging identity. At the same time he is experimenting within the realms of his own pair bonding instincts.

Brenda has reached the 30 year turning point and is dealing with the pain of coming out of an unproductive marriage and her role as a mother.

Fred has just turned 39 and realizes that he is no longer invincible and omnipotent. His first critical physical ailment has triggered the recognition that inevitable death is beginning to make itself known. While Mike, on the other hand, is 15 years of age, feels omnipotent, acts irresponsibly at times and is dealing with his first clumsy approaches towards females. He, like Don, is also faced with the difficult decisions of his future occupational and educational choices.

How does the group come into play with all these diverse age cycles and crises? The human primate learned over 100,000 years ago that his only chance for survival was to develop the biological and social means for operating within a group context. We must never forget that the basic drives and instincts that were displayed by our early primate ancestors are still with us and still exert incredible influence over our lives, notwithstanding that man had to create civilization in order to master this planet. The imperfections that have developed out of our adjustments and compromises with evolution have demanded that we find some way to fit in and work well with a highly productive group structure. Whether we wish to call this group a hunting party, tribe, clan, therapy group or nation makes no difference. The goal is the same as our ancestors . . . to find a better and more productive way to survive and flourish.

It was a tribal group that made it possible for our ape-like ancestors to learn how to hunt more effectively, copulate more efficiently, protect their young and sustain each other in a harsh environment. Today, we are still hunting in the woods for our means to survive. We are still seeking appropriate groups and tribes to affiliate with in order to sustain and guarantee our survival. We are still seeking to copulate, create, generate and maintain small familial groups. And all the feelings that are associated with this phenomena are still residing and bubbling below the surface, waiting to explode so that we can understand and sustain our existence.

It is within groups that feelings connected to intellect serve as the primary means of communicating with our fellow human beings. Without feelings, communication and group process, we would have ceased to exist a million years ago.

Evolution has provided us with the emotional means to bond with other human beings and without that bonding we would not have continued to exist. It was this bonding that brought the hunter home to the cave to feed his mate and his children. It was love and affection that motivated him to go out and conquer his universe in order to create a better life for his loved ones. It is this same evolutionary feeling, this bonding factor, that ties us all together to this day.

It is a shame that civilization has created a dampening effect to recognizing our emotional ties to one another. Evolution has not acted maliciously, but judiciously, however, in demanding that we emotionally bond deeply to only a few human beings while bonding less to others. Our energy input can only be stretched so far in developing and maintaining bonds of affection, kinship, ownership and family. With the explosion of human population, man has been forced to deal with competition and aggression in his immediate familial and occupational territory. It is within a therapeutic group context that we try to work through and resolve these deeply buried instincts. The therapy group can allow our strongest Id impulses to surface, be accepted and worked through. After all, our Id impulse is that realm of feeling that we have inherited from our primate ancestors. It has gotten us this far. To ignore it or try to squelch it is like turning our backs on our strongest motivating drives for survival and development.

Thus, the group as a whole, can facilitate enormous growth, creativity and production. However, the group is no stronger than its weakest link: which leads us to a closer look at the interdynamics and functional roles within the group structure. People in industry, business, politics and most important of all, the family, cannot function well or survive effectively unless they fully understand and appreciate the absolute importance of cooperation, division of labor and the allegation of functional roles. The National Training Laboratories[1] states:

"Cooperation demands maturity in the individual, understanding of the problems of human interaction, and competence in resolving these problems. Such qualities are not acquired automatically or by fiat."

While encouraging individuals to become Feeling People, we find it necessary for them to develop specific roles that nurture and support feeling contact and relationships in whatever subsequent group settings they may find themselves. We have already examined some of the dynamics of these various roles including good and bad mommy and daddy, good and bad siblings, peers, and extended relatives. We will now take a look at the subtle roles that emerge in group interaction, that have been closely researched in the absorbing and complex field of group dynamics.

No group can exist unless its members can be totally involved with one another and the process of the group itself. Therefore, the

---

[1] Leland P. Bradford, "Introduction", *Group Development, Selected Reading Series One* (Washington, D.C.: National Training Laboratories *National Education Association, 1961), pg. 1.

key to group success depends on the amount and kind of interaction that operates between the individuals. Because a group contains the qualities and dynamics of unique personalities, each person is able to explore himself in a deep and feeling way. Group members are also encouraged to become involved with, interact and observe others and the group as a whole. Since one of the goals of the Total Feeling Process is to help individuals relate in a more feeling, grounded way, we find that it is necessary not only to provide for the expression and connection of one's deeper feelings, but also to create an optimum environment for training in group dynamics and interpersonal processes, both for trainees and patients alike.

In order to facilitate this, we have borrowed heavily from the group encounter model which recognizes the importance of therapeutic confrontation and intervention, as well as the educational model which relies heavily on educational resources, dissemination of information and audio-visual aids. Thus, the Total Feeling Process strives to provide a comprehensive and complete therapy.

My own particular early training was extensive in group methods of education and treatment and I learned, first hand, the potential power for growth and health in group process methods. The combination of Group Development methodology, theory, and practice with Total Feeling integration has led me to the conclusion that a Feeling group with feeling dynamics is *Medicine* for what ails and hurts all of us.

Much of the scientific study of group behavior focuses on individual psycho-dynamics and leadership issues. In this section I should like to generally examine roles and their curative aspects for everyday living.

In order for people to relate productively to one another, they must first become aware of counter-productive roles and defenses and the underlying feelings that drive them. As roles that are alienating become stripped away, new behaviors can be uncovered and developed that are driven by libido and creative life urges. Since leadership functions naturally arise out of intensive feeling work on oneself, sooner or later it becomes necessary for members to practice and develop leadership skills. Because there is no sharp distinction in the Total Feeling Process between leader and member roles, it is the therapist's job to help the patient maximize his full unique potential and develop new and usually more appropriate feeling roles.

One of the assumptions in the Total Feeling Process is that the quality and amount of group interaction is the responsibility of the entire group. All members need to set goals for change and growth and develop and marshal their resources for achieving these goals. To facilitate this process members need to assume responsibility for their own feelings and lives as well as the feelings of their fellow group members. The individual is ultimately responsible for what he wants to do with his life but the group members assume the responsibility for encouraging and reinforcing feeling goals with each other.

As I have stated many times before, there is no compromise or substitute for a Total Feeling life. One does not "do" therapy for a given period of time and then go out and expect to live a feeling existence in an unfeeling world. People who have arrived at the advanced stages of feeling integration refuse to be intimately involved with anyone who is not totally committed to a clear, fully grounded feeling life. The novice or beginner at full feelings is still not living and feeling for himself. He often pursues feelings to please others while hoping desperately that if he feels enough, he will be "good" enough to capture a symbolic displaced love object. In many cases, he is not in a feeling therapy primarily to recapture his lost self.

The Total Feeling unrepressed person primarily wants himself. Secondarily, he will welcome and develop appropriate love relationships and, in some cases, ultimately, a feeling close family. He knows that if an individual stays locked into an unfeeling relationship, life style, or profession, that he is blocking and there is still much to be felt. Someone who has felt and resolved much of his core feelings will not waiver or give an inch to something that is unreal or symbolic. As a result, Feeling people do not want much contact with someone who is defending, blocking, acting out or non-feeling. If an individual in the group does not commit his entire soul to being and feeling himself, then core feeling people merely tolerate him and stay at a safe distance in order to avoid struggling with his sickness.

Anyone who is compulsively locked into programmed, symbolic, performative roles will resist or fight the feelings that will lead to roles that can be carried out in growth oriented, productive environments. One member states:

"My girlfriend only wants me to be her husband and the father of her kids. She's got this whole dream or scheme from childhood about the way life is supposed to be. She's out to 'capture' me, because she thinks that I am her only source of security. She wants me to be the daddy she never had while I just want to be me, not part of someone else's master plan.

I won't get that heavily involved with her, until she wants herself more than she wants me. I hate to have somebody so emotionally dependent. God, her clinging would drag me down, because I could never satisfy all that need.

My life *is* feelings and I am alive and growing here at the Center. This place is fantastic! . . . I learn so much here—I just don't want to be lost in some roles laid out by someone else that would deny and stifle me."

The girlfriend goes on to tell her side of the story and reveals how early role programming can effect a love relationship.

"The only relationship I have ever really known was the one between my mom and dad . . . My mother used to tell me to look for a man that was strong but I always knew somewhere that the woman had to have some kind of control in order to keep her man . . .

There was something missing in my mom and dad's marriage. I felt like both of them were hiding feelings from each other. Recently, I've wanted more feeling contact with my man and with my other friends . . .

My daddy would always tell me 'he'd do it,' meaning if I needed anything hung, fixed, whatever, he'd take care of it. When he would do something for me, it would be like he was showing me he cared for me through the things he did. If ever I needed anything done, Dad would do it . . ."

"One thing my mother would always tell me was to pick a husband that could support us (us meaning me and my children), a hard worker that would take care of us."

The seeds of conditioning are set early and parental ideas, values and beliefs influence and control one's actions. In this case, the parents were defining by word and deed what the roles of a man and woman should be. A problem arises when the old programming cannot be fulfilled according to the ideas of the parents and society. Present day reality challenges those old assumptions and change becomes mandatory. As each of the parties connects to the sources of their blind spots and parental conditioning, they will be free to relate to each other without the obstacles to real intimacy.

CONFRONTATION IN THERAPY

Most of the time a non-directive approach or laissez-faire style is used in private sessions and groups. If someone desires assistance in getting to, sustaining or deepening a feeling, he will convey the message to someone and they will help him to further his efforts. If an individual is asking for too much assistance, we know that he is symbolically acting out his dependency and needs to be pushed or reinforced to go into and develop his own feeling depth. The opposite can be just as true. If someone never asks for assistance, then he is surely acting off of pseudo-independence or a defensive counter-personal distancing mechanism towards other people. We all need assistance from time to time when going into some painful areas.

In order to release someone from defending a stereotypic, historical role and point the way to a feeling resolution, it is sometimes necessary to confront that individual in a private or group context. Confrontation is often an absolute necessity because it lays the bare truth out in the open for the person to feel its consequences. But confrontation should be used discreetly and at the proper time. This occurs when the individual is at the critical crossroads of real versus unreal existence.

To confront someone who is acting out and trying to satisfy symbolic needs requires certain skills and the ability to be real with that person. It is much easier to silently reject, withdraw or ignore the issues; but this is just another way of denying and refusing to deal with reality. One thing we must remember is that buried feelings are held onto with great effort and energy. As long as they remain repressed, however, they will continue to control that individual's life. Repression leads to alienation from self and others and practically guarantees that one's real needs will not be met.

Many individuals are afraid to confront one another, but when they finally do, the group becomes a powerful instrument for feeling change. A true confrontation is an explicit, powerful statement of reality to the person being confronted. This is especially true when it doesn't contain any historical material from the person doing the confronting. In other words, the confrontee doesn't have to defensively deal with the confronter's unfinished business from the past. He can deal exclusively with his own feelings without outside distractions and burdens.

Sometimes I have to confront someone's insanity quite hard but it is usually done at the same time that I am conveying my underlying caring for the real loving person locked inside. When my words reach their pain, they can't help but open up and let it all come pouring out. When it is all over, they are usually quite grateful, because I never intend any malice and I show pure caring for what is inside of them.

For example, during one particular group, a young female came over to the trainee sitting next to me and started spewing out her insanity. I had heard it coming from her a hundred times before and this time I reached my limit. I found myself confronting her quite angrily while she continued to defend, head trip and avoid her feelings. Finally, I started yelling:

"You're full of shit . . . You're not being honest with yourself! It's always something outside of you—your job, your boyfriends . . . You're always blaming them for your misfortune . . . You could change your job tomorrow, but you'd still be a miserable human being . . . It's not your job or your boyfriend . . . It's you!!!"

Occasionally, a confrontation fails to reach the deep realms of a highly defended person. The deep core feelings are kept at an inaccessible place, both to the confronter and the confrontee. This causes problems between group members because the relationship cannot go any deeper, due to those bottom line defenses. The behavior is saying "don't go any further or try to get deeper inside of me, because I will resist. Stay away or I will stay away." The feelings that are being defended are usually locked away in the deepest parts of the body and may represent very early annihilation and helplessness.

In a one-to-one encounter, the parties sometimes slip behind in their feelings. One person may be stuck and blocked with a feeling and may appear as if he is not all "there." He may look and act strange, be preoccupied or generally show deficiencies in relating to himself, other people and intimate partners. If this continues, it will have an effect on close ones and they, in turn, will exhibit random signs of not knowing what to do with the "absent," blocked participant. Many times the "missing" person will fall down on his interpersonal responsibilities and be incapable of communicating clearly or responding in an open, warm, giving manner.

It is at this point that it becomes common for other involved people to "trip off" of the central figure and perhaps become disturbed themselves. They may engage in destructive, escapist fantasies in order to protect themselves and perhaps, they will even feel guilty and secretive about having such fantasies. It then becomes necessary to set up a full scale feeling encounter so that the parties can clean out their accumulated feelings and get the relationship rolling again on the right track. Most of the time, when the blocked individual is confronted by the other person in a strong, firm manner, it is enough of an impetus to release him from the pains of his repression. The confronter, however, must be absolutely honest and care enough to help the other person plunge through his impasse.

Sometimes in group, the facilitator may test what unseen forces or hidden agenda are operating. An exercise or an intervention will be devised in order for the group to test its problem solving capabilities and move on to more mature stages of development. For example, if certain members are displaying rigid, autistic or stereotypically defensive behavior, then we know that they are not getting to certain feelings. We may use a modified technique called the "drop slip."* Each participant will be asked to write the name of one or two members whom they would like to confront. Some members put their own names down, because they feel a need to be confronted on certain issues. The slips are then mixed up and selected randomly

---

*I first saw this technique used in 1968 at Gaudenzia House, a drug rehabilitation center in Philadelphia. It has also been used by other such centers around the country.

and the person or persons who appear most often are then asked to take part in an open feeling encounter.

The results have always been positive and if conducted properly, the participants seem to be able to get to deeper, more relevant issues than that which can be achieved by more conventional methods. It also places responsibility on Community members to be more active and involved with their feelings and perceptions as well as relieving the therapists from being the primary source for facilitation of feeling and change. Since the trainers are also on call for being confronted, it gives them the opportunity to get to their own issues, thus providing a vehicle for further staff growth.

Many group exercises can facilitate group interaction and feelings by uncovering the dynamics that operate between individuals in a group setting. By exposing Community members to peer therapeutic feedback, a powerful tool for feeling integration is unleashed. A case in point involved a situation where the staff had been observing a great deal of "fringe" behavior. There always seemed to be some members of the group who were never fully involved. Because this was a part of their pathology, their sickness, the staff set up a group exercise to confront them in a non-threatening way.

Each person was asked to designate where he or she saw every other member, as well as themselves, in terms of group involvement: the "in" group, the "middle of the road" group, or the "fringe" group. At the end of the exercise, the members shared their perceptions and feedback with each other and then, physically moved into each of the three sub groups that was unanimously agreed upon by all the participants. The perceptions and feelings flowed quite easily amongst the people of the "in" group. Contact was non-threatening and involved. The "middle of the road" group also looked like they were working fairly well with each other—a number of them falling into heavy pain. The "fringe" group was having the most problems. It seemed as if the members of that group didn't wish to be there . . . They were having a tough time relating to one another, making contact and forming a cohesive unit. There was much anger, hostility and extremes of pathology in that group.

By confronting each other in such a way, the group was able to influence the behavior and feelings of their members in a very dynamic way. If one person tells you you're a horse, you can ignore it. If two people tell you you're a horse, you can still side step the issue. But if a whole group tells you you're a horse, you'd better start looking for a saddle! Hitting the floor and feeling the reality of such feedback can be a very powerful way to bring about change and growth.

One of the myths that gets perpetuated by those who have not been deeply involved in human relations type training is that pressure and intimidation is used to bring about change. I would agree that pressure is sometimes used, and there are some factors to be taken into consideration. First, there is a difference between feeling intimidated and being intimidated. Those who carry large overloads of fear are easily intimidated by seemingly innocuous situations. They feel threatened by fairly innocent stimuli, while others welcome a strong give and take confrontation. The second factor, which is very important, is that confronters need to tune in and really hear where the confrontee is at and judge when the time is right to make the confrontation. It must be remembered that our main goal is to facilitate and release feeling that can transform the way a person relates to life. There is a difference between a confrontation and a dumping session. Third, the confrontee needs to explain what feels right and works well with him, so that the confronter does not project onto him. Sometimes a person thinks that if something works well with himself, it will necessarily work well with others. This is not always the case and it is vital to remember that every human being is unique and must be approached specifically with general principles used judiciously.

Not all group encounters are concerned with defenses or pain. Some deal instead with physical stimulation. Throughout the animal kingdom, nurturance is supplied by various forms of touching, caressing, licking and petting. All infants come to know the human world around them by the tactile information received through the skin. This warm, human contact can be facilitated and consummated by all forms and degrees of physical touching. Because full body contact is a necessity for the adult as well as the infant, both grownups and babies need to feel the warmth and stimulation provided by other feeling human beings. Unfortunately, humans are easily distracted from this basic need and often become neurotic and withdrawn as a result of this physical deprivation.

We have seen many patients as stern, hard workers who never take time out to play physically with each other and their off-spring. When mommy and daddy play with each other, the children are the first to recognize a good, natural thing and they want to participate. My wife and I spend a lot of time playing physically with one another and fulfilling the need to make contact through touch. We explore, caress, stroke and massage our own bodies plus our sons' and this has helped to form a strong unbreakable bond of affection between us. Our oldest boy is quite grown up now and we still hug, kiss and play freely and there is much joy, laughter and spontaneity in our relationship.

An infant learns to "touch" the world, his universe, through the physical and emotional "touching" of his parents—his mother, in particular. Mommy and daddy are his universe for many months. When a child is deprived of this early nurturance, contact development is disrupted on the physical, emotional and spiritual levels. Many times this disruption can never be fully resolved and eradicated. The child will grow into an adult incapable of making full, strong contact with anyone or anything. The result can be an individual who marginally exists, lives on the fringe, makes either no contact at all or superficial contact with many in a desperate attempt to recapture the lost moments of physical and emotional deprivation that he endured as a child. When confronted with this reality in a group setting, either by a verbal encounter or a physical touch, the adult may break into intense feelings of deprivation. Upon integrating the deepest realms of this core pain, feeling and communication is usually restored and the individual is able to make flowing, open contact with those around him.

SELF CONFRONTATION

As one becomes more feeling conscious, he refuses to be exploited as much as when he was weak and helpless and subjected to the control and power of those who were not fully invested in his welfare. He takes more interest in confronting his own health and life. Issues surrounding diet, exercise, feeling time and real, rather than symbolic, priorities become the major concern of the individual rather than needing to elicit group pressure for change. As he becomes healthier, he may find that he won't buy things that are overpriced and that he cannot afford. He won't go over his head in debt, because he refuses to hurt himself by buying symbolic things that he doesn't really need and, ultimately, satisfy no one.

As one member put it:

"Much of the system is full of lies and pretenses. Inflation is running away, with people struggling and exploiting each other. My mother never raised me that way. She was full of integrity and honesty. She was never rich, but she earned my respect, because she never ripped anyone off."

As one learns to confront his own honesty and integrity, he learns to buy and sell with his feelings. Because a feeling human being demands that people keep their word and deliver what they have promised, he will do likewise. He never promises anything that he can't deliver and he expects the same in return. A total feeling person is a lover of justice and equality and will not involve himself in any enterprise that compromises his ethics and self-respect.

For some people there is difficulty in confronting the therapy itself. We have mentioned before that the program is not easy and it can be quite intense and demanding. Therefore, it is not for everyone. Sooner or later, those who have strong resistances to going deeply into themselves have to confront whether they should really be in this type of growth experience. This is especially true if someone insists on acting out destructively or irresponsibly onto other members. Highly entrenched symbolic behavior tests the tolerance of the more feeling members and, sooner or later, they may become quite frustrated in trying to get someone to give up unwanted or downright vicious actions.

Many patients have developed the most incredibly counterproductive, interpersonal defenses and if someone remains too incorrigible, we may ask them to take a vacation or a leave of absence to think things over. After a period of time if they are sincere in their determination to transform themselves and change the debilitating behavior, then they are reinstated, perhaps with a different structure of therapy.

Some people are just not internally strong enough to keep confronting and testing reality. A very powerful feeling may be on the rise and the person feels compelled to defend against it with antisocial, uncooperative, destructive behavior. One of the most difficult defenses to deal with is the flight from body feelings to unreal ideation. Many individuals who fear losing control and approaching their insanity create logical thought systems that, upon close examination, reveal extreme, unfelt, hidden fear. I have already discussed in an earlier chapter[2] this idea in everyone's ideation that consists of certain systems of cognition. These particular systems are acquired for defensive reasons and represent displaced projections onto symbolic objects and situations. This fear will cause people to either fight or flight.

Animals respond to perceived danger with either one of these self-protected devices, but human beings create complex rational belief systems to justify their actions. In most cases, the feeling and its true roots are inside the individual but in order to escape from the pain it is much safer to project it outside of oneself in order to minimize the threat and push reality further away. The entrenched unreal belief system is a real threat to a successful therapy because it appears unpredictably and is usually unamenable to negotiation. Prognosis is typically poor to fair and feelings are not the final arbitrator of reality.

GROUP NORMS

Implicit in the Total Feeling Process is a system of norms and unconscious expectations. First, there are the group norms which are both specific and general and shared by all group members who have integrated themselves into a feeling life. Second, there are individual expectations that each member holds for any kind of interaction and involvement with any other member. These expectations can be quite appropriate or simply extensions of one's deep early pain. In all instances they reflect either a relative degree of sensitivity or insensitivity.

The composition of a Total Feeling group depends on several variables. Any new member must go through an initiation/inclusion phase and this is usually fraught with some degree of anxiety and excitement. A total feeling therapy must inherently involve a degree of personal risk to all involved—the therapists, the program itself, and all group members—and sometimes this risk transcends or at least stretches the boundaries of typical and traditional therapeutic limits and norms. It must do this without a real threat

---

[2] See Chapter 7 on Paranoia.

of ultimate danger to those involved. To this extent, screening procedures must take into consideration how relatively constructive or destructive a potential patient may be. The question arises as to the degree of the patient's neurotic deviancies that are potentially damaging to the group process.

A case in point: a borderline paranoid psychotic may appear to be quite calm, placid and controlled on the surface, with all realms of affect deadened to any kind of expression. But since this is an expressive, emotive type of therapy, to scratch that placid exterior may unleash a torrent of violent, irresponsible, damaging rage. Those individuals who do not indicate enough ego strength to keep their violence within accepted, integrated forms of expression cannot be allowed to participate in group interaction. Such persons have such pent-up rage that they cannot discriminate between "here and now" authority and those insane love objects from childhood. Body and property rights must be protected at all times in an intense group interactional setting. This is not to say that a violent patient cannot be treated. However, his deviancy is such that for the time being, he is unfit to be with other individuals because he cannot guarantee their safety from his violent physical provocations. A classic double bind hypothesis holds true in this case. He will be rejected because of his irresponsible violence, yet he cannot get well unless he learns to express his violence in ways that are not dangerous to other human beings.

This situation is further complicated by the fact that many of these individuals are so highly defended that their capacity to feel is almost or completely blunted. Many highly repressed individuals want to feel with a great passion but they are driven to provoking other people to come down on them in a horrendous fashion just to facilitate some opening of those buried, locked-in emotions. Quite often, group members and therapists alike, resent having to be put into the position of a bulldozing blitzkrieg in order to extricate a tiny amount of feeling from a highly blocked individual. Translated another way, group members like and respect someone who has some potential to feel and takes full responsibility for opening himself up with the non-provoked aid of the therapeutic community. Thus, the manipulation of others to get to one's own buried emotions is frowned upon as a form of group and therapeutic deviancy. Someone who really needs help can ask for it in a very straight way without manipulating others into being horrendous pain-inflicting objects.

We are aware that all screening procedures are limited and only helpful to some extent. Typical diagnostic procedures do not suffice to provide enough information to predict group behavior. The staff and the group must have an opportunity to observe an individual's interpersonal behavior in order to make some kind of judgement as to his readiness for participation in a full feeling therapy. Therefore, the prospective patient must demonstrate that he possesses some capacity to feel and an ability to relate interpersonally, at least at a minimum level of success. He must also demonstrate that he is potentially a constructive rather than a destructive member of the community. Will he contribute or detract? Will he build or destroy? A careful assessment is made as to the amount of emotional impoverishment that a prospective client has been subjected to. If his early childhood went beyond the bounds of deprivation and entered the realms of extreme emotional and physical brutality and cruelty, then the chances are great that he may act out very strong retaliatory, revenge impulses onto the group or its leaders.

Likewise, those who have a history of extreme character disordering may present a therapeutic community with a type of pathology that can only be disruptive to its therapeutic flow and growth. If such an individual has insight into this behavior and shows a desire to rid himself of these displacements, then the therapy can help him. However, it can be very difficult to alleviate a person's destructive impulses when those same impulses provide a form of secondary defensive gratification and are so highly developed that they protect him from an excruciating, deep hidden pain.

Unfortunately, we have found that there are certain kinds of "rip off" mentalities that transcend cultural lines. These can even be manifested stylistically according to ethnic survival needs in certain sociological, cultural and economic settings. It is not my purpose to delve into the intricacies of ethnic characterological social forces but I will hint at them slightly, at the risk of opening up Pandora's box.

The "rip off" mentality can and does express itself in unique and culturally ethnic ways. I will state at the onset that these behavior characteristics were developed originally as unique social institutions and cultural expressions. Each ethnic group has its own means for protecting and defending itself in the face of survival

253

threats. When a particular repressed feeling is threatening to surface, some individuals who belong to distinct cultural groups will manifest culturally stereotypic behavior in order to protect themselves from that feeling. In many instances, they mistakingly displace that threat as being outside of themselves when, in fact, the real threat is a deep core emotion.

For example, an Italian who can trace his roots to Mafia methods of defense and retaliation may resort to those mechanisms when he experiences some deep threat to his personal being and identity. In certain Jewish sub-cultures, the syndicate, businessman, money manipulation mentality prevails. In such cases, a threat to one's self-esteem may trigger the con man, shrewd, gimmick promoter. Historically, the Jews who survived persecution were the one's who could buy, pay or bribe their way to freedom. So money signified the power to survive. The Black ghetto youth realizes that no one is ever going to help him unless he is physically and defensively superior; and thus, he uses his muscular strong-arm, gang tactic mentality to intimidate and secure his symbolic needs. This prowess serves as a secondary defense system and blocks the horribly intense emotional pain that lurks in the bellies of black people who historically have been deprived, tortured and ridiculed. The White Anglo Saxon defensive counterpart is the hurt, little boy, sneak thief, who, not receiving any warmth of love, must defend by sneaking around in the dark and stealing symbols.

The preceding list is by no means complete but it does point the way to cultural mechanisms of hiding and defending very deep hurt and pain. If such a defensive mechanism is "acted out" onto a therapeutic community, the results can be quite disordering and destructive.

It is important, of course, to always consider the limitations of our therapy and all other therapies. Some approaches have more success with certain populations and disorders and we are no exception. We have a highly ingrained sense of decency as well as innate capacities for feeling empathy and concern for other human beings. People who are socially motivated and wish to make full loving, feeling contact with others on a deep level are remarkably successful in the Total Feeling Process. These individuals possess considerable amounts of love, humanity, brotherhood and a potential capacity to connect to universal, unlimited reality. Their fineness and decency are easily tapped into and appreciated and they usually always leave other people feeling good about having contact with them. Their decency is contagious.

Of course, not all human beings are like the foregoing. It is a fact of life, though hard to accept, that not all people are decent, honest and loving. Quite the contrary. Due to severe infantile insults, some individuals are dangerously stupid and vicious and have long histories of inflicting varying degrees of hurt and harm onto others. I arrive at evaluations of people very reluctantly, but since everyone has to make evaluations of situations and people in order to make pertinent life decisions, I will admit that there are some people that I just don't like and respect. Consequently, I cannot do extensive successful therapy with them.

We have found that in many cases when a therapist is feeling conflicted or negative towards someone, if they feel deeper than their immediate reactions, they will lose the pains of the conflict. However, if negative feelings are consistent, then they can also accept that. One of our facilitators put it this way when confronting her own feelings toward an immediate patient.

"I find it very hard working with Bill. I don't trust him, because I know that he lies and sooner or later he's going to viciously pull some crazy shit. He doesn't really want to feel, he just wants to manipulate. He just does bad things. In other words, he's a son of a bitch and I find it very hard to care for him, yet I know I am a caring person."

The facilitator explored her own feelings on a much deeper level and was able to feel how "bad" she was treated by her own peers as a child. Her reactions toward the patient, however, didn't change over time and she found it very difficult to work with the client in question. Eventually, he did do something vicious to the whole group and left the program in a very unstraight way.

The problem of good and evil has existed since time began and it can be argued that evaluations of relative goodness and badness can depend upon at what point you are viewing the dilemma and what value system and criteria you are using. Many "evil-doers" use a system of denial. They take their evil and turn it around, making it appear to themselves, through their arguments, that what they are doing is good. Thus, we can say that whether something is good or bad, depends upon one's relative position in relation to a given situation and who is doing the evaluating. I am sure that Hitler and his followers believed that they were righteous, just like we Americans felt morally correct in our actions in certain wars.

We can, of course, assume that there is a supreme evaluation of what is good and what is evil and perhaps we should leave such matters to divine destiny to decide. But for many contemporary men and women, myself included, that does not close the matter. I believe that we have discovered a great truth in the deep core experience and it is my fervent contention and hope that one who has traveled the depths and heights of his core feelings will know absolutely whether he or she is really good or bad. I also believe that a Total Feeling person will be able to ascertain who else is inherently good and who is really bad.

Let me hasten to add that no one is either all good or all bad. Even very good persons occasionally have breakouts of "badness" or anti-social behavior. But that does not make them a bad person and even so called adjudged "bad" people have been known to have streaks of benevolent behavior. I would venture to say, however, that a feeling person has a system of boundaries that can be violated and that those boundaries have tolerance and trust limits. If those trust levels are stretched to those limits, then a feeling person must protect himself appropriately in order to keep the "bad" person out of his vital zones. This is appropriate and necessary behavior if one is to survive and maintain a sense of clear emotional groundedness.

Chapter 14 Transitions and Goals

It no longer is there —
the hope for the love
For I am adrift, alone.
It has happened.

I am not shatter proof
nor invincible
You can still hurt me
And send me to the depths
of my craziness.

More and More I feel
the aloneness
As the chord strains and snaps.
I fail and become estranged.
There is no one.

Yet, this bird will fly again
This soul shall heal.
My heart will guide my hands
to build that which was never
allowed
And whatever hinders my movement,
I will overcome with the will to live.

I   am   sorry
That it must be this way
Yet full love communicates,
So I say to you,
"Goodbye.
I must flight to live and survive.
I must go and leave you
to deal with your own craziness
and me with mine."

It is a shame for this little one,
my son,
For he cannot help it.

Feeling People

He is little, that is his only crime.
He will close down as the years pass
    to please the demons in his life.

        "I cannot save you, my boy."

They have unwittingly tried to drive me
    to be
As mad as they,
But I soar away
To be with you another day.

My son
You are the greatest gift of
    my soul, my life, my very being.
Where would I be without you?
You are the earth
    the essence of heaven
        Paradise.

You are softness and gentleness
HIS gift to me.
A miracle of wonder and joy.

        So precious and fragile.
        so valued
        and yet unable
        to be possessed.

        I will always love you
            and, maybe someday
        We will be together
            again
        The way
            it was
               meant
                 to be . . .

TRANSITIONS

The phrase, "Ladder of Success" is a euphemism that partly describes upward mobility in American culture. Everyone is on some sort of a ladder going somewhere. The fluidity of American commercial and professional life presents a realm of conscious choices and turning points. In therapy these choices can be painful or rewarding. Many patients show all the superficial signs of success in their jobs and personal lives, but inwardly find much of what they are doing to be meaningless and empty. Through feelings, they begin to actualize the next step in their climb toward self-actualization.

We call this period in time, when they are working through a particular issue or feeling, a transition. Perhaps all phases of the life cycle are transitional states that prepare one for the next step in life's journey. Therapy helps the individual to pass through each of these transitory phases and provides a vehicle for sifting, relieving and integrating the anxiety.

As a person feels more and deeper, he may find that the way he has been living his life merits questioning. An unreal person will be threatened with a life of full feeling and he may choose to convince himself that he is better off living symbolically. Others find that a feeling life is the way to full existence and happiness, but there is great difficulty giving up the illusory world that they have heretofore existed in. The fact is that we have only one life to live and if we should live a life split off from our core self, then we only half exist.

To compromise one's self for illusions and unfulfilling life styles is to set the groundwork for how one is to die. It is easy to believe that all the illness that plagues modern man is caused by foreign microbiotic organisms. I believe, however, that most of the diseases that beset man are caused by faulty, compromised, sick lifestyles. The way one chooses to live will determine how one will die.

"I want to live and be happy. I don't want to be dishonest and destructive. I have a right to be happy . . .

I had been married to the wrong person and we weren't compatible. Yet, it was so hard to admit that it was a horrible relationship and that in order for me to live, I had to get out . . .

I couldn't be me, living with a man who didn't feel and was a bullshit phony.

I've got to have my own life and be happy . . . Someday I'll find the right mate but I need to find the rest of me first . . . Getting out of this marriage was like saving my life . . . I'm worth more than that . . . I like myself more now . . . It's good to know that I made a mistake and I'm not a bad person."

This preceding example demonstrates that as one feels more of himself, he also needs to change the way he lives. This is true because of the crossroads that everyone has to face at different points in life. As one moves on and matures, he must confront the various losses that occur. Relationships change, people separate from each other, life cycle identity crises must be faced and resolved and all these issues require some form of emotional catharsis. Many people are not ready or are ill prepared for making changes to more advanced levels of living. If they are not ready, then they may go back to the old ways and explore some of the unfinished parts of that life. For those who have felt a large part of themselves, it is impossible to go all the way back to exactly the way it was. The amount of feeling that one has felt and integrated will correspond to the amount of change he will make in his life.

Many of these changes that take place may seem swift and in some cases, quite radical, but deep feelings change people's lives. It is important that changes in the way one lives and works should not be too impulsive, however. Many neurotics make changes out of symbolic, unfelt need and their choices usually end up disastrously. One must make his changes from a firm foundation of feeling rather than the whim of a passing displaced caprice. When a new patient wants to make a choice or a decision that seems to be blind or unconsciously self-destructive, we have to determine how resistant he is to giving up that choice for a time, until he has felt more. If he has made up his mind and is quite adamant in his decision, then of course, we let him go ahead even though he may be hurting himself. After all, he is an adult and is ultimately responsible for himself. But if he is not too defended and can be reached in time, we will try to have him feel more of himself and then he can make his choices from a clearer, more centered place.

As we can readily see, feeling often precipitates the transition from a non-feeling relationship and homelife to moving out and taking a chance for a better, more fulfilling life. When people discover that there is something better than being dead and dissatisfied, they move on with their lives. First, they may make a transition from the roles that they have played for others to seeking only themselves in an environment that allows for more feeling.

Jane: "At the time I left my home and my husband I was really into wanting to become myself. I knew how dead I was. I had had a taste of feelings and, although I wasn't really very far along yet, I had seen the group, seen people that were feeling and I wanted this for myself. I knew I couldn't have this if I continued to live the way I had been. I had to get away from my old life.

   After my intensive, I went back and realized that I couldn't feel around my husband and family. I was going backward instead of forward. I knew all the damage that had been done to me over the years. I'm even more in touch with it now, of course, but even then I knew it, and I guess, I had played with the idea of leaving him for awhile . . . It brought up a lot of fear and I broke down and started to cry. It was after that that I knew the difference between being so dead and feeling. I didn't want to be dead anymore. . . . After that I just moved out . . . found an apartment and was much happier. My rediscovery of myself started in earnest."

Deep core feelings also release a desire to be with other people who will help one to grow naturally and relate more openly. The following example is a young woman who found her life transformed by a deep feeling life style.

Toni: "I was walking around sad all the time. My friends were all moving away and I was feeling terrible. I had planned to see a psychiatrist and then I met some people who were part of the Feeling Community. Somehow I just knew that these people were right for me. They were so dynamic and feeling.

   It had been a year and a half since my father had died and when I met these people, my feelings about my dad and his death started coming out . . . I was looking for something I guess, a release . . . After I had been into therapy and felt a lot of my own sadness and pain, I found that there was no way I could stay in my old house with my mother. I couldn't be happy there . . . It was no good.

While I was in my mother's home, I was really dependent on her. Moving out, I'm on my own. Whatever I do now, I'm going to do by myself.

In therapy I also discovered that I really loved this group and the people in it, especially Melanie. She's gone now, but I think about her. With the first set of people at the Center, I knew that I wanted to open up. Some of them left and it took me awhile to make friends with this new group of people, but now I really like to be with them. . . . I have a new life now and new feeling people to enjoy it with."

Toni made a feeling transition from loneliness, sadness, loss, depression and dependency to deep warm intimacy with real true friends. She also developed her own independence and the determination to take care of herself and pay her own way. She now lives with other community members and is experiencing joy in her life for the first time. She has made a successful transition to a deep core feeling lifestyle, living with feeling people, making friends and supporting herself. Other people don't necessarily get this far. For some, just making a transition to deep feeling is enough and they stop short of feeling the emotions that would free them to make real friends, live in feeling households and work in a humanistic fashion. Others make a successful transition to feeling and a dyadic love relationship but can't make the transition to being a real part of a Feeling Community.

All therapies, jobs, potential sex partners, houses, neighborhoods, friends, etc. must contain an element of attractiveness for the individual to be drawn to it. This attractiveness usually holds out the promise of some kind of reward, which if high, will motivate the individual to move toward it. If the attractiveness is low, then that person will move away from it in order to avoid anticipated pain. As we have discussed in earlier chapters, intimacy or closeness also enters into the picture. Distancing becomes a problem in almost all human interactions along with the subtle or unconscious signal systems that people set up.

In the earlier example of Jane we can see that her transition from home and husband contained elements of the above. She wished to distance herself from her husband because their relationship was no longer attractive and was too painful to tolerate. She saw the depth of feeling in other Community members and she wanted this for herself. She also needed a place where she could be free to fully feel and she finally found one. Through the power of deep feelings, the therapy itself drew her in. She had to select something new while distancing herself from something old. With her new found life and self, however, she still had to deal with the problem of her own distance from others. Because she had been so pushed away by her own family, she had developed a mixed signal system. She wanted to come close to people but the defensive side of her pushed others away, thus creating a safe but not a completely satisfying situation. She was like a traffic light with the *Stop* and *Go* lights both on at the same time.

Fred, on the other hand, came into therapy because he wanted to find himself and get closer to his wife and son. His wife had been into the Total Feeling Process and had successfully negotiated transitions into deep feeling, community and work. What remained was the transition to being a successful marriage partner and parent. Fred "was" his defense system. He had kept everyone "out" for a long time but he knew that it no longer was paying off for him. Each new feeling breakthrough brought him closer and closer to his wife and child. But defenses are hard to die and soon after each feeling his old distancing roles would overtake him. He had a tremendous amount of buried rage towards his father and quite often his hostility would come out in subtle and diluted role playing ways. His wife and child would naturally respond to him with their own defenses and the distance would be set up again. In Total Feeling groups, because there is so much feeling going on, there is hardly an opportunity to defend. So Fred and his wife would contact each other at a full feeling level and they would be truly together again.

Fred needed to make the transition from being a hostile defensive distancer to a potentially full feeling intimate human being. His transition consisted of making more and more feeling connections. Both Fred and his wife are in the process of making the transition from a non-feeling, alienating marriage to a full feeling household.

Transitions can be facilitated by significant emotional breakthroughs. It is common for community members to cite specific groups or individual sessions as being the time that they really got in touch with something that changed their lives dramatically. Fred recalls the night in group when he first got in touch with and expressed his long suppressed anger. He, like others, was afraid to let his rage out because of that age old rationalization, "If I let my anger out, I'll wreck everything and everybody in sight." His family, as well as members of the group, were afraid of his unexpressed rage. He seemed like a volcano that could erupt at any time. Unexpressed feeling always acts as a barrier to closeness and as Fred began expressing his anger on soft pillows, in the safety and support of the Total Feeling Process, everyone felt more comfortable with him. That was the night that he made his transition into anger and became further involved with other people through real emotional contact.

Other transitions are obtained very slowly and painstakingly. In her early childhood, Jane had been literally "thrown away" by her mother and sister. She had not been abused physically but had suffered as the target of her mother's and sister's hatred. They brutalized her with absolute and total rejection. She was pushed so far away from her family that she suffered a lifetime of emotional and physical starvation for warm close contact. Her marriage only continued this pattern. Jane's therapy will take a longer time than most other people because of the extreme severity of the damage inflicted upon her. Often, children who are pushed away like this, learn to unconsciously push other people away and make themselves totally isolated. As Jane's buried pain diminishes, she will be able to come closer to people who can really care for her and she, in turn, will be able to return the caring.

Oh little one, so beautiful
and frail,
forgive me if I fail
though I do love you . . . . .
Release me from my guilt
For I am only too human
and blind.
So stupid am I
to be unkind,
yet they were brutal
to Me.

I would rather Die than inflict my
  brutality onto you
For you are my Life
  and Love.
Were I to die tomorrow
I would have lived Full
  knowing and feeling you,
    My Precious.

> *Destroy me: my wickedness*
>   *my weaknesses*
> *I bore thee out of*
>   *my ignorant youth.*
> *Yet now my soul cries for you and your pain*
>   *for you are my soul.*
> *You and I are*
>   *almost One and*
>   *the Same*
> *Yet different*
>   *though we be.*

There is a tendency for people to unconsciously raise their children exactly the same way that they were raised. The result is that the same behaviorial interpersonal and physical problems reappear throughout the lives of their offspring. Part of the therapy in the Total Feeling Process involves individuals making transitions in the way they feel and relate to their own children. Earlier transgressions and defenses can be felt and corrected as one becomes healthier and more grounded in a feeling lifestyle.

The following is a case in point.

Pat: "I wish I could have given to my daughter as a baby what I give to your baby boy." (crying)

Ther: "That was a problem a long time ago. You didn't like kids and yet, you had one so you couldn't give to her. Now all of a sudden, you've been freed up, you're liking yourself a lot more and you're feeling some regret because you didn't give her what you think she needed. Now things have changed for you. You're older and clearer and you're liking little children."

265

Pat: (crying very heavily as the therapist's words reach through to her heart.)

Ther: "You've grown a lot. You have some regrets though. You have some regrets about the past."

Pat: "I see how vulnerable and open little babies are and I feel sorry I didn't make it easier for Jackie. I made it harder." (crying very heavily)

Ther: "I think what you're saying, too, is you didn't own her before and now you're trying to re-claim her. Trying to make her your child again."

Pat: (crying very heavily and rocking back and forth)

Ther: "You really want a child of your own, something of your very own. You're making some claims now in life. There are things you want for yourself. Little Patty wants to come up in the world."

Pat: "I feel so inadequate (crying) as a parent. I'm just beginning to be a parent and I have a five year old girl. There are so many areas where I don't know what to do . . . I don't know what she's going through, I don't know what's happening with her (crying)."

Ther: "Therefore you don't know how to help her."

Pat: "I know. (crying). I want to help her . . ."

Ther: "You want to reach out and help her."

Pat: (sobbing) "I know she's got tons and tons of anger for me. I don't even know how to help her get that out. She's afraid to get angry at me sometimes . . . Lately, when I've driven down to my old neighborhood, where I grew up, I get sad. I kinda wish I could go back and relive my childhood. I would be so different."

Ther: "I think the comparison you're making now is like saying, 'I needed something different.' Let's hear the way you really wanted and needed it to be."

Pat: (crying) "I needed more space. I needed room (sobbing). I needed parents that could give me parts of themselves (sobbing), a sense of security. Parents that really cared. Parents that really wanted the most for me. Parents that thought I was special and smart and really gave me the confidence to be able to succeed in what I truly wanted to do . . ."

"I want to show my daughter *everything*. (cries more)
. . . They never showed me anything!!! (heavy crying) . . .
You never showed me anything!!! (patient picks up the bat
and starts hitting the punching bag) . . . You never showed
me anything!!! . . . You never gave me any options or alternatives!!! . . . 'There's only one way to go!!!' . . . (crying
and hitting bag) . . . That's not *true!!!* There are so many
ways to go!!! . . . There are so many things I could be!!!
. . . There are so many things I want to be!!!" (at this point,
she breaks into heavy crying with this realization).
Ther: "It seems like a whole world is opening up to you
. . . besides your just being a mother and a housewife . . .
so many possibilities now . . . so many different things you
can be . . . so many things you want to be . . ."
Pat: (crying) "I started to really feel that. I can be anything that I want to be."
Ther: "That's what you want for your daughter . . . that's
what you want for her."

As Pat continues to feel more and more of her own frustration
and pain from childhood, she will be able to actualize the kind of
life she desires for her own little girl, free of the contamination and
destructiveness of her internal defenses. Her transition from being
an inadequate, hostile, reluctant mother to becoming a concerned,
loving one will dominate her energies over the next year or two. By
finally emotionally owning her child, she has opened up a totally
new relationship for both of them.

LEVELS OF ASPIRATION

Many individuals who enter therapy bring with them a
deepseated fear that they are undeserving of a warm, decent relationship with a significant other person. These feelings of worthlessness, inadequacy and "one-downess" often effect the way they
relate to spouses, children, bosses, etc. Behavioral patterns, interpersonal dynamics, life style and work choices all fall short of their
potential due to an unfelt history of deprivation. When the flood-
gate to emotional catharsis is opened, transitions in life style, relationships, jobs, etc. suddenly flow.

For example:

Ther: "What's happening with you?"

Marilyn: "I just want to fully understand what's going on between me and Dan. This relationship is not like anything I've ever had with a male before because I never really felt decent. I don't feel decent all the time and there's a chance for me to be decent in this relationship."

Ther: "He's really appreciating you . . . the real you. He's really confirming who you are . . . the real Marilyn."

Marilyn: (crying) "I never felt decent before . . . It's very hard for me to take...very hard for me to take...something stops me from taking for myself . . . I have been treated like shit for so fucking long . . . for so long."

Ther: "Why did you let yourself be treated like shit? You must have seen yourself that way. You really see yourself as nothing . . . you let people treat you that way."

Marilyn: "I had a really bad reputation . . . It brought me right down . . . It didn't match me at all . . . My reputation does not match *me!!* (crying louder) . . . doesn't match my body or doesn't match me physically or emotionally . . . It just brings me down." (crying)

Ther: "You got down to a low level."

Marilyn: "I wouldn't let any of those guys in . . ."

Ther: "But you must have been very lonely . . . The only kind of males you knew were your brother and your father . . ."

Marilyn: "My father was a little irresponsible boy . . . I couldn't get anything from him . . . I had to go seeking . . . In a way I feel that the times that Dan and I have gotten close, I was seeking him out . . . yet what I'm trying to get, most of all, is myself."

Ther: "I think what was happening is that you were seeking him because you saw in him a quality . . . a quality you didn't have in yourself . . . didn't feel in yourself."

Marilyn: "Yes, I saw him as being very clear . . . I've seen some of my craziness since I've been working with him . . . his level of reality is really something . . ."

Ther: "Something to look up to . . .?"

Marilyn: "Yes, I definitely look up to Dan . . . There are a lot of good qualities in him . . . He's intellectual and he's really good with his hands . . ."
Ther: "Now you want to look up to yourself . . . you want to be in that same place that you see Dan."
Marilyn: (crying) "I never really said that though . . . I couldn't . . . He's a good man."
Ther: "You really respect him . . . Amazing how well you do when you have someone to respect."
Marilyn: "It's amazing what I respect myself for . . ."
Ther: "Sure, when you have a man that you truly respect, you can really respect yourself . . . Life is different now."
Marilyn: "It's not ever going to go backwards . . . from what I've seen it can't go backwards."

To elaborate further, all human beings are problem solving, goal seeking organisms. Each individual, in order to test his or her own feelings of inadequacy, will attempt to seek relationships and challenging experiences of greater and greater complexity. Each person will also paradoxically endeavor to simplify his life or reduce complex issues to their lowest common denominator. In other words, man will vacillate, back and forth, between conquering problems of ascending complexity while seeking ultimately simpler goals.

Now what does this mean? Every one of us seeks to overcome our own feelings of inadequacy and, at the same time, improve our relative present state of existence on this planet. I postulate that within each indvidual is a genetic and environmental memory of existing in a state of obscurity and that each person's motives to improve himself are based upon overcoming this past sense of obscurity.

Alfred Adler was astute in elaborating on the superiority and inferiority complexes[1]. However, the sense that I am speaking of is that each one of us desires to elevate his level of existence. We all want to improve and extend our lives beyond the circumstances of

---

[1] Alfred Adler, *Social Interest: A Challenge to Mankind*, (New York: Capricorn Books, 1964), pg. 96-126.

our own birth. In a sense, being a single sperm cell amongst millions of similar cells necessitates a motive or drive to signal ourselves out or make ourselves more sufficient than our brother and sister cells in order to survive. Genetically, the human organism continually seeks to adapt and improve itself in order to expand into ever new and strange environments. This would indicate that we still retain a cellular memory of our obscure beginnings as primitive organisms. This doesn't mean that the end goal is a fictional one of superiority over other human beings. But, rather, it represents a deep desire to attain something that is an improvement over one's previous upbringing. We are, in essence, competing against our own feelings of inadequacy and obscurity. This can be seen, at its most evident point, in those who are searching for personal identity.

If one's background and early childhood environment is seen as lacking in status and prestige, then a person will aim his sights on something outside of himself or onto a person that is deemed to represent a desirable level of aspiration. A young girl who experiences deficiencies in her early childhood upbringing may target a young prince as her romantic ideal. The obtaining and capturing of this romantic symbol of aspiration is, in a sense, seen as a symbolic capturing of an external manifestation of one's internal ambitions.

For example, a young woman writes:

"I have a lot of need and hope for a man for myself. It's important to me to be devoted to a single man and be very special to him. I'm seeking to learn about life and about myself through his eyes . . . I was very deprived of my Dad, as far as learning about myself and life, so I am trying to discover myself and all that I lost out on, through a man."

We can see many examples of people who are constantly seeking something outside of themselves that represents an improvement over their previous levels of existence. Marilyn was an example of this. The counterpart might be a young man from a poor family who may wish to marry a princess from a higher social class and thus, ostensibly, capture for himself a piece of his level of aspiration. Unfortunately, those who would marry across social class lines may end up feeling disappointed, because after capturing the prize, they still may experience themselves as being from "the other side of the tracks." Thus, they find it difficult trying to be something that they are not connected to internally. Those who come from emotionally deprived backgrounds, and this includes the rich and poor, seek to externally capture something that they did not get in childhood. Whatever the goal may be, it represents that level of aspiration that is seen as a desirable point of elevation beyond the pain of a deprived childhood.

One young man confides:

"I want expensive, materialistic things, such as a boat, to make up for my deprivation. As a child we had little or no material goodies. I, also, want to be in a position of power and importance. I never want to be in a position to beg. All these desires come because of my low life role in my family as a child."

It is noteworthy that certain individuals that come from emotionally deprived upper class families will seek some sort of gratification from people and symbols in the lower classes.

"I came from an upper, middle class family which was emotionally devoid of all feeling and 'love.' I have always been attracted to lower middle class, 'warm' friends, families that I could relate to, laugh with and love always."

Many people can work in concert and cooperation with one another if they all play a reciprocal role in fulfilling each other's strivings and ambitions towards certain goals and levels of aspiration. By collectively desiring to better themselves, they seek out even more complex relationships that help them to attain their goals. If a female who desperately seeks her own identity through a man wants to overcome and elevate herself from her own sense of childhood obscurity, she will need to undergo some sort of emotional transformation in order to meet the status level of the prince that she is seeking. This syndrome is filled with anxiety. As soon as this anxiety bursts forth into full transformative emotion, the person will feel freer from the deprivation and obscurity of childhood and perhaps, one step closer to the desired goal.

271

I postulate that one cannot properly integrate and attain those goals without some kind of emotional catharsis. In other words, without deep core feeling integration the young female will only fail in her attempts to capture her prince charming since she is, for all intents and purposes, still emotionally locked into feelings of obscurity from the past. Since this obstacle from the past is still present and active in her life, she cannot relate clearly and equally to her romantic ideal. It is like saying that a minor leaguer can never reach the major leagues unless he first conquers and overcomes his deficiencies. Deep core feeling and connection is the only lasting way to overcome the effects of one's past and become upwardly mobile. The more one feels of one's past, the more one progresses forward.

Unlike the young man's aspirations for wealth, it is not the attainment of external symbolic goals that is the measure of success. Rather, it is the recapturing and reclaiming of those lost and deprived parts of the self that internally catapults someone to a new level of aspiration and attainment. For many, reaching that level of aspiration is an on-going reality and, as soon as they do reach one of those focal points or goals, it is common for them to reach out toward another. Life becomes a cycle of desires, drives, and attainments followed by a new set of desires, etc.

For example, the young male who is seeking the princess because she represents a symbolic higher position in his cultural milieu, may attempt to achieve that status himself and perhaps surpass it internally, thus dispensing with that previous focal point. The princess, in other words, becomes no longer good enough for him and he moves on to a new level of aspiration.

Deep core feeling experiences help to facilitate this process. Instead of grasping at many symbolic dreams, people feel their buried pain, grow and proceed to conquer their own obstacles to future growth. There is an example of a thirty-one year old male who found himself locked into a position in life that was almost identical to his father's. He had the same value system as his father and made the same amount of money. Yet, he felt incredibly stifled by his father's values, which exerted considerable control over his everyday life. The more he felt the pain towards his father, the more he came to realize that his father's way of life was not working for him. He was able to integrate the feeling experience, change his aspiration level and move on to a new career which was socially, educationally and emotionally more gratifying to him.

This also happens many times in the educational sphere. A person might seek a college education in order to better him or herself and thus, function at a higher level or position. However, if that educational acquisition is not emotionally integrated, the level of attainment may be quite distorted. For example, one young male had two Master's Degrees but because of his own emotional deficiencies could not make more than $150.00 a week. At the same time, those same deficiencies held him back from a rewarding social and emotional life. If he was reoriented to seek his lost self, it might provide him with the elements of personality and character that would help him to improve both his social and professional life.

As I have already mentioned, the more people feel of themselves, the more difficult it becomes for them to remain in inhumane circumstances. The more that one feels, the more one wants to humanize his entire life. He senses his need to be treated as a unique individual and wants to treat others in this same fashion as well.

The world of work is an arena for the accumulation of much frustration and pain and if an employee or an employer feels that he is being treated within the confines of a role rather than as a person, he will harden himself to the painful influences of potential hurtful individuals.

It is quite evident that much Mommy and Daddy symbolism seeps into occupational relationships. The purpose of hardening oneself is to errect a psychological barrier that attempts to keep people from getting to these more vulnerable parts of themselves. This hard surface never works completely, however, because the effects of indignities do leak through to the reservoir of historical hurt.

When people are treated as human beings, then a job is not just something to endure, but it becomes an experience in self-validation and confirmation. If the boss cares, then the employees will care and vice and versa. If an employer approaches his work with enthusiasm, dignity and pride, his workers will thrive on his spirit and presence. If he is fully in touch with himself, he will enjoy being alive and he will bring his aliveness and energy to the job. His people will love being in his presence and they will work spontaneously and creatively.

People do not work just for monetary purposes and goals. They also seek rewards in more human terms. It is people who work and people are not unfeeling machines. Give them emotional rewards and they will find joy and richness in the most mundane and tedious of occupations. Boredom and drudgery for eight hours a day will kill anyone's spirit, but a humanistic atmosphere will cultivate and motivate people to work.

My mother and a deceased Uncle of mine had much pain in their lives, but they both possessed an indomitable quality for joy and laughter. In the most dreary of work circumstances, they could always bring enough joy and humor with them to completely humanize their situation. When Mom and Uncle Albert were there, the atmosphere was alive and people would come out of their shells. They both possessed an uncanny knack for brightening up a place.

The following is a poem that I dedicate to my Mother and Uncle:

Blessed are the comedians
For they bring joy and mirth to a dreary world.
Blessed are the clowns
For they remind us that we are all human beings.
Blessed are those who bring laughter
To those in pain and boredom
For they shall inherit my everlasting gratitude.
Blessed be my Mother and Uncle Albert
For you taught me to laugh and to make others laugh.
You made the world a better place for me to live in.
Your smiles, your spirit in adversity . . . . .
You always found
Time to share a joke . . . to brighten the day.

Blessed be you who bring the sunshine to everyone's
    faces and lives,
Blessed be you who taught me through joy and spirit
To humanize my life and work and, in turn, I give
    your gift to others . . . . .
Through you to me to others. May I never treat
Anyone just as a worker, but as a person.
May I treat everyone who labors in the field,
In the factory, and in the office as I would my
    own children, with total dignity as a
    unique individual.

Let me reiterate that feelings humanize people and people humanize jobs. When indignities and unfelt history harden people, deep core feelings make them soft and relaxed again.

There are other factors to be considered when focusing in on jobs. Status, advancement, prestige and self-image all play an important part in creating and maintaining an emotionally satisfying work environment for a clear individual. As one feels more and more of himself, his goals and directions in life become more grounded and more in keeping with who he is as a unique, feeling member of society.

Because we know that job, career and housing choices are always fraught with intense feeling, the Total Feeling Community provides a supportive environment for working through these transitions. We attempt to co-ordinate the creation, location and implementation of jobs, businesses and housing for all members who may need these services. For example, certain members may wish to work or live together. We encourage them to develop these relationships to fit their emerging feeling life styles and follow this up with support, counseling and problem solving. Often they will need a close check to insure that the participants are keeping up to date with their feelings and communication with one another. The reason that this is done is because new patients don't necessarily know how to live or work honestly with themselves and other people. It is common in a close, day-to-day setting to trigger off old habitual patterns of living and relating, so the community watches closely for signs of regression and neurosis.

Levels of aspiration can reflect the health and feeling depth of an individual. The following are a sampling of goals and levels of aspiration of clients that run the gamut from neurotic to fairly tuned in and self-actualized.

Irv: "I want (need) expensive materialistic things such as a boat, to make up for my deprivation. As a child we had little or no materialistic goodies. I want to be in a position of power and importance and recognized for it. I never want to be in a position to beg. I want to call the shots. Subserviance turns me off. I want people to need me and turn to me for help."

Mike: "My main goal has always been to get some kind of adventure. I never like things to stay the same."

Julie: "I want security . . ."

Jane: "I want a family . . ."

Marilyn: "I want someone . . . I want a man."

Lois: "Trying to find self and understand myself . . . sort out my feelings and feel good without having to look to others for attention and positive strokes. My family always used monetary values rather than true caring. I want to belong probably more than anything else . . . it is a feeling I rarely have had . . . I'm tired of being an outsider . . . I've always felt like an outsider even in my own family. My mother always told me how fair she was and in my heart I always felt that was bullshit. I have never gotten my fair share of love and attention from my family . . . I only got attention for negative behavior.

Patricia: "Right now the big goal in my life is to become orgasmic. The failure of my sexual organs to respond to my own touch and to the touch of men shows me what a failure I am as a person. My master plan follows that I will find a man whom I will have a successful relationship with because of the fact I can orgasm. I will make him feel like a man. All problems will disappear once we can reach a peak experience together."

Sandra: "My goals for myself are threefold. First, I want to develop and open myself to my fullest feeling capacity as a human being. I know there are still areas of myself I have not yet tapped into, areas which are vital to my identity. These are especially in the spiritual and cosmic realms right now. I guess, also, in this whole area of personal growth, I would include physical wholeness and health.

Secondly, I strongly desire to build a home for myself and my little family which is grounded in love, contact, warmth, growth and life. I see myself as being very instrumental in that. As opposed to a few years ago when I might have sat back and waited for my husband 'to do it,' now I am very much in touch with my own power and love and ability to mold humanely. I like that and I want to use it creatively to nurture a loving, supportive, growthful environment.

Finally, I want to help other people discover themselves and their full potential as creative, feeling human beings."

As we can see from the previous examples, many individuals focus outside themselves for self-actualizing goals and ambitions. Their energy is invested in material pleasures, security, other people, positions of power, sexual prowess, etc. They have lost themselves in their drive for symbolic, neurotic surrogates. Their ambitions for themselves as well as their transitional steps toward self growth will be contaminated with unfelt need and pain from the past. Only by feeling more and more of themselves will they be freed up to discover their true needs and potential as full feeling, creative human beings.

TERMINATION AND SEPARATION

In all human relations, as one passes from one transitional phase to another, there exists the potential problem of termination, that is how to end an existing relationship and in the case of therapy, separation of the patient from the total group experience. Clinically speaking, there appear to be five distinct phases or stages that termination goes through[2]. These stages are denial or flight, anger and hurt, negotiating and bargaining, grieving or mourning, and emotional insulation and psychological separation.

Denial is often the first reaction to the termination of an interpersonal relationship or separation from a therapeutic milieu. As one approaches very deep and meaningful early pain, he or she will respond in the present in a regressive fashion. This signals others that the individual is about to flee from painful internal realities as well as the present here and now symbols and triggers of that early reality. This anticipation of deep pain is a frightful prospect for many, especially if they are not in therapy or if they have been in therapy for only a moderate amount of time.

The more the defenses weaken, the more there occurs the prospect of frightening pain breaking through. What frequently follows is the person becoming totally unreal and unconscious to

---

[2] *Reading in Marriage and Family '76-'77* (Ross, Dushkin Publishing Group, 1976), pgs. 170-195.

avoid and deny the hurt. Such is the case of a young woman who had a great deal of trouble terminating an unproductive relationship. Her fear of her own internal, unintegrated pain led to a painful situation dragging on for over two years.

> Sara: "Tom was my first 'lover' and I had heavily transferred my mommy-daddy need onto him. I was very unaware of myself at the time so I only knew I was in pain, feeling lonely, depressed and totally miserable. My crying bouts, which would sometimes go on for hours, led to no resolution . . . only more depression.
>
> At every opportunity I would run back to him and try to become whatever he wanted. It seemed impossible for me to let go of him and the relationship even though I knew it was neurotic and destructive. I 'needed' him desperately. Or, at least, I couldn't stand the pain and loneliness without him. My communication skills at the time were non-existent and I was unable to even verbally clarify the relationship much less express my agony.
>
> After months of painful acting out and acting in with clinging and depression, a crisis finally precipitated our final break and the relationship ended. Soon after, I began analysis and was able to cognitively understand some of the pain that had been involved in my relationship with him."

Fortunately, Sara was able to break out of the heavy dependency and depression that was operating in her relationship with Tom. However, her bout with unreality and denial was not yet over.

> Sara: "My second major relationship began shortly after the termination of the first and resulted in marrriage. For three years I acted out incredible need for acceptance and love through the use of drugs and numerous extra-marital affairs. I was determined not to be in that heavy depression space again with a male, so I literally turned myself off to all intense feelings. Everything remained loose, superficial, non-involved and 'fun.' Unlike the first relationship, I was now able to verbally communicate some of my concerns. My husband and I spent hours talking about problems and goals in the relationship."

"But, eventually, I finally came to a point where I no longer wanted to act out or rely upon drugs to find whatever it was I was looking for. Whatever need I was acting out was not being met and I kept hungering and searching over and over again. Through my own analysis, I finally realized that it was me, real inner me, that was missing and all my acting out was a symbolic attempt to 'fill me up' with life, acceptance, womanhood, etc. My direction inward was clear at this time and my energy toward my feeling growth began to soar.

My husband, in the meantime, had been putting more and more energy into his professional identity. Emotionally, we were missing each other. I spent a few months questioning the relationship but felt very little pain at the idea of terminating it. I didn't feel much love for him. I didn't feel much of anything for him in the defended state I had been existing. A few tears and then very rationally I decided the relationship was going nowhere and it was time to move on. I did . . . with some fear, a little pain and mostly relief. The relationship had not been right, and at some level, I guess I had known that for a long time. Ending it allowed me to fully feel myself and begin to care for other people in a non-neurotic, clear way."

For those individuals involved in a feeling therapy, somewhere between the first and second year, early pain threatens to break into consciousness. Defensive patterns unconsciously develop and get acted out as a denial against feeling that pain. The individual may continue in therapy but there is an attempt to keep the experiencing of that deep core pain at a fairly safe, controlled level.

There can be a miscalculation by concerned others in the therapy group as to the ego strength of the flighting person. Group members will anticipate the loss of that member and may experience anger and hurt. This is usually preceded by a sense of disbelief. Because group members build up a set of expectations and beliefs about the terminating member, when that individual acts contrary to their hopes and expectations, there develops a subsequent sense of shock. An initial withdrawal of contact from the separating member may occur in order to match his flight responses. Random internal phenomena develops leading toward self-insulation in order to protect oneself against the pain of separation. Eventually, however, stronger feelings may surface and have to be dealt with.

Anger and hurt become an integral part of the inter-personal struggle with the recalcitrant exiting member. First, there may be subtle influence bids aimed at triggering that person's early pain with the hopes that he will return to the fold. This moment in group history is experienced as a crisis and threatens the very integrity and cohesiveness of the group. The group members may feel sorry and disappointed as they each go back and recall all their memories associated with the flighting individual. It is as if they have not given up hoping that they can get that member back.

This same phenomena occurs in family, marriage, and serious love relationships. Hurt, disappointment and pain may inevitably give way to anger and attack as each party breaks out old, previously held back grievances. There is an attempt to bring all the negativity in the relationship up to date. At this stage many people may become disillusioned and feel the pangs of failure. It is common to hear such phrases as "What did I do wrong?", "Where did we go wrong?" or "There must be something I could have done."

In order to protect themselves from the pain of disengagement, people may experience violations of their realms of intimacy. In male-female relationships the person who is experiencing violation may begin establishing strong boundaries against further intrusions. This can be anything from not sleeping in the same bedroom to not letting the other person see the injured party in the nude. Previously open areas of the same dwelling such as the bathroom and bedroom may suddenly become "off limits" as methods of retaliation.

In therapy, one strategy may be to "go with the resistance." That is, whatever behavior the exiting member may be displaying, the therapists can set up a situation where it becomes exaggerated. For example, a flighting member may be asked to drop out of groups for several weeks in order to dramatize the behavioral seriousness of the situation and also to emphasize the inevitability of separation. Thus, we can see we are entering a negative stage where much manipulating becomes apparent. Plea bargaining and negotiation takes place and usually futile attempts to re-establish once rewarding contact. Unfortunately, most cases of separation are never done pleasantly and are the direct result of people acting off their own painful concerns.

It is difficult for some individuals to accept and understand the necessity of assuming the total therapeutic task. If one does not internalize the absolute necessity of valuing the process of self revelation, feeling one's deepest roots, as well as honest and open communication with other human beings, then therapy can't be integrated into one's life. There's nothing fallacious about chasing and seeking one's dreams and goals but to lose and disregard oneself as a feeling person because of a fear of deep integral pain is a decision that leads to strongly questionable if not self-destructive ends.

Termination can threaten any relationship, therapeutic or otherwise, at any time when there are strong unreal violations. If striving for integrity and authenticity is strong enough, the ego will recognize the seriousness of all interpersonal effects and allow one to drop into his pain, resolve the core feeling issues and feel clear enough to come back and re-establish more self-actualizing contact in the present. This characterizes more stable feeling relationships and it also indicates the desire on the part of the participant to make the relationship permanent.

Those that are in more immature stages of development and experience themselves at a more primitive level of transition will treat most relationships as temporary. Thus, there may be a desire to drop into the feeling to alleviate internal tension but there may be no desire to establish firm contact in the here and now. People are left hanging and unresolved. This sequence of events is a direct indication of the participant's level of maturity. Unfortunately, that doesn't make the pain any less.

This bargaining phase of separation may be characterized by such phrases as "If you'll do this or stop doing that, then I'll become loving again." This type of negotiating rarely works towards permanence except when there's a mature commitment to the permanence of the relationship. In immature relationships the bargaining process can stretch out over incredible lengths of time or even over a lifetime without ever having real contactful resolution.

Stan: "I knew I couldn't stay involved with her, she kept seducing me then busting my nuts left and right. I'd

281

screw her and it would feel great, then she would turn around and do something completely off the wall. Okay, so I couldn't give her a total commitment . . . I knew she just wasn't the 'girl for me.' But things would be good, then she'd go out and fuck every guy in town. I knew she was doing this to get me angry and jealous. She wanted me all for herself but I didn't want her to kick me in the balls all the time.

Sometimes we'd sit down and talk and try to renegotiate our relationship. We would get into our feelings but I knew deep down inside me it would never be permanent. She knew it too. This kept going on for months and months. She couldn't accept my lack of commitment and I couldn't stand the fact that she was fucking strange males . . . guys she'd pick up casually off the street. She must have been very lonely, but we just kept missing each other and fucking each other up."

The breaking up of a relationship or separation from therapy can be discomforting for many individuals. Grief, mourning, anxiety, and anger get all mixed up. Sadness may be inter-twined with feelings of retaliation and bitterness. This process of grieving over the loss of a loved and valued one is not dissimilar to the mourning rites conferred upon deceased persons. Even after separation and death there is a periodic re-evaluation of the lost person's positive and negative traits.

In the case of Stan, his eventual breakup with his female partner led to a period of intense emotional release followed by periodic feeling breakthroughs and eventual complete acceptance.

Stan: "One day I said, 'That's it . . . I've had it!!' I guess I wanted her to redeem herself but it didn't happen. She didn't want to change and neither did I. She tried to get me back into the relationship afterwards but by then I was too turned off and said in effect . . . 'No, never again . . . Get out . . . Stay out of my life!!'

For about a month afterwards I grieved her loss. She was a great piece of ass, a hell of a companion and good friend, but a real bitch. I expressed a lot of anger on the punching bag and then I recovered.

282

For about a year I occasionally thought of her . . . Some of the intimate sex moments had been real good. Those were good times for me, fulfilling times, growthful. But I knew it wasn't the final step. She had been good for me and I was good for her. But we weren't meant for each other . . . not a 'soul' relationship . . . I just couldn't see myself nestling down in a cottage with her for the rest of my life or being the father of her kids. We just didn't fully have one another. Our directions were different."

In the case of separation, if the process is carried out in a messy fashion, participants may have to devalue the other person in order to sever the emotional attachment. If separating members are stuck at this anger stage, they may continue to rehash grievances for years to come.

Sylvia: "That Son of a Bitch . . . I tried and tried to make a home with him but down deep inside I knew I never really loved him. I just needed a daddy and I picked the biggest bastard I could find to prove what a shit I was. He gave me a nice house, clothes and kids but he didn't give me himself. Like a fool, I let it drag on for years hoping that I could fall romantically in love with him again. But I didn't know him at the beginning and I kept closing my eyes to how crazy he was because I was crazy.

In the back of my head I was hoping and praying I could find a Prince Charming. I hate my parents for filling my head with all that garbage. They never let me see the reality of their own relationship so I could deal with it. That made it hard for me to really see my husband and our relationship."

As "turned off" or as angry as an individual might be in a relationship, ambiguity may also be present. This is usually a state of vacillation where partners are not sure whether they are going to separate or not. In the case of an older person, dissatisfaction with an interpersonal relationship may lead to feelings of separation but ambivalence or guilt may aggravate the situation. The prospect of living alone is both exciting and frightening. Many such individuals are afraid to start all over again with new partners and friends and make the same mistakes.

In clinical practice, it is common to see many individuals strug-gle to stay in and maintain highly counter-productive relation-ships. A high degree of ambivalence is present and they are always in a state of tension, being pulled in many different directions at once. Unfulfillment arouses much anxiety and those who are neurotic thrive on it and become locked into one another's death-like sickness. Older people may feel that life has passed them by and they are too old to start over. Younger people share similar at-titudes. There is security in a known neurotic relationship and it may be easier to stay locked in one than be plagued by certain questions and feelings, such as "Who wants me with two kids?" or "Who can love a fat person like me?" or just generally "Who could possibly want me?"

All during these previous stages of separation, individuals gradually learn to insulate themselves from the realization of ultimate separation. There is often a need to ease pain by many dif-ferent devices, some more appropriate than others. As separation becomes a reality, everyone concerned has to walk through all of the feelings as best as they can. If the internal support system and resources are adequate enough, each person ultimately does accept the separation and then moves on from there to form newer and perhaps more fulfilling future contacts. If one is self-actualizing, each subsequent relationship should be an improvement over previous ones. This occurs because of the greater mental health of participants and much more reality oriented methods of object choice.

In the case of Sara, intense emotional growth led to her finally deeply owning herself and providing for herself the acceptance, love and development she had been sucking from others. She went on to develop a beautiful, loving relationship with a man and even-tually was able to expand that to children and a few close friends. Of course, being emotionally healthy does not necessarily mean one is devoid of all pain. What it does insure, however, is the abili-ty to accept and work through that pain in a responsible, produc-tive fashion and move on with your life.

Sara: "Marilyn and I had been involved on a very deep feeling level for a couple of years, working both "here and now" feelings and historical feelings. She became a poten-tial 'good mommy' for me in a primal context. Her warmth, sensuality and little girl spontaneity were totally unlike my own mother's and I found this filled a deep need in me while simultaneously triggering me into deep early deprivation feelings.

At the same time, she was like my little girlfriend-sister-daughter whom I took under my wing to teach about life. Our feeling progress paralleled each other for a time although we were at different levels of maturity and integration. Often we would be working similar issues and bouncing off of each other.

At roughly the same time we both began to hit deep birth issues and started to transfer negatively onto each other. I felt a need for her to really be there for and with me in the here and now. She, on the other hand, began to feel very threatened by the idea of an intimate relationship and began to withdraw. The more she withdrew, the more negative my transference became and the more she became threatened by my rejection.

This 'acting out' phase lasted around a month before I fully hooked into my birth issue and recognized how I had symbolically been 'needing' her and laying unreal demands on her. She had not worked through the heavy interpersonal issues I had and there was not any way she could emotionally respond to me from where she was. My primal need for her had blinded me to the reality of who and where she really was. I saw her the way I needed to see her. After working through this issue myself on a very deep feeling level, I attempted to communicate this with her but her own primal issues were coming up fast and furious which made contact impossible.

She continued to act out her fear and withdrawal and eventually a split in the relationship became inevitable. As she began to feel less and less, she turned to her outside, less intense relationships for support. The weeks went by and I became clearer and clearer on our relationship and the transference that had been involved. Contact was attempted a number of times, but eventually, I had to realize that our here and now relationship was gone. I was still able to 'use' her to work a lot of historical primal pain—physical and emotional need, anger at her inability to be there fully and finally, feelings of abandonment—all tied up with mommy—but the close relationship we had been striving for was shattered.

It took me a few months to fully feel all the transferential feelings involved with her but finally, I felt fully clear in the here and now and resolved with the past. The experience, although painful, was very growth oriented and I learned not only about myself and my issues with relating to females closely but I also learned how to 'work' a relationship in a feeling sense so that I didn't lose myself in it or have to block myself away from it. I felt it all—the highs and the lows, the joys and the hurts—and then I moved on, a lot wiser and deeper in myself."

Thus, we can see that people strive for wholeness and unity not only within themselves but with significant others. Perhaps the epitome of total integration occurs between male and female in what may be termed "the perfect match." Disintegration of relationships can occur because the relationship never completely formed and did not become a total whole. In essence, significant pieces were missing. The dissolution of that relationship occurs because the individuals involved may wish to start over again in an attempt to reach that point of wholeness, cohesiveness, and structural unity that we all seek. Sara's termination of her marriage was just such a case in point. This is not to say that people need to live in a state of near perfection but viable relationships have that sense of oneness and togetherness that allows the participants to feel that they are making it or have made it.

The Total Feeling Process believes that all human beings have the capabilities to be at one with themselves and near completion with at least one other person. Hopefully, through the process of deep feeling, members can overcome a lifetime of disintegration and alienation and arrive at a point where they feel cohesive with their environment and the people in it. To that extent, self-actualized groups and families are not just a mere dream, but a real goal to be actively sought and achieved.

Chapter 15   The Positive End of the Spectrum

THE TRANSCENDENTAL EXPERIENCE

Frances Clark[1] states that, "One of the underlying assumptions of transpersonal psychotherapy is that each human being has impulses toward spiritual growth, the capacity for growing and learning throughout life and that this process can be facilitated and enhanced by psychotherapy." Most abreactive or so-called feeling therapies place great emphasis on getting in touch, releasing fully and re-connecting to old or historic pain, thus repairing the lost self. The great focus of these pains is mommy and daddy, the immediate family and other childhood experiences.[2] Other cathartic therapies, in addition, stress here and now contact feelings and dream work[3]. These areas are extremely important and must be worked thoroughly to resolution and grounding. I believe these approaches are very effective, but they do not go far enough and thus, remain incomplete.

The Total Feeling Process takes its own place as a major contribution to the ever growing fund of human knowledge. I believe that the Center for Feeling People has evolved into something new and quite extraordinary: the full utilization of deep core feeling to tap into and connect to transcendental realities. Thus, there is a progression from rigid neurosis to self-actualization and then to self-transcendence. Let me explain.

First, we believe that anything that is inside of a human being is legitimate to feel and experience and that no one thing is more important than anything else. All human experiences have feelings that are attached to them and those feelings are waiting to be expressed, connected and integrated. For too long the field of psychology has tried to divest itself from all spiritual matters and has left such things to the clergy. The problem here is that most clergymen have never fully felt that which they have been preaching about and, as such, may be the least qualified to lead people deeply into their spiritual feelings.

---

[1] Frances Clark, Ph. D., "Transpersonal Prospectives in Psychotherapy", *Journal of Humanistic Psychology*, Vol. 17, No. 2. (San Francisco, CA Spring 1977), pgs. 69-81.
[2] Arthur Janov, *Primal Scream* (New York: Dell Publishing Co., 1970).
[3] Hart and Corriere, *Going Sane* (New York: Dell Publishing Co., 1975).

Most feeling or primal type therapists and psychologists have been afraid to take their charges into anything other than those so-called rational or tangible sources, such as mom and dad. But what about God, Jesus, Moses, the Ten Commandments and the Sermon on the Mount? Aren't they just as tangible? People do choose to invest a lot of their feeling selves into these grand and marvelous sources of feeling. Freud coined the term "love object"[4] to refer to those persons, places and things in which we invest our libido. Transpersonal sources are generally considered to be objects that are loved and revered by most of society and mankind in general. They represent values, ethics and ideas that are admired and cherished for their significance to each individual soul. These sources trigger the most powerful of human drives, the energy that moves man toward constructive, life supporting goals[5]. Through such sources many people have derived sustenance and meaning to their existence.

Most neurotics and all psychotics try to get somewhere without feeling their early pain. By attempting to move on to self-actualization and the transpersonal realm, without first dealing with the realities of their life is like trying to fly with a big load in your pants. Eventually, you have to crack up, or perhaps only reach a certain height and then believe that's as high as you can go. The reality of the load in your pants restricts you from flying as high as you might.

One basic assumption of the Total Feeling Process is that human beings are starving and thirsting after spiritual growth. Even after they have worked through and felt much of their early pain, there may still exist the need to reconnect to the cosmos. Many people were not allowed to feel all the wonderful meanings and significances of their own natural, spiritual heritage. Adults in our program are beginning to feel the insults and deprivations that were inflicted under the guise of organized religion; recognizing that alienation can be inflicted by institutions, clergy, and parents alike. When one begins to connect to the real meaning of the great faiths, there is a joyful recovery of something valuable, sacred and cherished.

---

[4] Sigmund Freud, *Introduction to Psychoanalysis* (New York: Washington Square Press, 1960), pg. 427.
[5] Eric Berne, Ph. D., *Layman's Guide to Psychiatry and Psychoanalysis* (New York: Simon and Schuster, 1968), pgs. 60-67.

One woman claimed that after a twelve hour marathon, she actually felt a healing force moving through her entire being. Another woman, a therapist, began to move into one of her own heavily defended areas. As time passed, she began to experience some strong Catholic feelings. There were several other Catholics in the room and they gathered near to her. It was like being at a high Mass. I began to talk to them and soon everything exploded. All the non-Catholics gathered around and began to tune into all the Catholic pain that had been held back for years. I knew that something special was happening as there was total group involvement with this issue. It was interesting to observe that the Catholics shared one thing in common: all their repression on a particular theme was exactly the same. The organized Church had actually closed these people down to the very feelings that could have made them firm, strong believing Catholics.

One woman explained it this way:

"As I listened to the words of the old Church hymn, I found myself again bowing my head in compliance with the words; 'Oh, Lord, I am not worthy that Thou shouldst come to me . . .' How many years have I had drilled into my soul that I was an unworthy sinner from the moment of my conception on: imperfect, born in sin, doomed to Limbo, even as a newborn. This was my heritage. And I had carried these feelings of being a blemished, imperfect soul all my life."

"As the feelings welled up past my heart, I longed for the freedom of innocence and purity and unblemished beauty which must be every infants' birthright. Yet, I found myself struggling with hundreds of years of Catholic conditioning and the legacy of Original Sin. Baptism would cleanse me but the core of my soul was scarred nonetheless. So they had told me and so I had carried this secret around like a chain binding my heart. How could I explode with life, . . . with love for God, . . . or any person? . . . How could I embrace the whole world in my arms in one ecstatic moment of love and union, if my head was bowed with unworthiness, shame and withdrawal."

"At different times during my feeling growth, I have experienced this innocence and sweetness in my soul. I know it is there. And yet, I still struggle with that piece of my faith which shackled me throughout my childhood. I have yet to break through this issue emotionally and reach the peak, cosmic experience, which I know must be there, with the Universe and God. When I turn inward with my religion to explore and feel its realities for me, I am still defended, chained, angry, unworthy, and confused. The mark of my religious upbringing continues to haunt me even as its joy and simplicity and love eludes my grasp."

A similar occurrence took place in the second half of the workshop when a strong persecution issue came up with a few of the Jewish members. They began transcending their usual ego boundaries and began to feel the pains of historical persecution. The non-Jewish members fed material into the episode until it was one of the most powerful emotional scenes I have ever witnessed. It seems that every Jew carries around deep inside of himself the exact emotional history of his people. The participants re-enacted slaughters from the concentration camps and pogroms by the Cossacks that their ancestors had suffered. There were continual references to God and the plight of the Jewish people. There it was, right in front of me, full and dramatic, being experienced and realized on a transcendent level.

One can understand the formulation of character traits of particular ethnic and cultural groups, simply by examining the various forms of repressions that were earlier applied to these people that have led to them adopting certain types of character armoring. Repression is something that happens early and is usually total, painful, with information coming in and being fully imprinted upon the subconscious mind. Later, during deep feeling release, it is those very same buried feelings that are re-captured and re-connected.

The feelings experienced during a transcendental recovery are usually very powerful. In many instances, they are more powerful than other emotions. This is true because the ego and body boundaries are usually transcended and the emotions contain all the energies of history, mankind and the cosmos. This helps a person to connect to brotherhood, universal love, ethical meaning in scripture and higher levels of values. Feelings of empathy, devotion, elevation, rejuvenation, sacredness, loyalty, and pride develop.

GESTATIONAL CONNECTIONS

A client once referred to me as being god-like. I must say, that initially, I enjoyed having those qualities ascribed to myself. I do see myself as god-like, but only to the extent that any beautiful child is god-like. Upon further investigation into this patient's ascription of such power to myself, I became aware of the element of fear and separateness in her voice. To the extent that she saw me as god-like, it made me qualitatively different from her and consequently, less human. There I was, the god-like creature, and there she was with all the other ordinary people, and never the twain shall meet.

As I made my intervention into her psychic pain, she exploded into a very painful gestation experience. When she was but three or four inches long inside her mother's womb, her father was indeed quite god-like, for he had the power of life and death over her. A little fetus is totally dependent upon the decisions of all-powerful, god-like parents to render the gift of life. So it was that this little person felt the agonies of waiting and hoping that her father would decide in her favor and grant her the full potential for human existence. Her mother had chemically transmitted to her that she was not wanted[6]. This was tantamount to maternal, psychic, intrauterine abortion. Her father, on the other hand, used all of his energies to convey to that little fetus that he wanted her and was going to do everything possible to support her growing existence.

Thus, we can see that the cosmological, in-utero world of that infant contained all the god-like qualities of ultimate survival or destruction: her mother being the diety that potentially destroys and her father being the all powerful savior god.

It is not surprising to see the subtle interplay and connection between an early gestational experience and elements of the transpersonal. After all, the womb is one universe inside and part of a much larger universe. We are all cells of a larger cosmological plan.

I have long believed that all humans have within their cellular structure the exact replication and memory of the creation and evolution of the Universe and that we will, in our lifetime, discover a

---

[6] William Swartley, Ph. D., *The Undivided Self* (London, England: Churchill Centre, 1978), pgs. 33-40.

very simple exact idea of the creation of that Universe. There is a point at conception when a fertilized egg explodes into a million particles and very much resembles what the beginning of the Universe probably looked like at its conception. We are also aware that all cells contain the genetic history of each organism and that history just didn't begin with the formation of man on this planet.

Theoretically, the Universe began very small, dense and extremely hot and went through several eras in the early moments. There was far more matter and anti-matter than now survives and these particles annihilated each other, leaving a residue of protons. The lighter weighted electrons began settling down and a quarter of the matter changed into heavier helium in the first few minutes. For hundreds of thousands of years intense heat kept the Universe in a constant frenzy. As the Universe expanded, it cooled and in a great flash of light the electrons at last joined the heavy particles to make the atoms of hydrogen and helium gas.

As the Universe grew, the flash faded to become the faint background of radio energy. Given the gas and the cosmic forces, everything else followed. Gravity drew the gas into the galaxies and over a billion years passed as this gravity shovelled vast clouds of gas together, making stars. The heat of this falling matter ignited the fire of the stars. Heavier stars exploded and the weak force helped to pull together the heavy elements while scattering them through space. Gravity helped build new generations of stars now enriched with heavier dust . . . The sun was one of them and in its skirts, gravity built planets from the dust including mother Earth, which bore life.

As energy erupted volcanically from the Earth, continents shifted and collided, creating wreckage that we now call mountains. From this surface energy, atoms combined and broke apart. Sunlight aroused the electrical force and out of that chemistry sprang life.

While physicists explore the origins of the Universe and the mystery of life in their laboratories, we can draw some strong inferences from the emotional discoveries of man himself while he explores his own deeper space. Several years ago, when I was into the deepest and heaviest realms of my feelings, I connected to some very powerful emotions and scenes. I spoke of these experiences with those who were closest to me and did not try to scientifically validate the events. The feelings themselves were deep and heavy to my very core and helped transform my life. I always wondered as to the mystical nature of my connections and I must confess that my critical judgemental mind has always questioned those findings. I think now I can explain them much more clearly.

There were several episodes that stand out in my mind and have made a lasting impression. Let me state, initially, that I will not take a strong religious view as opposed to strict dogmatic scientism. I have tried to integrate faith and reason and believe I have done so, quite well. The first episode was a full, explosive body-mind-feeling experience. I literally erupted like a volcano. Vast, loud, crying screams seemed to emanate from my hips and loins and I thought that my body would turn completely inside out. Several years later, I can still recall the physical sensations of that session.

I was screaming and crying as if I were flying through the Universe, from the lap of God, trying to go through my father's body and join my mother's egg to be born. I was a small round particle that I experienced as a soul and God was a vast source of incredible white light that, peculiarly, did resemble a wise old man. I was crying in pain while screeching through space, waiting for my mother and father to decide to bear me. I was totally dependent on them to give me a body and God was a source of pure love from which my life sprang.

Infant soul transcending through the Universe . . .
Screaming my way from the lap of God
And — Stop — Short
*   at mother and father*
Who must now decide to give this soul a body . . . . .

I must wait
*   in dependence*
And then finally, a miracle occurs:
Implantation of the sperm and the egg
*   forms a new little organism, ME*
*   that swims and moves,*
*   molding and developing over time*
Evolution of men and life.
Indescrible bliss of movement and growth.
I hear the music of the Universe
Its magnificence . . . . .

Its total bliss.
All that I've learned to appreciate
in beauty and in love
Stems from this feeling, this moment in eternity
This cosmic expansion
             creation
                      life . . . .

Now, it is easy to try to interpret this experience according to its symbolism. One can say that this is a symbolic representation of a particular phase of the birth process and I would certainly agree. I did start out as a small sperm cell in my father's vast universe of reproductive tissue. I did come from his lap and he was like God to me and I ultimately united with my mother to become a totally unique person. These mechanics of reproduction can be demonstrated and proven, but we cannot prove the existence of God. We can't even prove the existence of an idea. However, since the scene did have a strong emotional component, we cannot just dismiss its meaning. I surmise that the feeling part was also a memory of actual events that took place in the Universe and that these events are not mystical but physical. The mind merely created certain mental images of those truths that the body had already experienced and still remembered emotionally.

The findings of physics and astronomy follow parallel to the total feeling experience that I have just described. At other times I have exploded so much feeling that for a brief period of time, I felt as if God was totally inside me and that I was one with Him. For that moment, I was God and there was no separation. Another time, I felt Jesus enter my body and I exploded with incredibly beautiful, screaming, cleansing emotion. These were not hallucinatory episodes nor were they drug induced. They were pure, clear, rational feelings and I might state that they represented some form of encapsulated memory that I had never been exposed to in all of my formal or informal education during this lifetime.

I am not an advocate of the current ideas that surround beliefs in reincarnation. The general associations of reincarnation do not fit into what I believe to be purely physical phenomenon. However, I do believe that every human being contains the cellular memory of the history of his family, ancestors, race, species and evolution back to the creation of the Universe. Our minds try to create some form of image to account for what our body already knows and it does not matter if those images do not duplicate exactly how we and the Universe came into existence. The Universe is not perfect and could not exist as such and neither is the mind of man. What matters is that enough people have explored themselves deeply enough to arrive at similar conclusions and even though this does not constitute proof, it certainly presents some form of consistent logic.

MYSTICISM

Mysticism, then, is a feeling just like other feelings. Experiences that individuals have that can be classified as mystical have been greatly misunderstood by the psychiatric and psychological professions. I have heard many of my learned colleagues reject and discount the entire area of psychic, mystical phenomenon. To them it is as if this area of investigation is of no considerable significance and may even border on insanity and unreality. However, the mystical experiences of people of high repute and substantial psychological health make it necessary for us to at least explore this potentially rich source of human endeavor.

I am not referring to the areas of the occult but to those phenomenon that each one of us has that points to higher and richer meanings. Mysticism is the poetry and magic of life. Without it, human life would be subverted by the boredom and colorlessness of the mundane and dull worlds of obsessed pragmatists. Mysticism is the opposite of pragmatism and yet one cannot live without the other. Elements of pragmatism and mysticism exist in all of us and when we dilute and deny either aspect of ourselves we can expect to suffer from the pain of repression.

As I have stated many times throughout this book, all pain is derived from repression. When we see clients explode from their deep core buried self, the crying that ensues is the visible aspects of the mechanics of repression. The release and breakdown of repression produces a crying that leads to deeper feeling and insights. The mystical self can also suffer from the pain of repression, and once the repression is lifted, beautiful feelings emerge. I am suspicious of certain of my colleagues who stress and emphasize only one or a few particular areas of the human psyche? Yes, I believe it is important in the early stages of therapy that patients should uncover, feel and reconnect pains of early family life and deprivation. But it can be psychotherapeutically disastrous to keep trying to bend a patient into only those areas of feelings that the therapist is familiar with[8].

If craziness and insanity is the result of repression and blocking, then feeling eliminates the craziness. For example, it is common around the Christmas season for many people to go through varying degrees of insanity. They do this either through "shopping madness," being alone or being totally out of touch with the meaning, significance and spirit of Christmas. I postulate that the true feeling of the spirit of Christmas is of a mystical nature and, as such, by feeling that same spirit one is freed of the neurosis of Christmas. There is magic and beauty in the twinkling of Christmas lights and decorations. One gets a sense of mystery, destiny and higher cosmic realities. Poetically, it is even possible to sense higher mystical beings tuning into and being attracted to the beauty and energy of Christmas lights. "Yes, Virginia, there is a Santa Claus and he is real because he lives inside of you." If he did not live inside of you, you can be sure that the Grinches and the Scrooges would get a hold of your soul.

Thus, mystical feelings allow us to emotionally reach far out into space in order to grasp something more meaningful and powerful than that which we can imagine here on Earth. So I say to my repressed, atheistic colleagues, "Where is your joy and can you dance to a tune that goes far beyond your pitiful little selves?" Pay attention to your bodies, see how your skin and your arms want to reach out and touch the magnificence of inter-stellar space. Anyone can do it.

---

[7] Arthur Janov, *Primal Scream* (Dell Publishing Co., New York, 1974).

[8] John Lonsbury, "Inside Primal Therapy", *Journal of Humanistic Psychology* (Fall, 1978, Vol. 18, No. 4) pgs 19-28.

THE POSITIVE END OF THE SPECTRUM

Traditionally, psychotherapy has dealt primarily with painful psychopathology and has largely neglected the pleasurable or fun aspects of human existence. The capacity for fun and joy in one's life depends on a willingness to explore the full range of feelings. New patients cannot help but to keep walking into old painful situations. Joy is all around them, but they cannot see it or experience it because of an extreme overload of buried feeling. People who have been into therapy for awhile begin to open up to the full pleasures and joy of life. If fun is missing, then old patterns and feelings are still operating to dominate and control one's life.

The neurotic can't feel all of life because he was robbed of life's essences as a child. He settles for half existences because of the comfort and security that a defensive half life has to offer. It is a survival at the cost of passion, intensity, and a real strong drive and desire to live a full, exciting, passionate existence. The hum drum existence of depression replaces real living in a world laced with magnificent beauty and sensuous feeling rewards.

Full feeling is the release from a prison of helpless dependency on others. If one has never had real parents to care for and love him, then life will have been literally ripped from the heart. If a parent has been emotionally missing, then a major part of a growing child's life will be missing and can only be reconstructed by feeling the excruciating pain of that early loss.

Many parents only exist for their children as mere shells of people. They never let their children relate to the real person that is buried inside. The child grows up and recreates a zombie-like existence devoid of the inner essence of having a real feeling parent. He slowly dies inside and learns not to value himself and his feeling life. He structures his world to reflect his low self-esteem and worthlessness. Since he was not highly valued as a child he grows into an adult with little self-worth. He may even accept his failure at living with pseudo-grace and defensive resignation. Consequently, he finds it difficult to see himself as a growing, changing, becoming, organic, human being and he loses all desire to really move from the inside out. Passively he waits for the great movement to be initiated from the outside.

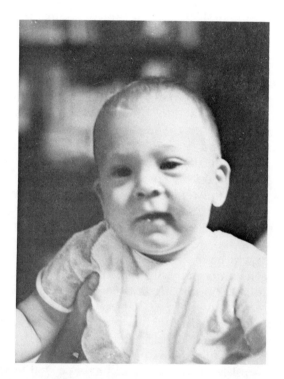

"You're my Buddha and my guru, the all knowing, wise, full of honesty and openness. It is through you that I learn about life and the Universe... You are my sweet baby boy..."

Many patients come into therapy from very insane, unfeeling lifestyles. They believe that they will go through a thing called therapy for six to eight months and come out feeling better and then return to their old life styles. There is such unrealistic hope in this system of logic. For someone to come from deadness to partial life and then to return to the deadness of one's previous existence again, is crazy. At best it represents a partial therapy and is witness to the split in the personality. It is like trying to be happy and turned on at a funeral. A person can only get as high as his environment will allow.

The task of recovery is to allow the patient to feel his anger at his own existence and also the old pain of not having his parents there for him. It is the subsequent release of feeling and the connection of insight that restores the essences of life's energy. The Total Feeling Process gradually pulls aside the defenses to deep feeling and for a period of time the client enters into a retrogressive phase of feeling. He is flooded with all the insults, deprivations, and unlovingness of his early life and their continuations into the present. He slowly gives up his hopes and his illusions about the extent of how "good" his parents, siblings, relatives, peers, etc. actually were and he becomes aware of their relative "badness" and their devastating effect on his emotional well-being. It becomes difficult to let go and give up the neurotic attachments of the past.

We must remember that he was able to half survive in his old milieu because of his defenses, but the more that he opens up and feels, the more he realizes how those people and situations contributed to his emotional downfall. During this phase, he goes through many changes that challenge all of his old beliefs about himself and the way his life has evolved and been influenced. Since he has been raised neurotically, he will live neurotically with neurotic people and struggle hopelessly to turn them from being bad to being good.

During this phase certain hidden elements of change have been at work. Even though he doggedly resists giving up past painful attachments, reconstructive influences are starting to take effect. A progressing consciousness leads him to be very aware of who and what is destroying him and he begins to differentiate the negative causes of his sickness from the positive reconstructive forces already at work providing a cure. He becomes more aware of what constitutes good parents, friends, family and group forms. There evolves an increasing awareness of another more positive way to live and the kinds of people with whom to live it. He soon begins to sense what constitutes the "good life" and starts to emotionally remove the obstacles to attaining that joy-filled existence.

Happiness and fulfillment become a possibility and as he unloads his pain, he moves closer to that realization. While he is still loaded with old feelings it may be difficult to let go and have fun and experience pleasure. Most neurotics need drugs (i.e., alcohol, pot, cigarettes, tranquilizers, etc.) to loosen up enough to enjoy sex, good company, conversation and laughter. If someone cannot make full contact in the present, it is because his unfelt past is still holding him back. Certain individuals have more pain to feel before they can enjoy the fruits of life. But as soon as that regressive phase reaches its peak and starts to diminish, new and more positive deep core feelings are experienced. The negative parental introjects give way to positive parental introjects and the patient begins to fully appreciate every aspect of his existence.

To discover what people really want and need to make them happy and capable of experiencing pleasure, we surveyed a section of the Total Feeling Community. We asked each member to write down, as a male or female, what they needed, wanted and expected from members of the opposite sex. After this task was accomplished a great many feelings came pouring out and the connections were quite revealing. A general conclusion gleaned from the data suggested that when these wants, needs and expectations were not met, fighting, arguing, withdrawal, and various forms of acting out would occur.

We have included several of the participants' responses in order to discover the trends.

> Carl: "I want to be looked up to and desired . . . I want my jokes laughed at . . . I want to be touched . . . I want understanding and concern."
>
> Irv: "I want warmth and honesty . . . mutual trust . . . respect and loyalty."
>
> Bob: "I like women to relate to my male power and not be afraid of it."
>
> Laura: "I want friendship from members of the opposite sex . . . I don't want to be one step down . . . I need a man who

really values me . . . I expect consideration."

Jane: "I want to be valued. I want to feel important—like I'm good for something. I want to be taken care of, emotionally and sexually."

Sarah: "I want total commitment to a contactful, fully feeling relationship . . . I need tons of affection and body contact. I want genuine caring and warmth for little me and gusty appreciation and enjoyment of big me. I want to play and be played with."

The women in the survey seemed more accepting of their little girl needs and spaces than males did of their little boy spaces. Most of the male needs were focused on here and now symbolic adult gratification (i.e., understanding, catering to him, wrestling, some touching and massage). Women also wanted to be catered to and wanted patience and understanding, but they specified a desire for cuddling and affection, playing, recognition of their softness as well as a need to be protected at times.

The males wanted acceptance for their power. They didn't want competition or castration. Women seemed to want that power to lean on and get support from and yet they also challenged it when they were struggling with their own power and insecurities. There seemed to be a need for and a fear of power at the same time, as well as a resentment (if there were heavy brother or father issues involved).

The women in the survey seemed to want to be "claimed" more than men who just want to be desired. Women wanted a friend in a male, where men were asking for loyalty. An equality factor existed with the women—"love and value me as much as I do you"—while men wanted to be respected more and looked up to. Part of a woman's view of being confirmed was to be "claimed" by the man she loved and desired. She wanted to be admired and desired physically by him more than any other female. In other words, seen as his "special girl." She wanted all of her to be loved as a woman. "Eat me up—all of me. Don't hold back your desire for me. Confirm my power and abilities. Be proud of me."

Men wanted to be looked up to and respected. They, too, wanted to be confirmed, loved and lusted after physically and sexually, especially their sexual organs.

301

We chose to seek out the wishes and desires that people had for members of the opposite sex because in the progressive reconstructive phases of therapy, people often seek out therapeutic love relationships with potential mates. This shows itself in a growing consciousness of good re-mothering and re-fathering by a peer partner. As the neurosis slips in and out, these love objects glide between being good and bad parents as the above needs and wants are met and answered. During this process the client is also discovering the goodness and badness of his own biological parents and this helps to strip him of his illusions and beliefs about himself, his life and his relationships.

We further explored members of the Feeling Community to discover what aspects of their life made them high. The responses were varied and ranged from here and now quiet times with nature and loved ones to intense feeling connection and release.

". . . wind in my face . . . when my husband and I are both clear and feeling great about ourselves and each other at the same time . . . after a heavy feeling when I really feel myself and I'm my own special friend . . . when I realize the changes I have made internally over the past few years . . . when I make some clear, beautiful contact with my kids . . . breaking through my heavy anger and rage and making a connection . . . after some very productive activity where I get many things out in the open, organized and accomplished . . . dancing and music . . . good and plentiful sexual contact . . . healthy foods clearing my body . . . laughter and jokes with my friends . . . being alive!! . . ."

Even exciting and dynamic human beings may go through periods of feeling relatively dull and lifeless. Energy can reach a low, emotionally dead, boring level and there may be a need to charge an individual's internal atmosphere—that is to turn them on to themselves, get them high, open and enjoying themselves. Lifting the spirit will occur through the dynamic interplay of people responding and contacting one another. Dull, lifeless humans sometimes forget that a good part of life can be a celebration of laughter and joy and that people can make contact through fun and play.

Intense feeling breakthroughs and resolution lead to the potential of a full peak experience which can represent a supreme moment in time for a particular person. It is one of the happiest, blissful, ecstatic, joyous moments of life. The rapture of the experience leaves a formative impression on the personality of the individual and serves as a reference point for recall, reassessment and re-affirmation.

"My biggest 'highs' have always been within the group setting—a feeling high. Those are the grandest of them all. I am on top of the world, the Universe—my heart swells with joy—I become a child of the Universe."

In Total Feeling marathon groups a peak experience usually occurs when every member has felt and resolved something very deep from their past and then makes full contact with all other participants, while feelings reach a peak crescendo. The sensations are so powerful that the members are literally "blown away" with happiness and contact. For those who have never delved deeply into themselves and experienced their full emotional potential, the idea of such powerful contact might seem bizarre or unfathomable. The language might appear exaggerated or unknown. But feelings have a language all their own, as uncensored and demonstrative as a little child. It is necessary to let the feelings speak for themselves.

Sarah: "I felt very open to everyone: no inhibitions, no defenses, just an outpouring of warmth. There was no holding back. I felt a real desire to make contact while at the same time feeling incredibly supportive of people, encouraging them to let themselves pour out. I felt caring and grounded, and later was very playful in the pool. For those moments I knew what it was all about . . . First, I made loving contact with my husband. I sat with him, looking into his face and crying with my love for him. Then I took his hand and we went around to share it with all the other people. The whole group was embracing in a circle of feeling. Everyone was crying deeply and every few seconds someone else would pour out with more feeling . . . It was ecstatic, exhiliarating . . ."

Pete: "Before I connected fully with the group, I felt irresistably drawn to a baby picture of myself. As I kept staring at the beautiful fat little baby, Me, I began to open up and tremendous rushes of feeling came pouring out. It was as if a volcano was erupting and blowing out of me. I began to scream and choke and cry like I had never done before. I was crying for that little infant, Me. I began wretching and screaming; nothing came out except pure, beautiful feeling. I felt as if I was turning inside out. I thought my asshole was going to fly out of my mouth and my eyes would bug right out of my sockets. The feelings kept coming and the more I looked at the picture, the more I screamed and cried. It was incredible! Nothing but pure energy, nothing but pure feeling Me, as I experienced the wonder of myself. I was all there. My wife looked at me and began triggering off into her own feelings. Others were blowing into feelings, just looking at me. I got up and took my wife's hand and we walked over to a couple of other people. Crying all at one time, we made deep eye contact and more feelings came pouring out. We embraced, held each other, cried, and then we all went over to other people and made more contact while feelings continued to pour out . . . Soon the whole group was in one huge feeling embrace and the intensity was astounding . . . We were all together in this whirling pool of intense emotion . . . Everyone was crying, embracing and sweating. We were one universal body . . . one soul . . . one universe . . . And then it went to a very high peak and we were soaring with each other . . . It was incredibly unbelievable . . . to be fully and jubilantly alive."

Polly: "The marathons are a chance for me to make loving, intense contact with people that I have learned to care for through feeling interaction. It is 48 hours of feeling, eating, playing, sleeping in the same room and being fully myself with others who wish to feel and live deeply and honestly. It is one of my most cherished times, for it not only gives me this concentrated contact with other feeling people, but it gives me a chance to work deeply with myself over a long period of time. The joy, the contact, the intensity are mind-blowing . . ."

Shana: "Saturday was filled with many different spaces. At one point I was tripped off by a song 'Having My Baby' by Paul Anka. The words filled me with longing for my own baby growing inside me and I was drawn across the room to my husband. 'I want your baby, my love . . . I want a little baby you or me . . . I want your love inside me . . .' As I cried these words to him, I was filled with unbelievable love and warmth toward this man, my husband. I felt opened up to myself and to him as I poured out my heart. He was feeling and expressing his own love for me and after a few minutes, we both spontaneously stood up, hand in hand, and began walking around to other people in the group sharing our love for them on a very deep feeling level. Their crying joined ours as we walked around drawing more and more people into our circle of love. Soon we were all together, looking in each other's eyes, loosening, melting away defenses, opening up our hearts with sobs of love and caring for each other. Eyes meeting, words mouthed above the crying, hugging, laughing, sobbing—an explosion of energy and contact. On and on it went, as I found myself, time and time again, reaching into my guts and exploding out my affection for these people. So much I have shared with them. And so much of themselves they have shared with me. I felt at that moment fully capable of loving . . ."

"This explosion of deep core feeling was catipulated, soon after, into a playful, joyful burst of child-like energy. The pool became a churning wild mass of splashing, laughing children as we released our joy with each other and opened up to more contact on a different level. The world of play . . . I felt playful and free and grounded in myself. I felt rich with all that I was becoming . . ."

CREATIVITY AND FEELING

When energy and feeling come to a standstill, frustration sets in and creativity becomes blocked. Many people who are very, very neurotic seem to lack spontaneity and creativity. I would postulate that the creative core of any individual becomes expressed, not from the tangle of neurosis, but from the clear, feeling spaces of the core self. That is why it is very common to see patients who unload most of their pain become much more creative in their everyday endeavors.

We can watch certain types of neurotics be totally uncreative and unimaginative in their personal lives and inter-personal relationships, yet at the same time be very creative, freed up and imaginative in their work lives. Thus, energy bound up in one area may not be bound up in another. Many others are very successful in their personal and interpersonal lives, but lack creativity and are blocked in other facets of their existence. Buried, unfelt pain creates neurosis, binds up feeling and blocks creativity. As more and more pain gets eradicated, it seems that creativity breaks out all over. A well-rounded and integrated human being is not only creative in the interpersonal and personal realms, but is quite expressive in other areas as well.

A feeling person creates, innovates and exists from a deeper and more meaningful level. He never does anything from his head alone. He will only be moved by primal energy from his deep intuitive self, his soul that creates. Craziness is nothing more than bound up feelings that block the true expression of one's deeper self. And it is deep core feeling expression that knocks away these blockages to creativity and release.

A free feeling human being will create music, art, film, pictures, buildings, stories, books, etc. from the very core of his being. Each new creative discovery can be a product of a released feeling. Every song, poem, picture, etc. has a feeling in it waiting to be recognized and felt. Since neurosis is also a form of inhibition of creativity, we witness many clients feeling totally shut down, with very little creativity seeping from their buried potentials. We have found that full potential can only be realized by the breakthrough of feeling.

Henry came into therapy because at the age of 28 his life had come to a standstill. He was a failure in almost every aspect. He could never succeed in establishing any kind of relationship with a woman. He held down a job that was not particularly exciting although he felt somewhat secure in it. Before entering therapy he contracted a skin cancer and after the cancer was removed, he was left with an intense fear that it would come back again and kill him. I don't wish to go into the feeling dynamics of his cancer, as I will save that for later, perhaps in some other book.

The point is that he had experienced some mild success and gratification from being a former professional musician. Much of his creative music, however, came out of his heavy depression. His songs were sad and filled with longing and pain. He knew that there was another side of himself that was not being expressed in his music. But, of course, he had to deal with first things first.

During the initial months of his therapy, he had no desire to play or create any more music. This is quite common. It would seem that he would have to clean up much of the emotional pain that was symbolized in his music, before he could create from the other unintegrated parts of himself. I have seen many people who are in the throes of unfelt suffering and agony become very creative. However, their creativity was merely a partial message as to their real suffering and unfelt pain. When they began dealing directly with that pain in a deep feeling way, their creativity would go into a state of limbo, only to come out again later in a different, more meaningful way.

The following is just such an example.

"When I was nineteen or twenty, I was leader of a rock and roll band. I was imaginative and somewhat entertaining, but I immitatively played other people's music. My improvisations on the saxophone were good, but nothing to rave about."

"I eventually gave up music and show business to go to college. I even sold my tenor saxophone for a night course. Years later during my training as a therapist, I blew into some feelings which connected me to the great alto saxophonist, Charlie Yardbird Parker. Somehow at that level I identified with him . . . It was enough to motivate me to head on down to a South Street pawn shop in Philadelphia to buy an alto saxophone, Charlie's instrument. I didn't play it much then but I kept it buried in my soul.

After exploding out much of my gut feelings, I went through a period where the poet in me emerged. I never ever knew he was there. In college, I had hated poetry. I couldn't stand reading other people's works, but when my own poetry started coming out, I flipped. It kept coming and coming, and each work was from a deep feeling. (I have included some of those poems in this book.)

Finally one night, 20 years after my sojourn as a professional musician, I broke out the alto saxophone and started playing. Within 3 or 4 days I was playing better than I ever had when I was younger. A friend of mine and fellow therapist joined me with his guitar and by the fourth night, eight or nine songs had come pouring out of me . . . all from the deep realms of that deep place that I call 'ME.'

I couldn't play anybody else's music anymore. I couldn't sing anybody else's songs either. It was absolutely amazing to me that I could sing at all. I didn't write the songs I sang. I sang them as they came out of my soul. Each melody, every lyric was stylistically different from every other. There was no redundancy. I didn't even go back and write the songs down. They were all put on tape, just as we made them."

"All this was accomplished on the fourth night after three nights of just playing around. I didn't know this stuff was in me. We made songs about my little son Adam, 'Anita Bryant,' 'Funky Depression,' 'Jamming,' 'My Girl Susan,' etc. It didn't stop there. It spread to other areas, such as 35mm photography, film and video work; we were even doing comedy. And, of course, I eventually began writing this book. It was a contagious epidemic of creativity and all of it came from feelings."

So, we can postulate that deep core feeling is the well-spring of all creation and creativity. I become totally dismayed when I hear and witness proponents of Eastern mysticism relegate feeling and human emotion to just one other faculty of the human creature. They fail to see that human emotion is the core essence of all human endeavor and creations. That is not to say that I don't agree with part of their position. Mixed-up, incomplete and unfelt feeling is not of core essence. If that is what the mystics object to when instructing their pupils "not to be a slave to their emotions," I would agree. Many people are slaves to their unexpressed, mixed-up, symtomatic feelings, but no one can be a slave to his free flow-ing, deeper and higher feeling self. It is impossible to be a slave to who one really is—that would be just another split. One is either himself or he is not. In that case he is something or someone other than himself. Since the self is endowed with the absolute and com-plete knowledge of the Universe and all of creation, we once again come back to the source which is ourselves and in complete connec-tion with all of existence.

Chapter 16 Dealing With the Future

DEALING WITH THE FUTURE

"Old age has its perils and these perils may be visited upon the self and others. A life without growth, feeling and critical self-examination may lead to the quagmire of stagnation and alienation[1]." Thus, one will inevitably age prematurely if he is entrenched in neurotic and outmoded value systems. If one is engaged in humanistic self-pursuit, he will mature into states of wisdom and be capable of generating that wisdom to the next generation to follow. A life of feeling keeps one vital, open and subject to the critical examination of debilitating, reactionary value systems.

To grow old gracefully is to allow oneself to be influenced and vulnerable to new and emerging values and ideas. If one were to resist such a need for change and accommodation, then that person might expect estrangement from his fellow man.

There used to be a saying, "Never trust anyone over thirty." Of course, those of us who were over thirty didn't wish to be generalized, discriminated and rejected by the young. But a reciprocal kind of thing began to happen coming from the other end of the aging spectrum. Many older folks, feeling the loss of their own physical prowess, develop near paranoic fears of the aggressions of younger people. What were once liberal minded, tolerant individuals, now become racially bigoted, near Hitlerian reactionary patriots. They make the character, Archie Bunker, look like Mickey Mouse.

While the old may fear rejection by the young, the young find themselves bearing the guilt-slinging attacks of the neurotically aged. Insanity in the aged is a real problem and comes about as a result of failure to take care of one's emotional business. In American culture, the aged demand care and respect but many of their children cannot give them these sentiments because they don't feel caring and respectful towards them. It is my awareness that all human beings want to love and respect one another but neurotic estrangement gets in the way. Through deep feeling all humans can share a common feeling humanity and level the myriad of human "manufactured" differences. This does not negate the fact

---

[1] E. H. Erikson, *Identity Youth and Change* (New York: Norton and Co., Inc., 1968).

that even though older adults might wish to make some kind of contact with their aging parents, those who have felt a large part of themselves soon learn that feelings have put them into a different world than the one inhabited by their parents.

Many non-feeling adults do not even realize that they are entrapped in their parent's destructive, domineering value system. One thirty-seven year old patient traveled 2,000 miles to see his parents and he reports on the conflicts:

"My father kept praising and attacking me and he didn't even know it. He would build me up, then tear me down. My mother criticized my long hair and when I got angry, she attacked me for using a four letter word. I couldn't wait . . . I felt I had to explode . . .

They kept slinging guilt at me. He would say, 'I'm your father, you owe me something.' My mother would cut off his balls and he, like a pussy, would stay with her and defend the bitch. It's incredible how crazy they are. They keep trying to interfere in my life and tell me how to do things even though I never ask them for help. They give me such aggravation. They show no *real* interest in where I am in my life, yet they keep pushing themselves on me. I don't need them yet they want me to need them just so they can feel valuable.

They can't even live and run their own lives . . . They hate and need each other . . . it's sickening. They attack my lifestyle and friends; they see evil in everything . . . It blows my mind how they are so hostile . . . They hate foreigners, blacks, chicanos . . .

My father is crazy. He thinks that this is his country and everybody else should get out. His mind sees everything as a con, a gimmick, a salespitch. 'Doctors are all crooks' . . . She complains about all his faults and constantly busts his nuts . . . It goes on and on . . .

How can I respect them? . . . They close their eyes to everything and try to control everyone . . . They are full of words, beliefs and myths, yet empty of any real feelings. They are incapable of growing from where they are. They are stag-

"Everytime I look into his face, I feel how much I needed my own father... How much I needed him. Without him I felt very alone..."

nant . . . dead. I know that I never want to grow old that way. God, help me if I do."

WHERE DO WE GO FROM HERE?

One of the questions we try to deal with in the Total Feeling Process is "Where do we go from here?" How do we take what we've learned and vitalize it in a society that is in desperate need of reform? How do we confront old value systems, old established modes of living and beliefs and change these into a more feeling oriented way of life? In the remainder of this chapter we will be taking a look at a few of the areas that are in dire need of revitalization and feeling consciousness. They are steeped in tradition, mythology, beliefs, values, taboos, prejudice, regimentation and specialization. In many ways they are "untouchable," yet they need, desperately, to be "touched" by those with insight, sensitivity and a creative dream of what it *could be* like. That dream of youth, to make it a better world does not have to die in a "quagmire of stagnation and alienation." It does not have to wither under the defeat and frustration of life's "hard knocks." Feeling can and does keep the dream alive—into middle age, into old age—hopefully, into reality.

FEELING EDUCATION

What is education? The moment that each of us is born, we are confronted with a major performance demand: be intelligent. This expectation is fostered on us by our parents and a society that highly values a supremely efficient brain. We are perceived as being able to function and survive more proficiently if our brains are highly developed and tuned. The I.Q. test is an index of how well one performs in various intellectual performance tasks and supposedly the higher the I.Q., the more intelligent one is.

Second to the brain, society and parents place high value on the body. The body functions in several ways. First, there is the aesthetic appeal, with great emphasis on appearance, good looks and a pleasingly symmetrical physique. Children learn early that the way they look and present themselves will gain them considerable attention. Little girls learn that seductiveness, cuteness and coyness are feminine skills that bring considerable rewards.

313

Little boys are rewarded for obvious displays of masculine behavior, such as hard muscles, agility, and potential penis size.

Another function of the body is to provide locomotion for proficiency at work. One needs a body to produce and provide support and nurturance for physical needs. Without a well trained adequate body a farmer cannot farm, a writer cannot write, a cook cannot cook. So the body carries out the purposes of the brain in order to serve the individual's purpose seeking goals. Thus, intellect and the body are sources of high attention reward from the crib onward and we spend most of our early years in a school setting in order maximize these qualities.

Yet, I have always wondered how many children actually liked school. In every setting where I have raised this question, the overwhelming response has been negative. Most, although not all, children hate school and the vast majority of adults that I have talked to look back at their own schooling with some disdain. "The only time that I liked school was when I was playing with the other kids" . . . "I do not have any fond memories of learning anything in the classroom. I really taught myself what I wanted to know."

Now, I know personally that I love learning and I also know that children crave and hunger to explore and learn. Then why is it that the same institutions that are supposed to provide an opportunity for children and adults to learn only elicit negativity from their clients? It would bother me if the readers of this book did not really want to read and learn from these pages, but were only doing so because someone required it. Likewise, it would be a shame if a student were forced into studying this work. Then it would be a resented performance task which could arouse extensive anxiety.

I am not advocating the abolition of forced performative learning tasks. I would prefer that the demand for learning arise from within the individual, however, rather than be imposed by an outside authority figure such as demanding parents or mass production learning mills. The schools that are being constructed today have the look and feel of high output factories. We are mass producing computerized scholars in an educational system that houses 30 to 50 children in a classroom. Individualized instruction is rare and the expenditure of teacher energy frequently falls into the categories of control, administrative paper work and hit and miss lecturing. Unfortunately this vast expenditure of human effort has fallen far short of the hopeful goals. Mass education has not

eradicated poverty, crime or warfare and it is doubtful if it even
has produced an enlightened population.

What has gone wrong? The world has neglected the most powerful of all the human faculties . . . Feeling. Human emotions have
been relegated to the bottom rung of the ladder. People don't even
know what real feelings are. They mistake intellectual descriptions
of sensations for feelings rather than experiencing the fullest and
deepest measure of their gut reactions. Most parents are quite unfeeling themselves yet they will delude themselves into thinking that
they are feeling. But the truth stands in evidence, because most
parents do not help their children nurture and explore their feeling
souls. They are so concerned with intelligence, appearance and
behavior, that they totally overlook their children's feeling reactions. They treat their offspring as inferior, non feeling objects,
rather than human beings with emotions that need to be felt and expressed. Most kids grow up wondering if anyone ever really *cares*
about how and what they *feel* inside themseleves. Parents and
teachers spend inordinate amounts of time on children's mental per-
formances yet practically no time at all on their emotional growth.

The Total Feeling Process hopes to reverse this deadly trend. As an
outgrowth of feeling exploration, we are encouraging an educational institution that is far different from the conventional educational establishment. Feelings must come first and the priorities
change. Education through feeling is very difficult for most
neurotics, because they are so used to the old ways that emphasize
smartness at the expense of feeling. They have learned to get attention and reward for being bright rather than for being a more sensitive, integrated human being. The moment that a person accepts
feelings as the prime value, he tends to respond to others by the
breadth and depth of their feelings. Thus, feeling people want to be
with other feeling people and they find it distasteful to be involved in
a non-feeling situation. The world is full of intellectualizers and
bright people who speak as if they were disconnected from
themselves. One can only come to such an end if he has been raised
in an environment where integrative core feelings were largely ignored and denied. Perhaps this is the travesty of American life, with
its soaring crime rate, general malaise and disillusionment. That is
why feeling education becomes the only alternative.

There are no degrees awarded for the attainment of certain
levels of feeling awareness, however. If feeling became a principle

value, we would be performing a revolution in the way people live and educate themselves. Knowledge would burst forth from the pleasurable wells of feeling experience and would remain a lasting, permanent part of the whole person. When insightful reality is experienced in this core fashion, the student will naturally gravitate to those areas of learning that he truly yearns for. Learning, in this sense, becomes a felt experience rather than a despised imposition.

Each one of us has been in formal educational settings for 5-6 hours a day for at least 10-20 years of our lives, having information drummed into our heads with little regard about how we have felt about what was being done to us. The rational myth behind this system is that the child will grow up and appreciate what parents and society have given him. If we must inflict this method upon our children, at least let us provide some form of feeling education to keep pace with intellectual inculcation. Otherwise, our children will grow up and perhaps even be educated, but emotionally and interpersonally they will be crazy. Affective research bears out that when one feels clear enough, he will seek out knowledge naturally and learn what is really appropriate for him to become happy.

Thus, at the Center for Feeling People, we are developing the equivalent to a feeling university without the connotation of a university. Someday we may even award degrees or certificates for levels of emotional attainment. Our society and our colleges do not give ritualistic confirmation for feeling, but perhaps that might be a future worthwhile endeavor. There is a dearth of tests to measure what one has learned in a given subject matter, but we have yet to devise equivalent measures of emotional achievement.

MEDICAL PRACTICES

The effects of a standard hospital birth have been discussed at length in the chapter on Gestation and Birth. The need for educated, emotionally clear parents who can establish an atmosphere of gentle sensitivity and support for their baby is a high priority if we are to help eradicate early trauma in future generations of children. Unfortunately, modern science has created a monster in the name of medical advancement. Yes, we have sterilized our delivery rooms and removed the high percentage of death for mother and child alike in the childbearing situation. But, in the process we have also removed the personal touching and caring that is so emotionally vital for a healthy child. Assembly-line hospitals, an increased percentage of unnecessary inductions and C-section deliveries, an irresponsible abundance and availability of anesthetic drugs to be showered and often pushed on an uneducated mother in labor, all contribute to the traumatizing and mistreatment of newborn infants. The motives for these technological advancements may have been positive but the end results have brought about an emotional national disaster.

And the problem does not stop in the delivery room. Nursery procedures are notoriously harsh, rough, loud and impersonal. Glaring overhead lights, tight binding, loud equipment clatter and a restriction of visiting rights by the parents leave the newborn infant vulnerable, alone and, more often than not, terrified.

Universally, pediatricians seem to agree that it is preferable to perform substantial amounts of preventative medicine on postnatal infants rather than on older children; the rationale being that children need time to accumulate overloads of pain and fear which might interfere with the carrying out of such medical practices. Unfortunately, this overload can result if little children are not allowed to integrate their early painful bouts with life.

A new baby is totally unsuspicious, innocent and susceptible. He does not have the cognitive and perceptive apparatus to anticipate pain. He knows what he likes and dislikes. Pediatricians, therefore, find that it is much easier to immunize infants during the first early months of life, rather than later on when they can perceptually see that they might be hurt. This early, traumatic situation can condition a person for life, especially if that early pain is not integrated properly. A two month old baby can go into a doctor's office relatively fearless, because he has not had enough time to build up negative associations with that situation. If he is mistreated enough over a period of time, however, without proper parental caring and support in the doctor's office, at the age of two he may show intense fear at the prospect of visiting the doctor. An insensitive population may pinpoint this fear at this point and argue that this is why it is better to immunize small infants over larger children.

Small infants are not necessarily more courageous than their older counterparts; it simply means that they don't have anticipatory anxiety. Many pediatricians argue, without batting an eye, that small babies will quickly forget early physical pain. But can we state unequivocally that infants forget bad experiences bet-

ter than older children? Contemporary research seems to negate
that fact.* In many cases it seems to depend upon how the parents
handle the situation. I, personally, did not like it when my little
boy was stuck with so many needles by an overly cautious medical
profession. I swore that he would never be stuck again until he
could adequately integrate the experience.

But what about the real prospect of contracting a dangerous
disease? Perhaps we really need more data on the infantile emotional components of disease susceptibility. To put in another way,
we do not have enough research data on the children of clear feeling
people versus neurotic couples. We can only make assumptions and
theorize that their immunity levels might be higher and their con-
stitutions sturdier. Can these sturdy babies survive without the implementation of some crude medical practice? Or do we subject
them to precautionary, painful medical procedures and run the risk
of subsequent emotional damage? Can loving parents overcome the
effects of medical insult, even when given for the child's own
"good"? The question here is will medical insult remain specifically
focused on that particular situation or will it generalize to the
parent/child relationship and thus, effect his overall personality?

One further area of early infant medical intervention surrounds
the practice of circumcision. I am choosing to explore this area in a
very personal way in order to share with the reader one person's
struggle in coming to terms with this ancient religious, medical and
social practice. It is one man's quest for what was right for his son
and himself and how he attempted to deal with this in a feeling way.

"For two days before the baby's circumcision, I was feeling
ambivalent and mixed. In my heart I didn't want my baby to
be cut and subjected to that pain. He was so helpless and
dependent. Did I have the right to tamper with something so
beautiful, pure and innocent? I talked to the nurses and doctors in the hospital about it and they unanimously and
vehemently advocated having him circumcised. The more I
talked to them, the more they were convinced that newborn

---

* Infants remember primarily psychoneurologically or perhaps, more accurately, biophysically. The older child
remembers conceptually.

infants do not experience or remember physical pain before six weeks of age."

"Inside of me, I couldn't believe them. I went through all the arguments for and against the procedure and I knew I had to make a decision soon. In Judaism, for a male to be uncircumcised, is practically a sin and a direct disobedience to God. The biblical injunction to have males circumcised at eight days of age was to reinforce and confirm the child's commitment and loyalty to Abraham's covenant with God. Could I go against this 4,000 year old inviolable, traditional law? Could I risk an act of disloyalty to the clan? As far as I knew, no Jew had ever openly rebelled against this savage ritual.

After I had eliminated all the hygienic and health fallacies of the benefits of the act, I was faced with the stark anticipation of the potential social implications. How would the child feel growing up with an uncircumcised penis, knowing that there was a physical difference between himself, his father and his peers? Would he feel strange, deprived and inferior without his "Badge of Judaism." Would he be rejected by women who have been conditioned to like the circumcised member? Many females have come to regard the circumcised penis as esthetically more appealing in the mature male. What about male liberation?

The pressure towards circumcision mounted. My wife had been raised a Catholic and in reality, the baby was a hybrid mixture of different stocks. It was incredible to me that my wife and I were both pretty much in the same place with the whole affair. After all the therapy and feeling that we both had been through and all the patients that we had worked with, we had to reach a fast conclusion because the 'Mohel' (one who performs ritual circumcision) was soon to be here. We had witnessed many people work through much early pain yet, in our experience, we had seldom seen core feelings that had to do strictly with physical pain. It was always the meaningful, associative emotional pain that seemed to have impact on the individual, rather than the physical aspects. In most cases, it was the painful meaning of the act, rather than the act itself. I, personally, had gone back and re-felt my own circumcision and the physical sensation did not compare with the powerful emotional meanings of that event."

I, personally, have seen patients go back and re-experience physical injuries manifested physically in the present. But in the Total Feeling context what they usually feel are the emotional meanings of those past events rather than the full physical pain of those injuries. There are some physical sensations, but the overwhelming pain is emotional. This does not negate the fact that, in some circumstances, emotional deprivation can intensify physical pain in a young child. In such cases, an adult regressing back to these early scenes will feel intense amounts of physcial as well as emotional pain.

There is no way that a baby can understand and integrate all the social, psychological and religious ramifications of ritual circumcision. But everything that occurs and that is present at that scene, including the meanings, gets recorded somewhere in his body, to be fully felt at a later date. What he does feel is extreme physical pain and his ability to overcome and integrate this experience depends upon how strongly his mother and father have been there for him during, before, and after birth and the circumcision.

"Both my wife and I had been there for our son during his gestation period and his birth. Would we now foul up the perfectly good foundation that we had given him during birth by exposing him to a barbaric circumcision? I knew that he would experience some pain with the event, but I hoped that his basic sturdiness would help him through.

The day of the Brith (a Jewish ritual circumcision and confirmation of Abraham's covenant with God) found me experiencing a great deal of anxiety, but I felt that we all would have to go through with it, so as to prevent him from having some social trauma when he grew up. I didn't want him to feel deprived and strange for not being circumcised. At the same time, four thousand years of tradition were leaning heavily on me as were the pediatric and medical professions.

The Feeling Community was present at the ceremony and everyone was experiencing dread. This was supposed to be a happy occasion, according to tradition . . . a celebration. It was more like a funeral. The Mohel arrived and experienced discomfort in this unusual setting. No one was celebrating and he tried to cheer us up, but to no avail. His jokes fell flat and the usual denial of what was about to happen didn't work.

I felt my anger rising and *subtly* directed at the Mohel. It wasn't really his fault. He was merely carrying out and obeying his tradition. We were both victims of an outdated practice that served an ancient purpose. I now know that that ancient purpose can be realized without the physical act of circumcision. It is not through a man's penis that he connects to the Universe and God, but only through his heart. My son's pain taught me that; unfortunately, too late.

If the beauty of God and the Cosmos is not felt in the heart and soul, then a meaningless ritual is not going to put it there. An uncircumcised and untampered penis is far more beautiful than a cut, bleeding one, with the child in pain. Circumcision is major surgery and when the Mohel performed his task, my child screamed from his own primal depths. He was hurt to the core and at that moment I was consumed with soothing him and taking away this awful pain. My wife and I began an outpouring of love onto him and in a few moments he was sucking for dear life on the one thing in the Universe that he could count on, his mother's breast.

He seemed to settle down in the warmth and security of her bosom. Would her love for him carry him through this awful experience? My mind was worried. What have we done? How will this brutality affect this once perfect and sturdy little human being? He had taken everything so well up to this point and seemed to have integrated it all. Would this be too much for him? It was too much for me. My wife was deeply wounded by the experience and many of the other group members were visibly shaken.

I waited over the next few days to see if there was any difference between the post and pre-circumcision. I wanted to see if there would be a change in his sleep pattern and the way he related to his mother's breast. Had there been such an outpouring of adrenalin that it would affect him for life? Could I remedy with love what had happened to him?

We did notice some slight changes in his behavior the next day or two. He seemed to defend himself with his legs as if he were trying to kick anybody away from him who might hurt him. He definitely was different and we were worried. The day after the Brith, I hit the floor in pain and the piece that I didn't have before came to me. I cried over the immorality of the act and felt that it would have been absolutely right for me to rebel against the commandment. I knew that I would have to fight with God, if necessary, and that I would . . . for myself, my wife, my son and for posterity, if need be.

It was wrong to subject him to the circumcision. I knew that now. His response had taught me. If he grew up uncircumcised, I would be there for him, helping him to accept and feel proud of his penis. I would confirm him and let him know that his penis was beautiful just the way it was and that there would be no sin against God nor would he be "cast out of Israel." If he wanted to be Jewish, Christian or whatever, that would be his choice and no authority other than himself could ordain him. If there was any ordaining to be done it would be by his parents and we would ordain him to be just himself."

We have no clear cut conclusions as to the effects of the circumcision on this baby, because we have not been able to separate the variables involved in molding his behavior at this present age.

"The psychological and stress consequences of early circumcision are just now coming under investigation. Yvonne Brackbill finds that circumcised baby boys show greater increases in heart rate in response to sounds than do girls and uncircumcised boys. Luther Talbert and his colleagues find that after circumcision, male babies show increased adrenal cortical hormone levels—hormones known to increase in response to stress. And after circumcision, T.F. Anders and R.J. Chalemian report, male babies change their sleep patterns, staying awake for longer periods of time than they did before the operation. Other researchers have found that male babies, at three weeks and at three months of age, cry more and sleep less than females and are harder to console when they get irritable. In short, infants are put under stress by the operation, and the potential effects of such stress should not be ignored[2]."

---

[2] K. E. Paige. "The Ritual of Circumcision" *Human Nature*, Vol. 1, No. 5 (May 1978), pgs. 40-48.

As this piece was written, it had been six days since the circumcision and it was concluded that there had been some effect as a result of the operation. An hour after the surgery, he opened his eyes and his mother saw fear in his face and eyes and his father noticed that he did not smile as often as he did after his birth. He seemed to be clinging more to his mother's breast. This may have been due to natural development but I have to consider the incredible insult that he had undergone.

The following are excerpts from the mother and other group members who were present at the circumcision. The emotional experience was intense for all involved and gave greater insight into the physical and emotional trauma of this early medical practice. The horror, anger and outrage that emerged from witnessing this barbarism gave rise to a more sensitized and aware group of people. It is sad that one has to learn through another's pain.

Mother: "Every time I think of the circumcision last week I shudder. My baby was so totally open and trusting and the act was so savage, brutal and inhumane . . . I felt my stomach sink as the Mohel arrived. I just knew it was going to be bad.

As he came into the house, a death-like silence filled the whole room. He seemed to be uncomfortable and kept cracking jokes, trying to make it a festive occasion. I will never know how *anyone* can consider a circumcision festive! When he set up the table with straps, I felt myself get sick and flash on Nazi Germany's torture chambers. My whole body started to react as I realized I was going to be handing over my baby to this treatment.

I know my husband and I had wrestled with what to do for days beforehand and with the advice of the medical profession, had finally decided to go ahead with the circumcusion because of social reasons, but at that moment all I wanted to do was grab my child and run. He was too perfect, too innocent and trusting to hand him over to pain. I had nurtured him, loved him and protected him for nine months. Now, how could I hand him over to this Mohel to cut his body—his perfect little body—no matter what the reasons?

My heart held the truth. My heart cried *'No!'* and now I have to live with the fact that I ignored my heart, my feelings, and hurt my baby boy. There is much pain here for me. I haven't felt all of it yet. There was pain for my child and I hope I can help him to feel and integrate that reality as he grows older."

Irv: "I felt a sharp pain in my groin, while the Brith was under way. The actual scissors' cut scared me—I felt very vulnerable. The Mohel seemed indifferent to the baby's pain, he even tried denying it, and this made me angry. I'm not very clear about the tradition and meaning of a Brith, but it seemed horrifying. I seek a reason for this operation, some justification, yet I find none.

After seeing the brith I have some insight into why I unconsciously touch my penis, perhaps to protect that area of my body from another savage operation. I guess being a Jewish male means suffering pain at eight days of age. I really don't know—'My Jewish red badge of courage.' "

Toni: "The Brith was a totally new experience to me. I found the vibrations in the room tense and full of turmoil. It seemed basically right to circumcise the baby, yet my eyes were full of tears. I did not like the way the Mohel handled the baby or the jokes he told. Jokes seemed inappropriate to the seriousness of the occasion.

I felt heavily for the baby and the position he was in, especially since it really seemed like the Mohel was unnecessarily rough and insensitive. I was impressed, however, by the way the Mohel was eventually able to calm and quiet the baby. I assumed if his vibes weren't right the baby could not have been soothed by him. I trust the baby's reactions to that man. He was soothed by the man's touch."

Dan: "I was talking to Fran and Estelle when the Mohel overheard me mention pain. At this point he (the Mohel) seemed very, very uptight and went into a big performance about how little pain the baby was in. What bullshit! For whatever reason we may use to justify circumcision, it still seems very insane to subject a newborn baby to such abuse. We all seemed to feel that way and the Mohel seemed insecure with what he was doing, on some level."

"Bob (the baby's father) appeared to be the most shocked by the procedure. It was like a part of him was being cut at the same time. I was picking up a lot of anger from him toward the Mohel and at the same time, some deep Jewish understanding that this is the way it must be. Sarah was also very hurt. A blow had been dealt to her new son. She looked kind of helpless, not fully accepting the infliction to the baby. I felt very uptight and I didn't like what was being done. It sort of runs chills up my spine thinking about it. I believe there must be a more humane way of circumcision, either radically changing the medical procedure for the baby's comfort or doing away with it entirely.

A newborn baby can't possibly understand or integrate what is being done to him like this. That's what is so inhuman."

Robbi: "I came in dreading the Brith. On one hand, I was witnessing a Jewish tradition and was joyous for the little male, but on the other hand, which went with my feelings, I did not want that child to experience pain in his genitals. I was experiencing a vulnerability in my genital area just in anticipation of his own pain. I thought the Mohel was insensitive—I hated seeing the baby tied down. There is no happiness in this ceremony—I couldn't watch.

He's very lucky to have parents who are there for him—I think this alone will make all the difference. Trust can be restored, but one day he will have to feel that pain . . . just how much of a difference will it make? I never want to go to a Brith again."

Wanda: " I couldn't stand watching the actual cutting. I cannot believe that this can really be good—it is a relic of the past—akin to the Chinese binding the baby girl's feet; the African tribesman mutilating his body. Every circumcision I've ever watched has made me very uncomfortable even before I was into feelings and understanding babies' feelings. If it was good and right it would not produce such a bad feeling in me."

"I am sure that a baby's real lasting pain comes from emotional deprivation. Yet, to watch the baby's little face was to know what pure pain is.

The Mohel's efforts at joking and reassurance didn't help much. It would be better to treat it as the grim event it really is."

Edie: "My reaction to the Brith was mixed. A part of me felt if this little boy wasn't circumcised, the emotional pain of being different from daddy and his peers would outweigh the physical pain that he went through.

When it actually came down to watching it be done, it was horrible. I still cry when I think about it. I'm not a male, but I can imagine how sensitive that area must be. It might have been a speck better had the Mohel been tuned into what the baby was feeling. I didn't like the way he handled the baby. He was much too insensitive and abrupt."

If we can learn from the pure, honest emotion of this situation, of one family's struggle, ambivalence and regrets in responding to their baby's early dealings with a medical intervention, then perhaps, there is some good to be derived from this experience. Perhaps, it can lead to an outraged population demanding of its medical and religious practitioners that they humanize their practices and respond to the baby as a full emotional human being rather than a non-feeling object with little or no rights

Chapter 17   To The Therapist

TO THE THERAPIST[1]

Stop, loved one,
for it all backs up
on you.

> *Stop and care for*
> *yourself.*
> *Enough of others . . . . . .*

>> *Stop, you can do*
>> *them no good*
>> *clogged in your head.*

>>> *Stop and release yourself*
>>> *from servitude and serve*
>>> *and tend to self, — Before*
>>> *it is too late . . . . . .*

Stop, the tension
  is here.
Shall I run
  to my cave and repair?

Stop, it's late but
  here I go to little me.
Back to the truth of
  my self. It is good
    to be true to me.

>> *Go and feel the truth*
>> *of your life.*
>> *As I sit in my chair*
>> *late of night, I see*

---

[1] This chapter is part of a series of papers presented to trainees who are seeking certification as "Total Feeling Process" therapists.

your pictures and I see
mine.

ME flows from the
pool, rich and full.
A burden lifts and
clears my head.

Once again I am
free and open. I'm
ready to take care and
love and be in the
world.

Oh, the beauty and love
Oh, the treasure of life.
I am here . . . . . .
Fully . . . .

INITIAL PHASE OF THERAPY

Many times a client will enter a feeling therapy without being anywhere near feelings. He may be incapable, in fact, at that moment of connecting to anything significant on a deep emotional level.

It would be utterly futile for any therapist to attempt to plunge this type of individual into deep feelings. Therefore, it is necessary to conduct therapy in a much different way than one would with an individual who is closer to his feelings. I believe that it may be inappropriate to introduce this type of client to the heavy onslaught of a 3 week intensive[2]. He may need to be guided into feelings at a very slow pace, with sessions spaced far enough apart to allow for the full integration of whatever material arises during each preceding session. In other words, in some cases, the typically out-of-touch neurotic may need a longer period of time between sessions in order to allow his insights to seep into his everyday life.

It is, of course, important to start softly and gently. The client may be very anxious or show signs of emotional deadness. He will

---

[2] Arthur Janov, Ph. D., *Primal Scream* (New York: Dell Publishing Co., 1970), pg. 79.

not really know the therapists or the community members and it may be frightening to open up deep hurts to perfect strangers. In breaking the ice, a supportive accepting approach is necessary to allow the individual to be and reveal as much of himself as possible. Remember that buried pain is excruciating and initial messages may be conflicted, ambivalent and contradictory. Not only might the client be in a very fixed stage and quite far away from deep feeling, but in some cases, he may have very mixed reactions to the therapy itself. He may be quite reluctant to communicate anything about himself that threatens to bring up real feelings. In other words, rather than delve heavily into his feelings, he may wish to escape from himself and his pain. Feelings may be undesirable "things" that need to be eradicated or defended. Close human contact may be needed but some clients may interpret any potential intimacy as very dangerous.

This, of course, implies that the therapist must be sensitive to whatever the particular stage of feeling of his client, so that he can fit the therapy to the client and not the client to the therapy. Intake diagnostic procedures should be geared "to feel the client out" in order to find out how he responds to certain therapeutic techniques. It is important to find out how much he is willing to communicate and try to accept him patiently, whatever his level of awareness or feeling. He may be in a state of blocking and control and to loosen him up will require some testing of his ego strength and internal support systems. If he exhibits very weak or non-existent internal support systems, it may be first necessary to help him strengthen himself for the feeling work ahead.

Initially, it may be profitable to test him within a counseling format, whereupon a face-to-face, free flowing, supportive encounter takes place. At this time the therapist might elicit information from the client that allows for the free expression of feelings towards the therapist and the therapeutic environment. We have to remember that we are subtly, and not so subtly, attempting to reinforce new kinds of norms that may be directly antagonistic, unfamiliar and antithetical to the client's previous norms. We are setting the groundwork and giving him permission to open up and feel whenever he is ready.

It is important to try and let the individual guide as much of his therapy as possible. Therefore, the therapist should respect his client's inner resources to discover ways to greater feeling. He should try and be there for the patient as much as possible, so that his client learns to trust enough to let out those little, tender parts of himself. The time will come when he will test his therapist's trust to the limits. He will challenge many times to see if *"this* authority figure" is safe. We must remember that, particularly at this early stage, he is very vulnerable and will be extremely sensitive to whether or not the facilitator or the group will hurt him again, just like he was hurt in the past.

Babies are born and hopefully treated as very special people. Their status is much different than that of a grown up. By the very nature of a baby's being, he attracts certain affectional responses from those who are charged with his care. He has all the charm and physical attributes that are necessary to pull love and warmth from those people who are involved in his early life.

In other words, an infant has the innate power to influence how other people behave towards him. If he is responded to as if he is a very, very special human being, all of his wants and needs will be responded to in a very positive fashion. Consequently, he will respond to life in a much more productive fashion.

It has been our experience in the Total Feeling Process that certain adults who were treated with some amount of specialness when they were tiny, grow up with a much more positive and trusting orientation to the therapy itself as well as to the therapeutic community. The more devastation and deprivation of those early special responses to the infant, the more he will exist as an adult in the deepest pits of pain, frustration and mistrust.

Severely disturbed people have a difficult time trusting. The very nature of their behavior behooves them to defend against that very early deprivation. This, in essence, makes for two different types of population: those who have received absolutely no love or warmth as infants and those who have received some. The ones who have received some warmth and love will stand a better chance of surviving and succeeding with their therapy and persisting throughout the long haul.

I have mentioned before that there is a difference in status between the infant and the growing, emerging child. A tiny infant, somewhere around the age of 3-5 months, gains a sense of power and omnipotence. This is primarily due to the very positive and special responses that he receives from his parents and significant other people. Any child who does not receive these special responses at that early infantile stage will not develop that sense of omnipotence and power. Instead, he will grow up with a need to obtain that power in perverted ways.

Another difference between these two populations is the relative stage at which parental "put downs" occur. Most children start receiving "put downs" at different phases of their development: gestationally, during infancy, the age of four or five, or early adolescence. For example, one mother said, "Oh, I liked my son better when he was a tiny little infant. He was so cute and adorable. But the moment he became a teenager, he grew hair all over his body and became quite coarse." This is a not so subtle "put down" and rejection of the child's masculinity and self-worth which became activated in the early adolescent period, although probably operating at a subliminal level during all of the earlier phases of development. I use the term "put down" because I think it has an important connotation. If a child is slighted, put down or attacked by one or both parents, it is difficult for him to tune into that sense of omnipotence and power. He is literally kept down. It is important to realize that the earlier the "put down," the more severe the pathology when that person eventually enters therapy.

Any adult who has experienced extreme deprivation and slights throughout his entire early life will become super-sensitive and perhaps, even paranoid as to his anticipated rejections and "put downs" by authority figures including therapists and community members.

Patients who have had severe rejection trauma are going to send out very early in their therapy, some strong hints that they anticipate rejection. It becomes very important to recognize those tendencies early and then to steer the patient toward feeling the very early, primary trauma instead of acting out the rejection scene in the here and now.

Psychotherapy is not a perfect process. Nothing in life is and even though we may be brilliant in our interventions, there is always the temptation to move a little faster than the client can go. If one risks an advanced intervention at a primitive stage, however, it is possible to lose trust and scare the client away. We all make mistakes and fortunately, mistakes in deep feeling work are not usually fatal. But, we must learn from our mistakes. We are therapists, explorers, experimenters and scientists all in one and we have our feelings and knowledge to help us understand what is happening.

Each therapist will have to judge for himself when to move in to help a client and when to confront his blockages. Often, the client may resist and the possibility of a struggle always exists. He will not only be afraid of his own insanity but his therapist's as well. No one is perfect and all therapists have their own craziness somewhere. On the one hand, the client may have a need for this new "authority" figure to be perfect and safe like his parents never were, while on the other hand, he also needs him to be totally himself, at all times, so that he can accept this authority as a human being with hurt, pain and feelings of his own. It is usually good for the client to see his therapist, now and then, in his own pain so that he will accept his own feelings more readily. Most therapists have been through much of their own on-going therapy and intuition will be the best guide when a possible intervention is at hand. Impulses should build enough so that one is fairly sure of what to do and what interventions to make. If one is not sure just yet, it is better to sit awhile and take one's cues from the client.

Besides the existential psychotherapy approach, the therapist may attempt to introduce the client to gestalt role-playing techniques, assertiveness training, deep breathing methods, meditation and sound, bio-energetics, and working rage with pillows, a punching bag or baseball bat. In these early stages of therapy, the client can also be introduced to the psychological workbook technique[3], use of music, and another method used extensively by Casriel Scream Therapy[4], the repetition of feeling phrases in an exaggerated fashion. In this latter method, the client is asked to repeat a phrase, over and over again, while increasing his breathing and the volume of his voice. He is then encouraged to let that phrase take him to other phrases, feelings and cognitive insights.

During these interventions, the facilitator will be able to note where the physical blocks to emotion are and then devise techniques that will help loosen up this armoring. He will have to sense when to initiate body work. This requires a careful analysis of where the client is blocking and armoring. The body possesses a certain wisdom about what it needs and if the therapist can an-

---

[3]Paul J. Hannig, "The Psychology and Treatment of Obesity" (unpublished Ph.D dissertation, 1974)
  Roberto Assagioli, M.D., *Psychosynthesis* (New York: Viking Press, 1965), pg. 104.
[4]Daniel Casriel, *Scream Away From Happiness* (New York: Grossett and Dunlap, 1972).

ticipate and read this need correctly, he can create a body exercise that will release more feeling. There are many standard exercises that can be improvised to the client's needs and each individual therapist will perhaps devise entirely new ones. One shouldn't be afraid to suggest a few experimental exercises, just to see how the client reacts to them.

For example, many clients, upon entering therapy, are very inhibited and this will show itself in the volume and intensity of their voice and breathing. By noting this, it is possible to provide exercises that will help intensify the client's voice volume, thus allowing access to deeper realms of feeling. The expression that exists in the client's eyes and face should also be noted as well as the way he carries his body. Alexander Lowen[5] has devised many diagnostic treatment tools for dealing with different types of depression as well as muscular and energy blockages. The reader is advised to research these resources.

INTERMEDIATE PHASE OF THERAPY

At ensuing sessions it is common for the client to begin to feel more fear and resistance to the therapy itself. He may have performance anxiety about his ability to get into his feelings or he may feel threatened with the presence of another human being. Many middle class patients are raised in homes where performance standards and expectations for a growing child are quite extreme. The child may feel as if he is worthless unless he meets these parental standards of behavior and accomplishment. If the patient has internalized and introjected these performance standards of his parents and yet feels that he must meet them, he may be a problem in therapy.

Novice clients are usually always dissatisfied with their performance in the early stage of therapy. It is common for them to think and believe that they must become full feeling human beings within two weeks. These fantasies can be very rigidly entrenched and resistant to removal by the most powerful of interventions. In many cases the therapist can be extremely gratified and satisfied with the client's progress, however the client himself is the one who has not measured up to his preconceived ideas of where he should be in his

---

[5] Alexander Lowen, *Bio-energetics* (New York: Coward, McCann and Geoghegan, Inc., 1975).

therapy. Thus, we see that there can be an incredible discrepancy between the expectations of the therapist and the client.

I might add that it is common to form these expectations previous to the actual beginning of therapy itself. For example, the therapy team, after the initial interview, may come to an evaluation that would suggest that if the patient opened up a little bit by the middle of the third week, the initial stages of therapy would be considered a success. These initial evaluations are based upon predictions that staff members make as to what the patient will accomplish within a given period of time. Another problem with expectations is when the staff interviews someone whom they see as being highly sophisticated psychologically. In other words, if a professional therapist comes into therapy after having considerable feeling work elsewhere, one might expect him or her to be less resistant and more open to deep feelings. Thus, the therapist's own preconceived ideas about that individual's depth of feeling might be shattered by a painful reality. Whatever the expectations, whether on the part of the therapist or client, it is important that the patient doesn't get so tangled in them that he gets further away from his feelings. So it is necessary to get him on the floor, as soon as possible, and turn his attention inward towards his buried feelings. Feeling music often softens up the most resistant defenses and, because in most cases, somewhere inside of him the client wants to feel and cooperate with the therapy, this can be a very useful initial tool.

If the individual has been deeply involved with a different kind of therapy, he will be used to a different approach and may need time to adjust to a new style and technique. He is not at home yet in this strange new setting and it may be some time before he feels fully comfortable just being himself. Everyone has inclusion needs and all of us handle it in our own unique way, so it becomes important to try to help this person ease himself into the process as smoothly as possible. Some people have so much heavy pain and rigid defenses that inclusion is very difficult and it will initially be up to the therapist to see if it is at all possible for this new client to fit in. Remember, however, that the welfare of the entire group is very important and each person may have certain emotional gifts and attributes to bring to the group. If someone indicates that he will only be a detriment to the group progress and never become a productive, constructive member, then it may be necessary to refer him elsewhere. No one says you have to cure the whole world.

As a therapist, you will have your own resistances to working at times. You may not want to attend a particular group or a particular client's session. If you have been doing therapy for a long time you may even build up your own internal resistances to the therapy itself. Your moods and feelings will also go through many changes, and therapists, just like the clients, become frustrated and disillusioned with the process and progress. Because a good part of your life and existence will be invested and involved with this individual, you will be going through feelings that may be very fascinating and painful for both of you. Remember you are a part of a small fraternity of people whose life's work takes them into the most challenging, frightening and creative parts of the universe: the human psyche of feelings.

Keep in mind, that sometimes these feelings of resistance toward a particular client, may be the precursors of some feeling interactions to come between you and your client. It is important that you both work these issues openly and honestly within an analytical and feeling framework. This will further enhance the building of rapport and trust. You are also advised to keep track of the client's potential super-ego transference. As I mentioned earlier, if the client suffers from feelings of fear, self-doubt and inadequacy, he may project onto you, the therapist, a dissatisfaction with his "performance." He may imagine that you are evaluating and criticizing him and even that you may dislike him.

Unfortunately, many clients are highly defended and entrenched in transferential projections and will try hard to pull the therapist into their struggles. This is a form of helpless, manipulative seduction and may be unconsciously geared to arousing an angry response from the very person that can help him. The client is so defended that he is saying, in effect, "you must do something bad to make me feel." This is a common trap in therapy and it is very difficult to help this type of client take adult responsibility for his own therapy. Adult helplessness needs to be desymbolized and recognized for what it is . . . a helpless dependency to be saved and rescued, loaded with fear, hostility and a form of denial.

When this material arises in therapy, the therapist can supportively help the client trace these feelings to their proper source. The therapist's role, at this point, is to keep the patient on track as far as external reality versus the client's mixed-up internal reality. If both therapist and client are not alerted to and aware of these possible projections and able to work them through, the therapy itself, may be jeopardized further down the road.

Projection can be a constant source of irritation to the therapist and it is necessary to respond to this phenomenon in a direct and non-threatening way. Most patients are inclined to construct projections based upon their own inner historical feelings. I have mentioned elsewhere that these projections may be a super-imposition of an inner reality onto an external source. For example, a client may say "this room is spooky." There may be no objective facts that confirm this statement, but the client's inner workings extend outward and attribute malevolent forces to the room. The room becomes the object of the patient's internal fears. It is as if the client becomes attached in a symbiotic and symbolic fashion to that object. In this case, it is the room. The therapist may challenge this projection and help the client to see that, "It's really me and not the room that is feeling spooky."

Many times these projective phrases disguise the true feeling of fear that lurks deep within the belly. Defensively, it is safer for a person to locate the object of fear outside of himself, so that he can learn to cope and deal with an external stimulus rather than feeling the pain that lurks in his core. It is the therapist's job to refocus the patient's attention from outside of himself to the deep sources of pain within him.

Paranoid patients commonly project interpretations of malevolent forces outside themselves, whereupon they only feel a faint glimmer of their own internal pain. If they can feel the full force of their internal traumas, then they may reduce the potential threat of external sources. This would, ultimately, free them up to operate within a larger framework of human relationships and existence in general.

Fear is the hallmark of projection and neurotics expend enormous amounts of energy repressing their internal fears, thus focusing all their attention on outside distractions. If they can begin to say, "It is not really him, it's me," then they can become freed up from struggling with bad daddies, bad mommies and other malevolent, evil forces. The extent, breadth and scope of one's capacity to project will determine the parameters of his life space. If a woman projects that people are frightening, work is frightening, school is frightening, going out of the house is frightening, then she falls victim to her own projections and must live within the narrow confines of her own home and, in some cases, her own secluded little room.

The extreme of this condition is schizophrenia, where patients will feel safe and secure only in their own little worlds. They never venture out to make contact with those fearful projected objects and situations. The bottom line of the schizophrenic's pain is the excruciating damage and horrendous, murderous onslaught of early gestational parental insults. Once a therapist understands the painful routes of his patient's projections upon him, he need not get caught in the trap. And, let me say it quite succinctly, the projecting individual is, in fact, laying a trap for the unsuspecting therapist or other objects of his malevolent fears.

This type of individual is so highly tuned and sensitive to the prospect of being hurt that his radar detection system actually creates boogie men and women. In most instances, this manufacture of the external malevolent force has actually nothing to do with external reality. The point is, he sees it as if it does. To him, the external evil is absolutely real and his inflexibility resists any argument to the contrary. His very survival depends on being able to recognize that external threat. He must be primed and ready to perceive and protect himself from any potential source of pain and hurt. He is so primed and energized to see it that, in most cases, he creates it. It is like a self-fulfilling prophecy, whereupon the unfinished past must be recreated in the present in toto.

Every therapist at one time or another has been, or will be an object of projection. If he is in tune with the deadly game that the projector is playing, he can respond to it in a very appropriate fashion. I must confess that I am hard put to say what is an appropriate fashion. At times, I have responded to people laying projections onto me with incredible anger. At other times, I have been cool as a cucumber. If someone is really out to ruffle my feathers, I'm sure they can succeed in doing just that. But, if they are sincere about getting to the roots of their projected behavior, I can and do remain very calm and supportive of their endeavors.

At the beginning and also throughout the therapy, it is so important to allow the client to feel support for his efforts to get well. This supportive feedback helps to reinforce his positive efforts toward self-growth and health. This, of course, does not mean that one has to be phony or dishonest. The client can appreciate straightforward reinforcement yet also know that when the time is right, you will confront his craziness in as equally a forthright manner. Do not be afraid to add input to his deep feelings, high or low, in order to trigger and deepen his capabilities. He will want to know that you are competent and able to be inside with him when he is joyful and proud as well as that you can see and respond when he is in the agonizing throes of pain. This is deep level facilitative interpretation.

By now the fragile, unfamiliar stages of therapy are diminishing and the therapist is getting a pretty good idea of what his client needs. The time may have come to push a little bit harder and perhaps even insist that he do some of the exercises he may have initially resisted at the beginning. Communicate to him that it is okay to go all the way with his feelings. You are with him now, giving him support plus your energy and believe me, he will need it. His behavior and issues are clearer now and he is discovering that all behavior, no matter how disturbed, makes sense and can be tracked logically to its core feeling roots. This last point deserves repeating. Eventually everything makes sense and is explainable at a deep core level.

At this point you have gathered enough data on your client to predict what serious problems will arise in his therapy. You are beginning to see how he transfers, projects, displaces and controls himself and others around him. You are beginning to become familiar with how he acts out his unfelt, unresolved pain and you can formulate appropriate interventions.

Acting out one's early feelings in the here and now is a fact of therapy and the client may or may not be aware that this is what he is doing. Even if he has some awareness of his acting-out, he will find it very difficult to curtail his behavior and actions. It is important to remember that he is in pain and seeking relief in his own typically unfeeling way. This behavior is often difficult to tolerate. The only thing one can do is to wait until he feels all of the pain, remembering that the healing process of the therapy is always at work and just being present at one's sessions and groups has a curative, healing effect.

If the therapist has a clear picture of the individual's primary family dynamic, then he can use modified forms of psychodramatic and role-playing techniques in a group setting which may bring the client's hidden agendas to the forefront. In this way everyone has a chance to see him and understand his background a little better.

Because he is still more unfeeling than feeling, he may still be afraid of what he is not in touch with and will seek to control both the therapist and the group until he feels the pain connected with his defensive maneuvers and manipulations. Do not hesitate to offer feedback on what you observe and your personal feeling reactions. If you hold back too much for too long the issues may pile up and become too difficult to disentangle.

At times a therapist may feel uncomfortable or dissatisfied with superficial, upper level, incomplete feelings. There is always the desire to want someone to get in as deep as possible because we know of the curative and transformative powers of deep core feeling. As a consequence, we tend to highly value that kind of experience. But this does not mean that we can push someone to those depths, before they are fully ready. Someone has to have first relinquished enough of their defenses and built up considerable feeling capacity before deep, full feeling is possible. And even then, there will be times when defenses will block full feeling explosion. This may test your patience, as a therapist, to the limit and by all means explore the limits of your own patience and expectations. But if your patience has run its course and you've reached the end of the road, it may be time for a full scale therapeutic "crunch." This can be a very exciting, challenging and dangerous point in the therapy. The defenses of the client come full force, face-to-face with the power of a therapeutic onslaught. In most cases, the patient wants his defenses to crumble in order to feel the full force of his own feelings but there are times when it is "touch and go."

One further point to mention is the fact that feeling people and feeling therapists respond positively when someone is getting into deep curative feelings. Because of this you may feel conflicted or ambivalent about ending a session at its prescribed time. We all like to see the outcome of a completed feeling and are pulled toward allowing it to run its course. On rare occasions, if it is a particularly heavy breakthrough, you may find that you do want to extend your boundaries and stay with your client over the allotted time schedule. However, therapy does have time limits and, as a general rule, these limits must be adhered to. It is important, of course, as the therapist, to provide ample opportunity for clients to go deeply into feelings over extended periods of time whether it be in private sessions, groups or long marathon weekends.

CONCLUSION

Psychotherapy is a very demanding profession. Not only do we as psychotherapists have our own personal problems to work through, but there is the added pressure of professional identity as well as political and legal problems. We may also need to take a closer look at therapist competency. It has been my experience that academic training plus local licensing procedures do not guarantee professional competency or ethics. Fifty to ninety percent of the clients who have entered this therapy have had difficult and counter-productive experiences with many other highly credentialed professionals. Presently, the Center for Feeling People is investigating the criteria for professional competency.

I cannot and will not demean my own academic background or my memberships and certifications in many different professional groups. Furthermore, it is absolutely necessary to recognize that a truly qualified academic background can be very compatible with personal qualities of sensitivity, honesty, openness and general therapeutic skill. However, formal academic background can, at times, serve as a hindrance to one's personal therapeutic effectiveness if this is the only expertise brought before a client. Sensitivity, motivation, intelligence and desire in combination with a strong theoretical, experiential and academic background provides the necessary attributes for a truly effective psychotherapy. Add to this an individual who is grounded in his professionalism and personal ethics and we have a full scale definition of a competent and professional therapist.

The Total Feeling Process has its own therapeutic code and may be in variance with other schools of thought. Through extensive research we have tried to verify and validate the methods of this therapy with other established therapeutic modalities. I have found that it is easy to be seduced by one's own enthusiasm about this form of treatment, however. One might even be tempted to brag. I have tried to give credit to those therapists and theorists who have been instrumental in developing my philosophy and I hope I have succeeded. It is not my wish to hold myself out as a "personality." Rather, I prefer to remain somewhat in the shadowy background and let the therapy stand on its own as I feel it can.

Over the years, at times it has been a struggle coming to terms with all of the different types of therapies and growth programs that exist in this country but I have tried to take in and assimilate all that information. Likewise, I have been greatly influenced, both positively and negatively, by every client who has entered this training. What is now evident is that there are some people who benefit enormously from deep feeling work. There are others who are just not ready or appropriate for this kind of treatment.

Those clients who have endured have taught me much while I, in turn, have exposed them to the powerful curative force of their own feelings. Feeling People try to be real. They are beautiful and I love them . . .

For information about the Center, contact:

Paul J. Hannig, Ph.D.
10170-4 Larwin Ave.
Chatsworth, CA 91311
(818) 882-7404